SUCCESSFUL COACHING

Updated Second Edition

**A Publication for
the American Sport Education Program
and the National Federation Interscholastic
Coaches Association**

**Rainer Martens, PhD
ASEP Founder**

Human Kinetics

Library of Congress Cataloging-in-Publication Data

Martens, Rainer, 1942-
    Successful coaching / Rainer Martens. -- Updated 2nd ed.
        p.   cm.
    "A publication of the American Sport Education Program and the
National Federation Interscholastic Coaches Association."
    Includes bibliographical references (p.   ) and index.
    ISBN 0-88011-666-8
    1. School sports--Coaching--United States.   I. American Sport
Education Program.   II. National Federation Interscholastic Coaches
Association.   III. Title.
    GV711.M355   1997
    796'.071'273--dc20   96-31259
                                                              CIP

ISBN: 0-88011-666-8 ✓

Table 12.7 on page 119 was adapted, from M.H. Stone, H. O'Bryant, and J. Garhammer, 1981, "A Hypothetical Model for Strength Training," *Journal of Sports Medicine* 21:344.

The **Facilities Inspection Checklist** on pages 161-164 was adapted from the *American Coaching Effectiveness Program Level 2 Sport Law Workbook*, Human Kinetics, pp. 40-41, and *Athletic Business*, November, 1985, pp. 36-38.

The **Preparticipation Physical Evaluation** on page 170 and the **Medical History** on pages 171-172 were adapted, with permission, from *Preparticipation Physical Evaluation*, 1992, by the American Academy of Family Physicians, the American Academy of Pediatrics, the American Medical Society for Sports Medicine, the American Orthopaedic Society for Sports Medicine, and the American Osteopathic Academy of Sports Medicine.

Table 15.1 on pages 173-174 was reprinted, by permission, from *Preparticipation Physical Evaluation*, 1992, by the American Academy of Pediatrics.

The **Injury Report Form** on pages 178-179 was adapted, by permission, from the National Safety Council.

Acquisitions Editor: Jim Kestner; **Developmental Editors:** Jan Colarusso Seeley and Linda Anne Bump, PhD; **Assistant Editors:** Lynn M. Hooper and Julia Anderson; **Editorial Assistant:** Coree Schutter; **Copyeditor:** Molly Bentsen; **Indexer:** Barbara E. Cohen; **Graphic Designer:** Keith Blomberg; **Graphic Artists:** Tara Welsch, Angie Snyder, Yvonne Winsor, Sandra Meier, Ruby Zimmerman, and Denise Lowry; **Cover Designer:** Jack Davis; **Photographer (cover):** Wilmer Zehr; **Illustrators:** Dorothy Hagstrom, Gretchen Walters, and Barbara Cook; **Printer:** United Graphics

Printed in the United States of America   10   9   8   7   6   5   4

Human Kinetics
Web site: http://www.humankinetics.com/

United States: Human Kinetics, P.O. Box 5076, Champaign, IL 61825-5076
1-800-747-4457
e-mail: humank@hkusa.com

Canada: Human Kinetics, 475 Devonshire Road, Unit 100, Windsor, ON N8Y 2L5
1-800-465-7301 (in Canada only)
e-mail: humank@hkcanada.com

Europe: Human Kinetics, P.O. Box IW14, Leeds LS16 6TR, United Kingdom
(44) 1132 781708
e-mail: humank@hkeurope.com

Australia: Human Kinetics, 57A Price Avenue, Lower Mitcham, South Australia 5062
(088) 277 1555
e-mail: humank@hkaustralia.com

New Zealand: Human Kinetics, P.O. Box 105-231, Auckland 1
(09) 523 3462
e-mail: humank@hknewz.com

Contents

Preface to the Updated Second Edition

The first edition of this book, *Coaching Young Athletes*, is the most-read coaching book ever written in North America, with nearly 100,000 copies sold since it was released in 1981. Why change the title of such a successful book? Because many coaches and sports administrators interpreted "young" in the title to mean prepubescent children, not teenage athletes. Thus, by changing the name to *Successful Coaching*, with no reference to age, I hoped to encourage coaches at every level to read this book.

The first edition of this book was the text for the Level I Course of the American Coaching Effectiveness Program (ACEP). Although many community-based sports programs offered the ACEP Level I Course, others told us that the program was more comprehensive than what they wanted to offer for their volunteer coaches. Thus, we reorganized the ACEP curriculum to create a *Volunteer Level* for volunteers who would probably coach for only a season or two while their sons or daughters participated in a sport. We also created a *Leader Level* course for those who want to pursue coaching as a vocation or serious avocation. (In Appendix A you will find a complete description of the Volunteer Level, the Leader Level, and the more advanced Master Level, as well as the many resources that comprise the comprehensive curriculum.)

Released in 1990, the second edition of *Successful Coaching* was revised to be the text for the ACEP Leader Level Course. It was a comprehensive introduction to the art and science of coaching. The book introduced a positive coaching philosophy; the principles of coaching as digested from the fields of sport psychology, sport pedagogy, and sport physiology; and useful advice from the field of sport management.

The second edition retained the highly practical, understandable, and concise content of the first edition, but it also contained significant changes that came about through the constructive suggestions of many coaches and sports administrators. I rewrote the sport pedagogy part to make it even more practical for developing instructional plans. I added a chapter to help you understand how athletes learn sport skills.

I also revised the sport psychology and sport physiology parts to include important new findings from these sciences since the first edition was written. Perhaps the most significant change was the deletion of the sports medicine section. I removed sports medicine not because it was any less important, but because it was so important that for the Leader Level we created a separate course and book called *Sport First Aid*.

Finally, I added a new section called sport management. It included highly practical chapters on managing your team or program, managing risk, managing your stress, and managing time. Not only will these chapters help you coach more successfully, they will help you grow as a coach and individual.

In 1990 the National Federation of State High School Associations (NFSHSA) joined with ACEP to form a single national interscholastic and club sport coaching education network. Working together, ACEP and the National Federation Interscholastic Coaches Association (NFICA) formed a special version of the ACEP Leader Level, known as the National Federation Interscholastic Coaches Education Program (NFICEP), and the second edition of *Successful Coaching* was its text.

ACEP continued to grow, and in 1994 we expanded our mission, developing programs for parents and sport administrators. To reflect this expanded mission, we also changed our name to the American Sport Education Program (ASEP). Today, ASEP's program has blossomed into a 16-course curriculum, and the original ACEP program has been designated SportCoach. The partnership between ASEP and the NFSHSA has continued to grow, and this book is being released in conjunction with revisions of our Leader Level

Sport Science and Sport First Aid courses to reflect the latest knowledge in sport sciences and sports medicine. This updated second edition of *Successful Coaching* is the textbook for the Leader Level/NFICEP Sport Science Course, now called the ASEP/NFICEP Coaching Principles Course.

In addition to updating the content of *Successful Coaching*, we have responded to cries from coaches, administrators, and parents for more practical information about how to prevent athletes' use of tobacco, alcohol, and other drugs. I have deleted the Drugs and Sport chapter of the second edition of *Successful Coaching* in favor of the latest entry to ASEP's SportCoach curriculum: the ASEP/NFICEP Drugs and Sport Course. Today, ASEP and the NFSHSA continue to work together providing coaches with practical, essential information for becoming successful coaches.

The first edition of this book has been used to educate coaches in almost every sport at every level—team and individual, women and men, contact and noncontact, beginner and advanced. On occasion administrators have said, "I like the book but I wish it had more examples for our sport. Our coaches won't relate to examples in those other sports." Obviously it is not possible to write this book for each sport, nor do I think it is necessary. I have provided representative examples for all the categories I listed. Furthermore, *Successful Coaching* is about the *principles* of coaching, and most of the principles apply to all sports. Even if a specific example does not directly fit another sport, I find coaches can readily apply the principle to their sport. In fact, some coaches tell me they find it helps their understanding to make comparisons across sports.

Much has happened in coaching education since the release of the first edition of this book. More than 150,000 coaches have completed ASEP/NFICEP courses. Sport administrators across the country are much more aware of the need for coaching education. National, state, and local organizations are taking steps to implement coaching education programs, especially the ASEP/NFICEP curriculum. Colleges and universities are rejuvenating their coaching curriculums through cooperative efforts with ASEP. And perhaps the most encouraging development is that more and more men and women who are choosing to make coaching a vocation or serious avocation are eager to acquire this education.

I authored the first edition of this book with three special friends—Robert Christina, Jack Harvey, and Brian Sharkey. Although Drs. Christina and Harvey did not contribute directly to the current edition, their contribution through the first edition permeates this revision. I also wish to express my thanks to Brian Sharkey, my former mentor, for authoring the revision of Part IV, "Sport Physiology." Ted Miller spent many hours helping me locate resources and finalizing the details of the manuscript, for which I wish to thank him. A very special appreciation goes to Linda Bump, who contributed significantly in developing the content of several sections and to Jan Colarusso Seeley, who served as my editor. Finally, I wish to thank the hundreds of coaches and administrators who have shared with me their knowledge about coaching and their ideas about how to make this book more helpful.

Becoming a Successful Coach

Welcome to coaching! If you've not coached before, you have many new experiences awaiting you. Perhaps you've already daydreamed scenes of your athletes carrying you off the field on their shoulders after winning the championship and your friends and neighbors congratulating you for masterminding the perfect season. Or perhaps your daydreams turn to nightmares—you see yourself making a tactical blunder, and some loudmouth spectator ridicules you. Then you lose your temper and say things you regret. If you have coached before, perhaps these daydreams and nightmares, or similar scenarios, are real experiences for you.

Like any profession, coaching has its highs and lows, but if you are prepared, they can be mostly highs. If you already have the teaching skills of an educator, the training expertise of a physiologist, the administrative leadership of a business executive, and the counseling wisdom of a psychologist, you can throw this book away; it won't help you. But if you don't, join me to find out what makes a coach successful.

Is success winning games? Yes, in part, winning is an aspect of successful coaching. But successful coaching is much more than just winning games. Successful coaches help athletes master new skills, enjoy competing with others, and feel good about themselves. Successful coaches not only are well-versed in the techniques and skills of their sports, they know how to teach these skills to young people. And successful coaches not only teach athletes sport skills, they also teach and model the skills needed for successful living in our society.

Being a successful coach is an enormous challenge. And good intentions are not enough to be successful; you need all the knowledge you can get. *Successful Coaching* will help you acquire this knowledge by teaching you more about sport science and sport management. It does not discuss the teaching of techniques or tactics for specific sports, although both are certainly important. Successful coaches need to know about both (a) sport science and management and (b) techniques and tactics. In the past coaches emphasized the latter because little was known about the former. But that's changed now, and *Successful Coaching* will give you a firm foundation in the practical application of sport science and management.

In this introductory book you will learn about three sport sciences—sport psychology, sport pedagogy, and sport physiology—and about sport management. Don't worry if you come across terms, like sport pedagogy, that are new to you. I'll introduce these sport sciences to you in understandable and, I hope, entertaining ways. I don't want to lose your interest because of needless scientific mumbo-jumbo, but becoming a successful coach does require you to learn some new terms. Just as carpenters must know about miter boxes, soffits, and wainscots, modern-day coaches need to know about aerobic and anaerobic training, intrinsic motivation, muscle glycogen, optimal arousal, plyometrics, and risk management. In this book you will find out about all these things and much more in language you can understand and in ways to help you become a successful coach.

Most coaches have learned the skills of coaching through years of trial and error. But, oh, how some of those errors hurt! *Successful Coaching* will help you shorten that learning process—and reduce those painful errors—by drawing upon the wisdom of experienced and knowledgeable coaches and the research of hundreds of sport scientists who have studied sport over the past 40 years. The unique emphasis of this book is the integration of sport science research with the practical knowledge acquired by highly experienced coaches.

This book, of course, does not contain all the information you will need to be a successful coach. There is much more to learn. This book is only a starting point, a foundation for building your knowledge of the sport sciences and management. As the text for the ASEP/NFICEP Coaching Principles Course, it is followed by a series of more advanced texts in each of the sport sciences that com-

prise the Master Level. (See Appendix A for complete information about the American Sport Education Program courses.) But even after you study at the Master Level, much will remain to be learned. These books are only one source of information. Another way you can learn is to watch and talk with other coaches. They can teach you both effective and ineffective coaching practices; what you must do is distinguish between the two. *Successful Coaching* will help you do that by providing you a foundation in sport science and management.

Of course, another important way for you to learn is from your own experiences. As you coach, examine your experiences periodically and think about what you are learning. What can you do differently to coach more successfully, and what do you want to do the same because it works well? Some coaches have 20 years of experience, but have learned little because they do not think about and adjust to their experiences. Other coaches may have only a few months of experience, but learn much quickly and adjust to successful and unsuccessful coaching practices.

It won't take you too long to read *Successful Coaching*, but it may take some time to know its contents, and perhaps even longer to put into practice what you know. Just as an athlete doesn't learn to play shortstop overnight, you won't learn the skills of coaching in a day. You will need to read and reread parts of this book, practice the skills described, observe other coaches, and learn from your experiences through thoughtful analysis. As you undertake this self-study, you will see that successful coaches are those who can learn new skills, who are flexible enough to change old ways when change is needed, who can accept constructive criticism, and who can critically evaluate themselves. Throughout *Successful Coaching*, I will ask you to do all these things. In fact, I am going to urge you to put forth the same effort to become a successful coach that you will expect from the athletes you coach.

Part I

Developing a Coaching Philosophy

Chapter 1
YOUR COACHING OBJECTIVES

Chapter 2
YOUR COACHING STYLE

Your success as a coach will depend more on your coaching philosophy than on any other factor. By philosophy I mean the beliefs or principles that guide the actions you take. It is the foundation on which all your knowledge about sport science, sport management, and techniques and tactics will be built. Your coaching philosophy will determine how wisely you use this knowledge.

Part I is devoted to helping you develop your coaching philosophy by asking you to think about the two most important decisions a coach makes. The first decision, discussed in chapter 1, is de-termining which objectives you will seek to at-tain when coaching. In chapter 2, I ask you to think about the coaching style you will use to achieve your objectives.

How you make these decisions will form two vital parts of your coaching philosophy and, to a large extent, will determine how much success and enjoyment you and your athletes will have. Obviously, no one can make these decisions for you; however, I will encourage you to consider several important issues as you develop your coaching philosophy.

Chapter 1

Your Coaching Objectives

One of the two most important decisions you will make as a coach concerns the objectives you will seek to achieve with your athletes. Stop for a few moments to think what your objectives will be, and write them down. In this chapter we'll first consider the objectives you have for your team or athletes and then will consider the objectives you have for yourself.

Three Major Objectives

Coaches often list many specific goals they hope to achieve when coaching their athletes; usually their goals fall under three broad objectives:

- To have a winning team
- To help young people have fun
- To help young people develop . . .
    a. *physically*, by learning sport skills, improving physical conditioning, developing good health habits, and avoiding injuries;
    b. *psychologically*, by learning to control their emotions and developing feelings of self-worth; and
    c. *socially*, by learning cooperation in a competitive context and appropriate standards of behavior.

Which of these objectives is important to you? Winning? Having fun? Helping young people develop? Perhaps you believe all three are worthwhile. But are they equally important? What if you must choose between them (which at times you will)? Coaches often must decide whether to pursue victory at the possible expense of an athlete's well-being or development. What will your priorities be?

Assessing Your Objectives

The short questionnaire here will help you decide about your objectives for winning, having fun, and helping young athletes develop.

Read each statement and the three options that follow. Decide which of the three you feel is most important and write the number *3* in the blank next to that letter. Then decide which option is least important to you and write *1* in the corresponding blank. Put *2* in the remaining space. Although in some cases you may think all three choices are important, indicate which is the most important and which is the least important of the three. Try to answer each question as you honestly feel.

1. The best coaches are those who
   A. Give individual help and are interested in young athletes' development.   A. ＿＿
   B. Make practices and games fun.   B. ＿＿
   C. Teach athletes the skills needed to win.   C. ＿＿

2. If a news story were written about me, I would like to be described as
   A. A coach who contributed to the development of young people.   A. ＿＿
   B. A coach for whom athletes enjoyed playing.   B. ＿＿
   C. A winning coach.   C. ＿＿

3. As a coach I emphasize
   A. Teaching skills that young people can use later in life.   A. ＿＿
   B. Having fun.   B. ＿＿
   C. Winning.   C. ＿＿

   Total   ＿＿   ＿＿   ＿＿

Now let's score the test. Add up the scores in each column. Each total should be between 3 and 9; the higher the total, the more you emphasize that outcome. The first column shows your priority for the development of young athletes, the second your priority for having fun, and the third the ranking you gave winning.

Most coaches' scores indicate they believe winning is least important and helping athletes develop is most important. Did you answer the same way? Is it true of how you coach?

A Philosophy of Winning— A Winning Philosophy

No single decision is more important in determining how you coach than your priority for these objectives—especially the significance you give to winning. Some coaches who say winning is least important don't behave that way when they coach. For example, coaches who play only their best athletes, who play injured athletes, or who scream disparagingly at athletes who have erred demonstrate that winning is more important to them than athletes' development.

Be honest. Do you at times overemphasize winning? Do you at times make decisions that reflect more concern about winning the game than the development of your athletes? It is easy to do in a society that places so much value on winning!

Many coaches face a dilemma about their objectives when they coach. Society clearly rewards winners. Yet society also looks to sport as a means to help young people try out life, build character, and develop leadership skills. Coaches who want to help young people develop physically, psychologically, and socially through sport often find they are evaluated only on their win-loss record. Perhaps altruistic at first, too many veteran coaches are conditioned by the organizations for whom they coach to pursue the objective of winning regardless of the cost.

This must change, and coaches must take responsibility for making the change. While society may be fickle about its objectives for sport participation, coaches must resist the forces that encourage them to win at all costs. Coaches now more than ever need to be clear about their objectives when coaching.

I want you to consider the following objective as the cornerstone for your coaching philosophy. It is an objective that many national sport organizations, experienced and successful coaches at all levels, professional educators, and physicians endorse. It is an objective I hope you will endorse as well, and more importantly, one you will put into practice! The objective is this:

**Athletes First,
Winning Second**

What I mean by this is quite simple: Every decision you make and every behavior you display is based first on what you judge is best for your athletes and second on what may improve the athlete's or team's chances of winning.

Athletes First, Winning Second is the philosophical foundation for the Bill of Rights for Young Athletes, which is presented on page 6. Take a moment to study these rights. Think about how your coaching might deny an athlete these rights, and then about how you can coach to help ensure that each athlete is given them.

Athletes First, Winning Second is an objective simple to state, but not simple to implement. Today many sport organizations are led by administrators who demand that coaches reverse this objective—Winning First, Athletes Second—either because winning is their personal objective or because these administrators are pressured by others. Coaches who skillfully help young people become better humans but fail to win an often unknown quota of games are considered losers, and all too often are fired. This is the regrettable reality in sport today, but it must and will change. In the final analysis, it's not how many games you win, but how

BILL OF RIGHTS
FOR YOUNG ATHLETES

Right to participate in sports

Right to participate at a level commensurate
with each child's maturity and ability

Right to have qualified adult leadership

Right to play as a child and not as an adult

Right of children to share in the leadership
and decision-making of their sport participation

Right to participate in safe and healthy
environments

Right to proper preparation for participation
in sports

Right to an equal opportunity for success

Right to be treated with dignity

Right to have fun in sports

Note. From *Guidelines for Children's Sports* (pp. 15-31) by R. Martens
and V. Seefeldt (Eds.), 1979, Reston, VA: AAHPERD. Copyright 1979
by AAHPERD. Reproduced with permission from the American Alliance
for Health, Physical Education, Recreation and Dance, 1900 Association
Dr., Reston, VA 22091.

many young people you help to become winners in life.

So what do you do now if you are in this situation? If you believe the *Athletes First, Winning Second* is the right priority, resist the temptation to abandon your principles because the pressure to win threatens your job, or worse, your self-worth. Resist transferring this threat by threatening the well-being of your athletes. Stick to your principles and seek to convert those who are pressuring you to win to your objective—*Athletes First, Winning Second.*

Striving to Win

Having *Athletes First, Winning Second* as your objective does not mean that winning is unimportant. The immediate short-term objective of any contest is to win. Striving to win within the rules of the game should be the objective of every athlete and coach. To play sports without striving to win is to be a "dishonest competitor," says Michael Novak in *Joy of Sports.* Striving to win is essential to enjoyable competition.

"Winning isn't everything, it's the only thing," said Vince Lombardi, or so we are told. Actually Lombardi did not say it quite that way; that was a reporter's mutation. What Lombardi actually said was, "Winning isn't everything, but striving to win is." And that statement more accurately reflects his coaching philosophy.

Does it make sense that the emphasis on winning should not be on the winning itself, but on the striving to win? It's the pursuit of the victory, the dream of achieving the goal more than the goal itself that yields the joy of sports. Many outstanding athletes candidly say that their best memories of sport are not the victories themselves, but the months of preparation and anticipation and the self-revelation before and during the competition.

Commitment

Competition and the striving to win are significant in another way. Today we hear much about our alienated youth, their lack of commitment to our established institutions, and their lack of desire to achieve excellence. Sadly, many young people are not finding activities in their home, school, or place of worship worthy of their commitment. But America's youth are being turned on by sport; they find sport a challenge worth pursuing. And what is that challenge? It is the competition—the comparison of abilities and efforts, the striving to win, and the recognition for excellence achieved.

Larry Smith was one of these "uncommitted" youth. He was too lazy or disinterested to do his schoolwork; he usually sat around the house watching television and eating, which resulted in his becoming overweight. But for some reason Larry went out for football, where at last he found a challenge. To make the team and meet the maximum weight limit, he needed to improve his grades and lose 10 pounds. His parents and teachers had tried to get him to do both for months, but had failed. Now he did them of his own accord!

Recently a 16-year-old youth with mental retardation received an award on national television for his outstanding accomplishment as a swimmer. What was remarkable about this young man was that at the age of 12 he could not speak or perform the basic self-help skills

of feeding and dressing. But through the Special Olympics, he learned to swim and compete—and this challenge brought him out of his inner world. He learned not only to feed and dress himself, but also to speak and, even more remarkably, to teach other young people how to swim.

In discussing some of our schools' problems, the noted educator James Coleman observed that humanity's great accomplishments come about when individuals make an intense commitment to something, when only their total concentrated effort may result in success—but even then success is not guaranteed. Sports attract that type of commitment and often result in great personal accomplishment.

WINNING vs. ETHICAL BEHAVIOR

Ethical Behavior

The element of competition in sport has value in yet another way. Through sport young people can develop morally—they can learn a basic code of ethics that is transferable to a moral code for life. Competitive sport—where winning is a valued prize—provides opportunities for high levels of moral development to occur.

For example, Sharon is playing a recreational game of tennis with Susan, who hits the winning point on the baseline. Knowing that the shot was good, Sharon so declares it. Susan wins. Now that's not so hard to do when you're playing tennis only for fun, when there is little at stake.

But imagine Sharon playing the same game, and winning means the prestigious city championship and a trip to a national tournament. It takes a great deal more character to make the proper call now.

One value of competitive sport is that such moral decisions are required often, and young people face opportunities to learn, and adults to model, appropriate ethical behavior. To make an appropriate moral judgment at the expense of a valued victory is a real test of character as well as an opportunity to build character.

Keeping Winning in Perspective

Striving to win is important in sport. That process can bring out the best in young people—in their performance, commitment, and moral development. For sport to provide these benefits, you must maintain a proper perspective on winning: *Athletes First, Winning Second*.

Remember that striving to win the game is *an important* objective of the contest, but it is *not* the *most important* objective of sport participation. It is easy to lose sight of the long-term objectives—helping athletes develop physically, psychologically, and socially—while pursuing the short-term objective of winning the contest, because the rewards for winning are immediate and powerful. Winning or striving to win is never more important than athletes' well-being, regardless of the mixed messages our society sends. Ask yourself, Will I be able to keep those long-term goals in sight not only during practice but in the heat of a contest, not only when I am winning but when I'm losing, not only when I have the support of my administrator but when he or she pressures me to win?

When winning is kept in perspective, sport programs produce young people who enjoy sports, who strive for excellence, who dare to risk error in order to learn, and who grow with both praise and constructive criticism. When winning is kept in perspective, there is room for fun in the pursuit of victory—or, more accurately, the pursuit of victory is fun. With proper leadership, sport programs produce young people who accept responsibilities, who accept others, and most of all who accept themselves.

Your Personal Objectives

I hope you are coaching because you care to help young people through sport. You also are likely to have other objectives: to earn a living, to demonstrate your knowledge of the sport, to gain public recognition, maybe even fame. You may be coaching for the social contact, the love of the sport, to have fun, to travel, or to be in charge. All these objectives and many others are appropriate personal reasons for coaching, and you need to achieve some of your objectives or you are likely to quit.

Coaches sometimes deny their personal objectives. They may feel that the only socially acceptable reasons to give for coaching are altruistic statements about helping athletes. It is good to have these altruistic motives, but it is entirely appropriate to seek to fulfill your personal objectives in coaching as well—as long as they are not achieved at the expense of your athletes' well-being.

To help you examine your personal objectives, I've listed some common reasons for coaching on the following page. Indicate how important each of these reasons is to you by checking the appropriate box. Add any other reasons that you have in the space provided and rate them too. Now think carefully and honestly, and try to identify any reasons that may cause conflict between what's best for you and best for your athletes.

For example, if personal recognition or power is among your personal objectives for coaching, you need to guard against placing your objective above the interest of your athletes. You will be especially vulnerable during intense competition to pursuing your own goals at the expense of your athletes. This risk can be managed, but you must come to know yourself well and entrench firmly in your mind the philosophy of *Athletes First, Winning Second*.

Successful coaches know the differences between their objectives for the contest, their objectives for their athletes' participation, and their personal objectives. Successful coaches strive to win each and every contest, although they may know that a victory is unlikely. Successful coaches help athletes develop physically, psychologically, and socially. And successful coaches strive to achieve their personal goals without jeopardizing their athletes' well-being. Indeed, successful coaches find ways to achieve all three objectives.

Personal Reasons for Coaching

Reason	Not at all important	Somewhat important	Very important
To be involved in a sport I like	☐	☐	☐
To earn a living	☐	☐	☐
To help secure a teaching position	☐	☐	☐
To have power	☐	☐	☐
To be in charge	☐	☐	☐
To be with people I like	☐	☐	☐
To give something back to the sport	☐	☐	☐
To gain public recognition	☐	☐	☐
To enjoy myself	☐	☐	☐
To demonstrate my knowledge and skill in the sport	☐	☐	☐
To travel	☐	☐	☐
To help athletes develop physically	☐	☐	☐
To help athletes develop psychologically	☐	☐	☐
To help athletes develop socially	☐	☐	☐
_____	☐	☐	☐
_____	☐	☐	☐

Chapter 2

Your Coaching Style

The second important decision you need to make is about your coaching style. That style will determine how you decide what skills and strategies to teach, how you organize for practice and competition, what methods you use to discipline players, and, most important, what role you give athletes in making decisions.

Three Coaching Styles

Most coaches lean toward one of three coaching styles: the command style, the submissive style, or the cooperative style.

Command Style (The Dictator)

In the command style of coaching, the coach makes all the decisions. The role of the athlete is to respond to the coach's commands. The assumption underlying this approach is that because

the coach has knowledge and experience, it is his or her role to tell the athlete what to do. The athlete's role is to listen, to absorb, and to comply.

Submissive Style (The Babysitter)

Coaches who adopt the submissive style make as few decisions as possible. It's a throw-out-the-ball-and-have-a-good-time approach. The coach provides little instruction, provides minimal guidance in organizing activities, and resolves discipline problems only when absolutely necessary. Coaches who adopt this style either lack the competence to provide instruction and guidance, are too lazy to meet the demands of their coaching responsibilities, or are very misinformed about what coaching is. The submissive-style coach is merely a babysitter—and often a poor one at that.

Cooperative Style (The Teacher)

Coaches who select the cooperative style share decision making with athletes. Although they recognize their responsibility to provide leadership and guide young people toward achieving

the objectives set forth, cooperative-style coaches also know that youngsters cannot become responsible adults without learning to make decisions.

Coaching Styles Evaluated

Which style best describes you: command, submissive, or cooperative? I consider the submissive style to be no "style" at all and urge you not to adopt it. The command style has been prevalent in the past and is commonly seen among professional, college, and high school coaches. Many novice or inexperienced coaches adopt the command style because it is the one they have seen modeled by their own coaches or others. Some coaches adopt this style because it helps them conceal their own doubts about their capabilities. If they don't permit the athletes to question them, if they can avoid explaining why they coach as they do, then their inadequacies won't be uncovered—or so they think!

On the surface the command style appears effective. Good athletic teams need organization. They cannot be run effectively as participant democracies; the team cannot vote on every decision that needs to be made. Indeed, the command style can be effective if winning is the coach's primary objective and if its authoritarian nature does not stifle athletes' motivation. But this risk is one of the major limitations of the command style. Rather than playing because they are intrinsically motivated, athletes may play for the praise of the coach or to avoid his or her wrath. Coaches who use the command style also prevent athletes from fully enjoying the sport. The accomplishments are the coach's, not the athletes'.

The command style is increasingly being rejected today by coaches of young and adult athletes alike, for it treats athletes as robots or slaves, not as thinking human beings. Coaches are recognizing that the command style alienates all but the highly gifted athlete and that it diminishes their own satisfaction in relating to athletes.

The command style is not compatible with the objective of *Athletes First, Winning Second*. If your objective is to help young people grow physically, psychologically, and socially through sport; if your objective is to help athletes learn to make decisions; if your objective is to help young people become independent, then the command style is not for you.

It is obvious by now that I favor the cooperative style of coaching, because it shares decision making with the athletes and fosters the *Athletes First, Winning Second* objective. Some people think adopting the cooperative style means you abandon your responsibilities as coach or that you let athletes do anything they want. That's not the case at all!

Cooperative-style coaches provide the structure and rules that allow athletes to learn to set their own goals and to strive for them. Being a cooperative-style coach does not mean you avoid rules and order; failing to structure team activities is neglecting a major coaching responsibility. The coach faces the complex task of deciding how much structure creates the optimum climate for athletes' development.

Imagine handling a wet bar of soap. If you hold it too tightly, it squirts out of your hands (the command style). If you don't grasp it firmly enough, it slips away (the submissive style). Firm but gentle pressure—the cooperative style—is what is needed. The cooperative-style coach gives direction and instruction when they are needed, but also knows when it is useful to let athletes make decisions and assume responsibility.

We know there is more to being an athlete than just having motor skills. Athletes must be

able to cope with pressure, adapt to changing situations, keep contests in perspective, exhibit discipline, and maintain concentration in order to perform well. These ingredients are nurtured routinely by cooperative-style coaches, but seldom by command-style coaches. The cooperative approach places more trust in the athlete, which has a positive effect on self-image. It promotes openness in the social-emotional climate and improves both communication and motivation. Athletes are motivated not by fear of the coach, but by a desire for personal satisfaction. Thus, the cooperative style is almost always more fun for athletes.

There is a price to pay, however, in choosing the cooperative style of coaching. This style requires more skill on the part of the coach. It means that coaches must be in control of themselves. It means that choices seldom are absolutely right or wrong. Cooperative-style coaches must individualize their coaching much more than command-style coaches. Finally, you may at times have to sacrifice winning in the interest of your athletes' well-being. When I discuss sport psychology and sport pedagogy, I will show you how to use the cooperative style.

Helping Athletes Become Responsible and Independent

I encourage the cooperative style especially because it is conducive to helping athletes learn to become responsible for themselves and therefore more independent. Too many coaches in the quest to win deprive athletes of assuming responsibility for themselves. Coaches deny athletes this opportunity not only by making all the decisions for them in practice and contests, but also by controlling most aspects of their lives to keep them eligible for competition, out of trouble, and financially solvent. Such coaches may claim they are helping their athletes, but more likely they are making certain they don't lose the athletes' services.

The most difficult aspect of coaching is this: Coaches must learn to let athletes learn. Sport skills should be taught so they have meaning to the athlete, not just to the coach. Coaches must learn to involve athletes more in what coaches are teaching them—both the motor and mental aspects. Athletes need opportunities to initiate learning and to make mistakes and learn from them.

Outside of sport, coaches should help athletes become complete citizens—academically, financially, socially. But coaches need to walk a fine line between helping athletes with these aspects of their lives and controlling them. Coaches should help athletes learn the skills of living, but must give athletes enough independence to make mistakes and to learn from them.

Coaches who are successful in helping athletes become responsible and independent are not dictators, nor are they on ego trips. Successful coaches serve as guides and partners in sport and life. Through the courageous act of sharing decision making, coaches can nurture the development of responsible, independent members of society. In the final analysis, this achievement is far more significant than winning any contest.

What Makes a Successful Coach?

In chapter 1, I mentioned that successful coaches must have good knowledge of the sport sciences, sport management, and techniques and tactics. I also stated that successful coaches rank their program objectives in the right priority. And I tried not to be vague about what I thought were the right priorities! In this chapter I have recommended that to be successful, coaches adopt a coaching style compatible with those objectives. Now I will briefly describe three other attributes of successful coaches to which I have alluded:

- Knowledge of the sport
- Motivation
- Empathy

Knowledge of the Sport

There is no substitute for knowing well the techniques, rules, and tactics of the sport you coach. Some people believe this knowledge is less important for teaching beginning athletes than advanced ones but this assumption is false. In fact, to teach the fundamentals well to beginners requires as much knowledge, if not more, than to coach professional athletes. (Actually they require different types of knowledge.)

Not knowing how to teach skills risks injury and frustration from repeated failure for your athletes. The more you know about the basic skills of your sport and about teaching these basics in the proper sequence, the more success and fun you and your athletes will have.

Moreover, your ability to teach these skills will earn you great respect from the athletes, for they value them. This respect gives you credibility that you can use in teaching athletes other important things, such as ethical behavior, emotional control, and respect for others and themselves.

Having once played a sport is, of course, the most common way coaches acquire knowledge about techniques, rules, and tactics. But that may not give you all the knowledge you need, nor does not having played a sport mean you can't acquire the knowledge about it. Most communities have sources of information about a variety of sports. Technique clinics are frequently offered in larger cities—check with your school athletic director or coach or your community youth sport administrator for information. Many books and videos are available for most sports (see Appendix A for resources available from the American Sport Education Program). You can learn, too, by watching other coaches. Just remember that all methods are not appropriate for athletes of different ages or skill levels.

Motivation

You can have all the skills and knowledge in the world, but without the motivation to use them, you will not be a successful coach. You need only to come across a youngster who has the ability but not the motivation to develop into an excellent athlete to see full well the importance of motivation.

Sometimes coaches have the motivation to be successful but not the time. Or rather they don't have sufficient motivation to make the

time for doing what is necessary to be a successful coach. I encourage you to have the motivation; young people need the time.

Empathy

Empathy—what is it? It is the ability to readily understand the thoughts, feelings, and emotions of your athletes and to convey your sensitivity to them. Successful coaches possess empathy. They can understand athletes' joy, frustration, anxiety, and anger. Coaches who have empathy are able to listen to their athletes and express their understanding of what was said. They don't belittle, chastise, or diminish the self-worth of their athletes, because they know how it feels to experience the loss of self-worth. Coaches with empathy more readily communicate respect for their athletes, and in turn receive more respect. Empathy: You need it to be a successful coach!

Your Coaching Philosophy

You now have spent some time thinking about your two most important decisions as a coach: what your objectives will be for your athletes' participation, and what coaching style you will adopt to achieve these objectives. These decisions are fundamental to your coaching philosophy, but a comprehensive philosophy requires much more. The key is to know who you are and to continually evaluate how your coaching experiences fit into your value structure. (You can learn more about developing your coaching philosophy in chapter 1 of *Coaches Guide to Sport Psychology*.)

Now to close Part I, take a few moments to evaluate yourself by completing the questionnaire "What Kind of Coach Am I?"

What Kind of Coach Am I?

Below are seven items that summarize the major issues we have considered in chapters 1 and 2. Circle the answer that best describes you.

1. The order of priority for my coaching objectives is in the best interest of my athletes.
   (1) Seldom   (2) Usually   (3) Always   *3*

2. My usual coaching style is
   (1) Submissive   (2) Command   (3) Cooperative   *2*

3. My motivation to coach is
   (1) Low   (2) Moderate   (3) High   *3*

4. I am able to keep winning in perspective.
   (1) Seldom   (2) Usually   (3) Always   *3*

5. My knowledge of the techniques, rules, and tactics of my sport is
   (1) Weak   (2) Average   (3) Strong   *2*

6. My knowledge of the sport sciences (sport psychology, physiology, etc.) is
   (1) Weak   (2) Average   (3) Strong   *2*

7. My ability to convey empathy is
   (1) Weak   (2) Moderate   (3) Strong   *3*

Now add up the numbers you circled and evaluate yourself according to the following scale.

Total: _____

7-10 points Warning! You are hazardous to the health of young people. Please reconsider your desire to coach or reread this chapter and determine if you can improve your score. If you choose to continue to coach, please read the remainder of this book carefully at least three times.

11-14 points You are on the right track, but you can definitely improve by learning more. Read this book at least twice.

15-18 points You are well on your way to being a successful coach, but there is still room for improvement. Determine where you need to improve and read this book at least once.

19-21 points You're what athletes need. Don't ever quit coaching! You might just read the remaining chapters to see if I made any mistakes!

Part II

Sport Psychology

Sport psychology is concerned with understanding why athletes and coaches behave as they do, sometimes in relation to each other. It is a complex topic because human behavior is complex.

Over the past 20 years, sport psychologists have learned much that is of value to coaches, but coaches have not found it easy to gain access to this information in practical, understandable terms. The four chapters in Part II will help you learn the basics, and when you're ready to learn more I encourage you to read my book *Coaches Guide to Sport Psychology*, the ASEP Master Level text.

Although many aspects of sport psychology will help you become a better coach, none are more vital to coaching than learning how to communicate with your athletes and understanding what motivates them to play sports. In chapters 3, 4, and 5, you will learn about the basics of communication, have an opportunity to evaluate your communication skills, and then learn how to further develop those skills. In chapter 6 you will learn about the complex factors influencing athletes' motivation and, by understanding these factors, how to help athletes optimize their motivation.

Successful coaches are good sport psychologists. They are skillful communicators and motivators. Study Part II carefully to help you become a good sport psychologist and a better coach, but remember that human behavior has few absolutes. These chapters offer recommendations as guidelines, not laws. They must be understood and used not as a replacement for, but in conjunction with, good common sense.

Chapter 3

Evaluating Your Communication Skills

Coaching is communication. Every act of coaching requires you to communicate. Successful coaches are masterful communicators. Did you know that when coaches fail—are fired—it is far more often the result of poor communication skills than a poor win-loss record?

As a coach you must be able to communicate effectively in countless situations, including ones like these:

- When a parent speaks to you about a child not playing enough
- When you explain to athletes how to perform a complex skill
- When you present your team to the school pep assembly
- When you feel compelled to speak to the official who just made a call you're sure was incorrect

The purpose of this chapter is to increase your awareness of the importance of communication in coaching and to help you evaluate your own communication skills. Although coaches must be able to communicate equally well with athletes, fellow coaches, parents, administrators, and the public, I will focus on the communication process between coach and athlete. All of the principles put forth, however, are completely applicable to any communication.

Three Dimensions of Communication

Let's begin with some basics about the communication process. Three dimensions of communication are illustrated in Figure 3.1. First, communication includes not only *sending* messages, but also *receiving* them. Many coaches believe they are quite skilled at sending messages, but they are often weak at receiving

Sending	——————	Receiving
Verbal	——————	Nonverbal
Content	——————	Emotion

Figure 3.1 The three dimensions of communication.

them. Coaches not only must be skillful at sending clear, understandable messages, they need sharp listening skills to understand what athletes are communicating in return.

Second, communication consists of *nonverbal* as well as *verbal* messages. Gestures of hostility, facial expressions of joy, movements of intimidation, and acts of kindness are all forms of nonverbal communication. It is estimated that over 70% of communication is nonverbal. People tend to demonstrate greater control over the verbal than they do the nonverbal, and this is true as well of coaches. Because coaches are often intently observed by players, administrators, and the public, they must be especially attuned to nonverbal communication.

Third, communication has two parts: *content* and *emotion*. Content is the substance of the message, and emotion is how you feel about it. Content is usually expressed verbally, emotion nonverbally. Pressure-packed competitive sports challenge coaches to be in control of both the content and the emotions they communicate.

Coaches are typically more skilled in the sending, verbal, and content dimensions of communication than in the receiving, nonverbal, and emotion ones. But through practice and effort, coaches can develop the latter set of communication skills equally well.

How You Communicate

Communication with your athletes consists of six steps (see Figure 3.2):

1. You have thoughts (ideas, feelings, intentions) that you wish to convey.
2. You translate these thoughts into a message appropriate for transmission.
3. Your message is transmitted through some channel (verbal or nonverbal).
4. The athlete receives your message (if he or she is paying attention).
5. The athlete interprets the message's meaning. The interpretation depends upon the athlete's comprehension of the message's content and your intentions.
6. The athlete responds internally to his or her interpretation of the message.

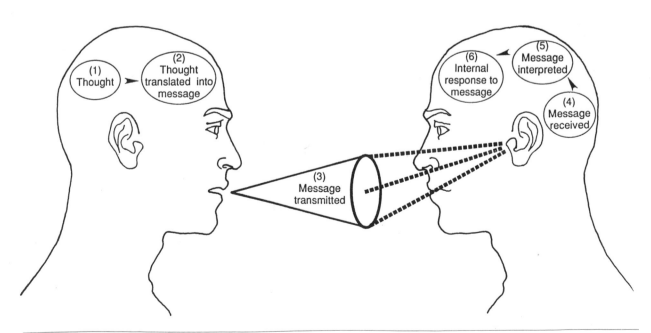

Figure 3.2 The communication process.

Sometimes this sequence of events flows smoothly, with you and the athlete clearly understanding the messages that both of you are sending. But sometimes problems develop in one or more of the six steps. Let's look at two examples.

Example 1

COACH (shouting): *"How many times do I have to tell you to use a cross-over step?"*

JOHN (meekly): *"Sorry. I forgot."*

COACH'S INTENTION: *To give John feedback about a technique error and to encourage him to remember the right technique in the future.*

JOHN'S INTERPRETATION: *"He thinks I'm lousy. I want to do it right, but there are so many things to remember. The harder I try, the more nervous I get and the more mistakes I make. I wish he'd get off my back."*

What went wrong in this communication? The coach's intention was good: to give constructive feedback. But the method he chose to transmit the message was not, in either content or emotion. John received the message negatively, and instead of its helping him to correct his error, it added to the pressure he felt.

The same message expressed to another athlete, however, might be interpreted to mean, "Darn, I did it wrong again. Coach is upset. I don't blame him. I ought to be getting it right, and he's just trying to help." Even though the coach was not skillful in delivering his message, the second athlete understood the coach's intent and interpreted the message positively.

Example 2

COACH: *"I thought you really played well today, Denise."*

DENISE (with a tone of disbelief): *"Uh, huh. Thanks."*

COACH'S INTENTION: *To praise Denise for a good performance in hopes that she will repeat it.*

DENISE'S INTERPRETATION: *"Coach is only saying that because we won. When we lose, even if I play well, she yells at me and the team."*

The coach's thoughts were good, and she accurately transmitted the message she intended to send. Unfortunately, Denise's perception of the message's intent, not the content, was skewed. This may have been the result of previous messages that led her to believe that winning is more important to the coach than the players are. Because the coach had lost credibility with Denise, a well-intended message was received negatively.

Why Communication Is Sometimes Ineffective

The reasons for ineffective communication between coach and athlete include any or all of the following:

- The content you wish to communicate may be wrong for the situation.
- The transmission of the message does not communicate what you intend it to because you lack the verbal or nonverbal skills needed to send the message.
- The athlete doesn't receive the message because he or she isn't paying attention.
- The athlete, lacking adequate listening or nonverbal skills, misinterprets the content of the message or fails to understand it.
- The athlete understands the message content, but misinterprets its intent.
- The messages sent are inconsistent over time, leaving the athlete confused about what is meant.

Ineffective communication is not always the fault of the coach; the problem may lie with the athlete, or with both coach and athlete. But you can do much to avoid problems of miscommunication by developing your own skills. We will discuss these skills after you evaluate yours.

Evaluating Your Communication Skills

From interviewing and observing hundreds of coaches, I have identified eight communication skills that coaches need most. These eight skills, or rather the lack of them, are presented here through caricatures. Read the description of each coach and then rate yourself on the skills discussed. Circle the number that best describes you. If you have not coached before, answer according to how you communicate in a leadership position.

Pretentious Pete

Never admitting to an error, Pretentious Pete finds he doesn't get the respect he demands because he doesn't show any for his athletes. When he speaks, they tune out because what he says never amounts to much or is negative. Pretentious Pete has not yet learned that he cannot demand respect; it must be earned.

Do you have credibility with your athletes, or are you like Pretentious Pete? Rate your credibility.

1	2	3	4	5
Very low				Very high

Norma Negative

Most of the words and actions of Coach Norma are negative, sometimes almost hostile. She frequently criticizes her athletes, increasing their self-doubts and destroying their self-confidence. Norma Negative is slow to praise, as if she believes it is not "coach-like" to say a kind word. When an infrequent kindness is uttered, it is usually overshadowed by other negative comments.

Are you primarily positive in the messages you deliver, or are you like Norma Negative? Rate the degree to which your messages are positive or negative.

1	2	3	4	5
Negative				Positive

John (The) Judge

John Judge continually evaluates his athletes instead of instructing them. When a player errs, The Judge, as he is known, places blame rather than providing feedback or information about how to correct the error. When the players do well, The Judge cheers them on but doesn't

know how to instruct them to achieve advanced skill levels.

Do you give ample feedback and instructions, or are you like The Judge? Rate the extent to which the content of your communication is high in information or high in judgment.

1	2	3	4	5
High in judgment				High in information

Fred Fickle

You are never sure what Coach Fred Fickle will say next. Today it's one thing, tomorrow

another. Last week he punished Bill for fighting but not Mike, his star goalie. He tells players not to argue with the officials, but he does so regularly.

Are you consistent in your communication, or are you like Coach Fred Fickle? Rate the consistency of your communication.

1	2	3	4	5
Inconsistent				Consistent

Gabby Gayle

Coach Gabby is the most loquacious person you ever met. She gives instructions constantly during practice, and when she's not yelling advice to her players during the contest, she is muttering to herself on the sidelines. She is so busy talking that she never has time to listen to her athletes. It has never occurred to her that her players might like to tell her something rather than always being told.

Are you a good listener, or are you like Coach Gabby? Rate how good a listener you are.

1	2	3	4	5
Not good				Very good

Stan Stoneface

Stan Stoneface never shows emotion. He doesn't smile, wink, or give his athletes pats on the back. Nor does he scowl, kick at the dirt, or express disgust with them. You just don't know how he feels, which leaves his players feeling insecure most of the time.

Do you communicate nonverbally, or are you like Stan Stoneface? Rate your nonverbal communication skills.

1   2   3   4   5
Weak   Strong

Professor Gobbledygook

The Professor just isn't able to explain anything at a level understandable to her players. She talks either above their heads or in such a roundabout way that they are repeatedly left confused. In addition, The Professor, who is used to dealing with abstractions, is unable to demonstrate the skills of the sport in a logical sequence so that the athletes can grasp the fundamentals. Are you able to provide clear instructions and demonstrations, or are you like

Professor Gobbledygook? Rate your ability to communicate instructions.

1   2   3   4   5
Weak   Strong

Jerry Jellybean

Coach Jellybean just doesn't seem to understand how the principles of reinforcement work. Although he gives frequent rewards to his ath-

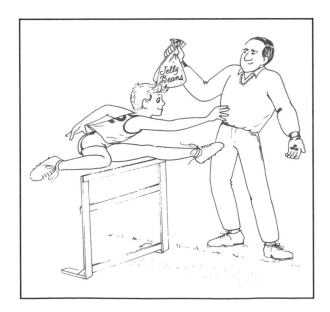

letes, he reinforces the wrong behavior at the wrong time. When faced with misbehavior, he either lets the infraction pass or comes down too hard.

Do you understand the principles of reinforcement, or are you like Coach Jellybean? Rate your skill in rewarding and punishing athletes.

1	2	3	4	5
Not skilled				Highly skilled

Coaches' Communication Awards

Now add up your eight ratings and write your total score here. _____ Find the category your score falls into and accept the award you deserve.

36-40 Golden Tongue Award. You are destined for success.

31-35 Silver Tongue Award. Good, but you can be better. Read on.

26-30 Bronze Tongue Award. OK, but you have plenty of room for improvement. Read on carefully.

21-25 Leather Tongue Award. Given to those who frequently place their feet in their mouths.

8-20 The Muzzle Award. Until you improve, wear it. Read the next two chapters every night for a month.

If you are not a recipient of the Golden Tongue Award, the next two chapters will help you develop the communication skills you need to earn it.

Chapter 4

Developing Your Communication Skills

In the last chapter you evaluated yourself on eight communication skills that are vital for coaching success. In this chapter I present information to help you improve six of these communication skills:

- Developing credibility when you communicate
- Communicating with a positive approach
- Sending messages high in information
- Communicating with consistency
- Learning how to listen
- Improving your nonverbal communication

The seventh skill, applying the principles of reinforcement, is discussed in chapter 5, and the eighth, instructional communication skills, is examined in chapter 9.

Developing Credibility When You Communicate

Can you think of someone who has very little credibility with you—a fellow worker, a neighbor, a politician perhaps? Do you know coaches like Pretentious Pete? You don't put much stock in almost anything those persons say. Why not? It's probably for one of these following reasons:

- You believe they are not knowledgeable about what they say.
- Usually what they say makes little sense or is of no importance to you.
- They often distort things or simply lie, so you have little trust in them.
- They constantly speak negatively.
- They speak to you as though you were stupid or less important than they are.

Your credibility is probably the single most important element in communicating effectively with your athletes. Your communication credibility is reflected in your athletes' attitudes about how much they can trust what you say. At the outset, youngsters will give you credibility simply because you occupy the prestigious role of the coach. From then on, however, it is up to you whether you maintain and build this credibility or diminish it. You can build credibility in a number of ways:

- By being a cooperative-style coach
- By being knowledgeable about the sport, or at least honest about whatever knowledge you possess
- By being reliable, fair, and consistent
- By expressing warmth, friendliness, acceptance, and empathy
- By being dynamic, spontaneous, and open
- By using the positive approach—the next communication skill I'll discuss

Communicating With a Positive Approach

One of the most important skills you can learn, for coaching or any other aspect of life, is to communicate with a positive approach. The

positive approach emphasizes praise and rewards to strengthen desirable behaviors, whereas the negative approach uses punishment and criticism to eliminate undesirable behaviors. The positive approach helps athletes value themselves as individuals, and in turn it gives you credibility. The negative approach increases athletes' fear of failure, lowers their self-esteem, and destroys your credibility.

Using the positive approach does not mean that every message should be full of praise and gushy compliments. Too much praise leaves youngsters doubting the sincerity of your messages and reduces the value of your rewards. It also does not mean that you turn your back on athletes' misbehaviors. At times athletes should be punished, but even punishment can be given in positive ways (see chapter 5).

The positive approach is an attitude that you communicate in both verbal and nonverbal messages. It is an attitude that communicates a desire to understand, an acceptance of others, and an expectation of mutual respect. It is the attitude of a cooperative-style coach.

Bad Habit

But why do so many coaches behave like Coach Norma Negative? One reason is that they have simply fallen into the habit of telling athletes only what they do wrong rather than what they do right. Is this true of you? Think not only about the content of your messages, but about the emotion they express as well.

Breaking habits is difficult, especially ingrained habits such as the negative approach often is. If you are uncertain whether you use the positive or negative approach, or about the degree to which you use them, ask a fellow coach or friend to observe you for a constructive evaluation. *Warning:* This takes courage and a very good friend.

If you know you are in the habit of using the negative approach, you need to do three things to change to the positive approach.

- You must want to change.
- You must practice the positive approach not only when coaching but in all your communication. The positive approach is often most difficult to use with those to whom

you are closest, so practice with a friend or significant other. (Who knows, learning to be a successful coach may help your relationship.)

- You need to monitor yourself or get help from someone whom you will permit to tell you when your bad habit rears its ugly head.

Unrealistic Expectations

Another reason coaches use the negative approach is that they have unrealistic expectations about acceptable and unacceptable behaviors. Sometimes coaches forget that 14-year-olds are not 28-year-olds, or that one 16-year-old is not as skilled as another. When coaches have unrealistic expectations, they seldom view their athletes as successful. If coaches communicate their judgment of failure to athletes—and sometimes they do—athletes will feel frustrated and unaccepted.

It is important for coaches to have realistic goals not only about their athletes' performance abilities, but about their emotional and social behavior as well. Remember, it's natural for kids to "horse around" and have fun.

Being realistic in your expectations and remembering that people aren't perfect will help you be Coach Paula Positive rather than Norma Negative. And just remember: If athletes behaved perfectly they wouldn't need you as a coach!

Short-Term Success

The third reason coaches use the negative approach is that they honestly believe it gets the best results, possibly because so many college and professional coaches model it.

The negative approach does work. It can help athletes learn the skills you want and motivate them to achieve. But when criticism is frequent or continuous, the strong negative emotion it creates in athletes often also interferes with learning and motivation. Athletes start playing it safe, taking as few risks as possible to avoid the coach's wrath. The negative approach is effective only for a limited time; after a while athletes "turn off" and the coach loses credibility.

Sending Messages High in Information

Some coaches seem to think that a whistle, a cap, and the title "Coach" qualify them as John (The) Judge. They constantly give verdicts to their players, telling them whether they did something right or wrong—usually wrong. But it's not enough to tell athletes that they did something wrong; they need specific information about how to do it right. Successful coaches are not judges; they are skilled teachers.

Some coaches communicate like The Judge for the same reasons they adopt the negative approach—sheer habit and imitation of other coaches who engage in this practice. Other coaches become judges because they lack the technical knowledge of the sport necessary to give athletes the information they need. When this occurs, coaches may become judges to cover up for their own deficiencies. Command-style coaches are especially likely to communicate like The Judge.

Being a judge is dangerous; it assumes you always know what is good and bad, right and wrong. Too often judgmental coaches label something as bad or wrong, only to learn later that *they* were wrong.

Let's take an example: A boy is late to practice, so the coach makes him run 15 laps as punishment without letting him explain. Later, the coach learns that the boy's mother was late getting home from work and that he was responsible for babysitting his little sister. Under these circumstances, the athlete behaved responsibly.

Consider another example: After a girl strikes out by swinging at a ball a foot over her head, the coach yells, "For Pete's sake! What's wrong with you? Don't you know a ball from a strike?" Although the batter made a poor judgment in swinging, the coach's message is highly destructive and provides no useful information to the athlete.

Remember, sport tends to evaluate participants enough through competition. Usually athletes know when they have played poorly. Who needs to be told you made an error when the ball goes between your legs and the game-winning run scores? Athletes need some room to make mistakes—that's part of learning.

Provide evaluation when it's clear that athletes don't know what is correct or incorrect. If a behavior is good, praise them for it and tell them what is good about it. And if it's wrong, give them specific instructions on how they can improve.

The last season that legendary coach John Wooden coached UCLA basketball, two psychologists recorded all of his verbal communication with the team during practice. Nearly 75% of Wooden's messages gave specific instructions to the athletes. His remaining messages were 12% requests to hustle, 7% praise, and 6% scolds.

Another study found that Little League baseball coaches who provided specific instructions were evaluated more positively by their players than were coaches who gave general encouragement. This was especially true for players who were low in self-esteem. Youngsters so dearly want to learn sport skills that not only will they respect you for helping them learn, they will respect themselves for their learning.

Habitually communicating in judgmental language also tends to make people around you feel uneasy. They become cautious, even defensive, always wondering how you are evaluating them at the moment.

Although there is a time to communicate your evaluations, they should not dominate your interactions with athletes. Save evaluation for instructional sessions when you can put it into a constructive framework.

One final caution: Do not evaluate the athletes' selves. Instead, evaluate their behavior. Rather than saying to a youngster who has made a tactical error, "What's wrong with you, Joe?" it is better to say, "That was the wrong decision, Joe," commenting only on the behavior.

Communicating With Consistency

Communicating with consistency while coaching is a real challenge, for each of us has a little Fred Fickle in us. It is so easy to preach one thing and do another, or to do one thing one day and the opposite the next. Or your brain may tell you to say one thing verbally, but your emotions express something else nonverbally. When youngsters receive these mixed messages, they become confused.

Look at it from the perspective of the athletes. A coach asks them to show emotional control when playing, but then she throws a temper tantrum at an official. A coach asks players to respect their teammates, but treats them without respect. A coach teaches that physical fitness is important, but does nothing to keep himself fit. A coach tells athletes to be self-confident, then turns around and destroys their feelings of self-worth by yelling at them for their errors. A coach penalizes a bench sitter for being late to practice, then ignores the same behavior by a starting player. When coaches behave in this way, it is no wonder that youngsters think of them as hypocrites!

Failing to keep your word is another form of inconsistency that can have devastating results. For example, you may promise your athletes a reward for a good practice but then fail to deliver. A few such occurrences and athletes learn not to trust you, which lessens your control over them. If you don't provide a promised reward, you lose the power to use rewards in the future, and you may be forced to resort to punishment as a means of control.

Athletes, however, are not out looking for inconsistencies in their coaches. Because of the great respect they have for the position of coach and those who hold it, most athletes begin with the attitude that the coach can do no wrong, and are therefore slow to see inconsistencies. Because of this deep trust, it can be a shattering experience when an athlete does recognize a coach as a hypocrite or a liar.

Of course, few coaches intend to be inconsistent or hypocritical; usually they are just careless. It is easy for coaches like Fred Fickle to forget the influence they have on the athletes under their charge. It is so important to remember this: *Be as good as your word.* If you want your communication to positively control and influence your athletes, then you must be consistent.

Learning How to Listen

Are you a good listener? How much of what is said do you actually hear? If you are like most untrained listeners, you probably hear less than 20%.

Although listening may seem deceptively easy, it is actually difficult. Coaches are often poor listeners because (a) they are so busy "commanding" that they never give others a

chance to speak, and (b) they assume that they know it all and that their players have nothing to say that needs to be heard. "Athletes should be seen and not heard" seems to be their attitude.

Poor listening skills cause breakdowns in the communication process. After repeatedly failing to get you to listen, athletes will simply quit speaking to you, and are less likely in turn to listen to you. Coaches who are poor listeners also often have more discipline problems. Athletes may misbehave just to get your attention—a drastic way to get you to listen.

Improving Your Listening Skills

You can do a number of things to improve your listening skills.

- Most important, of course, is recognizing the need to listen.
- Concentrate on listening. This means you must give your undivided attention to what is being said. Has someone ever accused you of not listening? Although you may have heard the words and could repeat them, you were not really listening. What the accuser sensed was that you were not "with" her or him psychologically.
- When you listen, search for the meaning of the message rather than focusing on the details. Especially in disagreements, we are inclined to listen for and respond to details that we can attack or refute, failing to listen to the major point of the message.
- Avoid interrupting your athletes. We sometimes interrupt others because we anticipate what they will say and complete their thoughts for them. Then we respond to what we thought they were going to say, but perhaps later discover that the intended message was quite different. Many of us also interrupt those who speak slowly, because we are too impatient to hear them complete their messages. Remember that you can listen considerably faster than a person can speak.
- Respect the rights of your athletes to share their views with you. It is important to listen to not only their fears and problems, but also their joys and accomplishments.

Your response to athletes' views is important in shaping their attitudes.

- Repress the tendency to respond emotionally to what is said (but don't be like Stan Stoneface). Think about why an athlete said what he or she did and how you can respond constructively. (I know this is easier said than done, but isn't that true of most complex skills?)

Active Listening

Educators distinguish between two types of listening—passive and active. Passive listening is what we typically think of as listening—being silent while another person speaks. Although passive listening is sometimes desirable, it has limitations in that the speaker is not sure whether you are paying attention or really understand what he or she is saying. Although passive listening communicates some degree of acceptance, athletes may think you are evaluating them. Silence does not communicate empathy and warmth.

Active listening, as opposed to passive, silent listening, involves interacting with athletes by providing them with proof that you understand. Here are some examples of how it works:

One of your players is worried about meeting your expectations for an important game.

PLAYER: *"Do you think we can beat this team?"*

COACH: *"They are a pretty good team, but we have a good team too."*

PLAYER: *"But what if we don't play well?"*

Now you must interpret these questions. Is she really worried about the team winning, or is she worried that she may not be able to play well enough herself? In active listening, you don't just guess at your player's meaning; you work to find it out. You do this by feeding back to the player what you think she means:

COACH: *"Are you worried how you might play?"*

PLAYER: *"Well, a little."*

COACH: *"As long as you try to do the best you can I'll always be proud of you."*

The coach's reassurance lets the player know that her acceptance on the team is not contingent on her performing well, but only on her trying. Here is another example:

GYMNAST: *"What's the worst injury you've seen on the high bar?"*

COACH: *"I saw a fellow fly off and break his neck."*

The coach may have answered the question without thinking about what was really being asked. The player may have been expressing concern about the possibility of his own injury. Active listening by the coach might change the conversation this way.

GYMNAST: *"What's the worst injury you've seen on the high bar?"*

COACH: *"I've not seen too many injuries. Are you worried about getting hurt?"*

GYMNAST: *"Sometimes I think about it."*

COACH: *"With today's better equipment and the use of a spotter, the chances of serious injury are really small."*

Active listening is a tremendous skill that brings together many of the ideas we have discussed in this chapter. Active listening, however, works only when you convey that you accept your athletes' feelings and that you want to understand and help. Otherwise, you will come across as insincere, patronizing, or manipulative. Because active listening lets athletes know that their ideas and feelings are respected and understood, they will be more willing to listen to you in return.

Improving Your Nonverbal Communication

If you have ever needed to communicate with someone who does not speak your language, you know both how important and how effective nonverbal communication can be. It is estimated that 70% of our total communication is nonverbal. In the world of sport, especially team sports, numerous situations arise in which effective nonverbal communication is essential to good performance. It is equally important to your role as a coach.

Categories of Nonverbal Communication

Nonverbal communication, or what is also called body language, falls into five different categories.

- *Body motion*: Includes gestures and movements of the hands, head, feet, and entire body. A tilt of the head, a furrow of the brow, or a shift of the eyes can communicate a great deal in the context of an ongoing interaction.
- *Physical characteristics*: Physique, attractiveness, height, weight, body odors, and the like. Your own physical condition, for example, communicates the importance you give to physical fitness—not only for young people, but for persons throughout their lives.
- *Touching behavior*: Pats on the back, taking someone's hand, putting an arm around a player's shoulders, and so forth. These are appropriate touching behaviors that communicate positive reinforcement.
- *Voice characteristics*: The voice's quality—its pitch, rhythm, resonance, inflections, and so on. Often it is not what we say but how we say it that conveys our real message. For example, the comment "You played a nice game today, Bill" can be said sincerely, with looks of approval and voice qualities that tell you truly mean it. Or it can be spoken sarcastically and with a sneer, indicating you mean just the opposite.
- *Body position*: The personal space between you and others and the position of your body with respect to theirs. An example of communication through body position is the "cold shoulder," which tells you someone does not want to talk with you.

Are you aware of each of these dimensions of nonverbal communication, and are you effective at both sending and receiving nonverbal messages through each? Whatever skills you have in nonverbal communication were prob-

ably derived in on-the-job training—the job of daily living. Teaching nonverbal communication skills by written or spoken words alone or learning nonverbal skills without practicing them is not easy.

Your first step, then, is to recognize the importance of nonverbal messages in the total communication process. One way to develop nonverbal skills is to observe the feedback others give you as you both send and receive nonverbal messages. The value of that feedback depends on your sensitivity and receptivity to it. The more sensitive you become to nonverbal cues, the more likely you are to be able to express your feelings and attitudes nonverbally and to understand athletes' feelings and attitudes. This is an important aspect of developing empathy, which was discussed in chapter 2.

You as a Model

Once again, keep in mind that your every action in and out of the playing arena is a form of nonverbal communication. I reemphasize this point because many coaches forget that all their behaviors communicate, not just the good ones.

Perhaps one of the most important things you communicate by your actions is respect, or lack of it, for people and the sport. How you walk, how you approach others, your gestures, and both what you say and how you say it all convey your attitudes about sportsmanship and other people. Impressionable athletes who hold you in high esteem are influenced by everything you do.

Your actions can teach athletes much more than just the skills and rules of your sport. Lead the way in congratulating opposing teams after both victories and losses. Show athletes how you want them to behave after having played well or poorly, after having won or lost. Model how they should react when you think the team has been treated unfairly.

Young people, I find, are more influenced by what I do than what I say. You know the axiom: Actions speak louder than words. So if you want your athletes to display good sportsmanship, it is not enough to just tell them—you must show them!

The "house rules" developed by the YMCA say it well:

Speak for yourself
Not for anybody else.

Listen to others
Then they'll listen to you.

Avoid put-downs
Who needs 'em?

Take charge of yourself
You are responsible for you.

Show respect
Every person is important.

Note. From "Introduction: The YBA Philosophy," *YBA Director's Manual* by J. Ferrell (Ed.), 1977. Copyright 1977 by the YMCA of the USA. Reprinted by permission.

Key Points to Remember

1. Having credibility with your athletes is essential for effective communication.

2. You can establish and maintain your credibility by being a cooperative-style coach, being knowledgeable about the sport, being fair and consistent, being friendly and dynamic, and using the positive approach.

3. By using the positive approach, you emphasize praise and rewards to strengthen desirable behaviors rather than relying on punishment to eliminate undesirable ones.

4. You can be more helpful to your athletes and maintain better relationships with them by not judging them constantly. Instead, give specific instructions on how to perform skills.

5. You can avoid destroying your credibility and confusing your athletes by being as consistent as possible in your communication.

6. You can improve your listening skills by not always being the one to talk and by recognizing that what your athletes have to say is important.

7. When you communicate to athletes that you heard and understood what they said, you are using active listening skills.

8. Being skilled in nonverbal communication skills like body motion and position, touching behaviors, and voice characteristics is highly important to your role as a coach.

9. Your every action is a potentially important nonverbal message because your athletes see you as an example of how to behave.

Chapter 5

Principles of Reinforcement

Two terms are often used to describe the consequences arising from our behaviors: reinforcement and punishment. When the consequence of an action causes it to be repeated, that consequence is *reinforcing*. Reinforcement can be either positive (giving a reward) or negative (taking away something undesirable). The key is that the likelihood of the desired behavior is increased by the consequence. For example, an athlete is more likely to hustle in the future if he or she is named Practice Player of the Day (positive reinforcement) or is exempted from putting away equipment (negative reinforcement).

When the consequence of a behavior decreases the likelihood of its being repeated, the consequence can be seen as *punishment*. In this instance, a player who failed to hustle might be required to put all of the day's equipment away. This concept of behaviors and their consequences is the first principle of reinforcement.

This and other reinforcement principles can be a valuable part of your communication skills if you apply them correctly. Although the principles themselves are easy to understand, they require skill to apply with athletes. They are easier to use with laboratory pigeons and rats, with whom these principles were first developed, but humans don't behave like pigeons or rats (not most of the time anyway).

Why are the principles of reinforcement more complex to use with humans? One reason is that we do not necessarily react to positive and negative reinforcements in the same way. For example, having to sit on the bench for swearing may be punishment for some players, but it may provide others the recognition they seek from teammates. In short, reinforcements are relative, not absolute. What's reinforcing to me may not be to you.

Also, reinforced behavior cannot always be repeated at will if the athlete does not possess sufficient skill. For example, being praised for hitting a home run may instill a desire to hit more home runs, but this does not mean a player can do so repeatedly. (In fact, the player may begin to seek more positive reinforcement by swinging for the fence too often, to the detriment of his or her overall hitting.)

A third reason the principles of reinforcement are complex is that you must consider all the reinforcements available as well as how people value them to understand how they will behave. For example, though your spouse may yell at you for spending too much time with your team, this negative reinforcement may be far less than the positive reinforcement you get from coaching the team.

I want to impress upon you the complexity of the principles of reinforcement because some psychologists have touted behavior modification as a quick fix. This is untrue! Yet your understanding and application of what is known about behavior modification can be a valuable part of your communication skills.

For the principles of reinforcement to work, you must be consistent and systematic in their use. If you fluctuate in what you reinforce, athletes will behave erratically in response to your mixed messages. In the remainder of this chapter I present the principles of reinforcement most relevant for coaches. For these principles to become effective communication tools, you must study and practice them regularly.

Using Rewards

Rewarding athletes is not as easy as it sounds. You must first consider what behaviors deserve rewards. Next you need to distinguish planned rewards from accidental reinforcements. Finally, you must understand the principles affecting the frequency, timing, and type of your rewards. Let's look at each of these issues.

What Should I Reward?

Reward the performance, not the outcome.

When a player hits a line drive to the shortstop, who makes a great diving catch, the performance is good (line drive), the outcome is not (an out). When another batter hits an easy fly ball to the leftfielder, who loses the ball in the sun, and the batter ends up with a double, the performance was weak (easy fly ball), but the outcome was good (a double). Rewarding the double reinforces luck, not skill, and not rewarding the line drive may cause the player to change his hitting method in search of a more favorable outcome.

Although coaches may know they should reinforce performance and not outcome, in the midst of competition this principle is too often forgotten. Coaches begin to think about winning and losing (the outcome) more than about how athletes are playing (the performance).

Reward athletes more for their effort than for their actual success.

When athletes know you recognize they are trying to hit the ball, make the shot, or run as fast as possible, they do not fear trying. If athletes know you will only reward them when they succeed, then they may begin to fear the consequences of failing. This causes anxiety in some players.

Reward little things on the way toward reaching larger goals.

If you wait to reward only the achievement of major goals, you may never reward a youngster; reward intermittent steps. (See the section on shaping on pp. 38-39).

Reward the learning and performance of emotional and social skills as well as sport skills.

Reward your athletes for showing self-control, good judgment, and the ability to handle responsibility (but you have to give them responsibility first). Reward them, too, for displaying sportsmanship, teamwork, and cooperation.

Accidental Reinforcements

Sometimes athletes' behaviors are reinforced accidentally. For example, after once pitching a no-hitter in baseball I noticed a flat rock just behind the pitching rubber. For the next 10 years I placed a similar rock in the same position behind the rubber before each game, but I never pitched another no-hitter. You see how superstitions can be created in sport. Athletes may attribute their performance to behaviors or objects that were accidentally associated with their performance, but in no way caused it. These superstitions are hard to die, which attests to the power of the principles of reinforcement.

How Often Should You Reward?

Reward frequently when youngsters are first learning new skills.

Generally, the greater the frequency, the faster the learning. One caution, though: Rewards given insincerely or too freely lose their value. Recognize that when athletes are learning, reinforcement and punishment are information. They tell your athletes exactly what you like or dislike, and the informational content of the consequence becomes even more important than the reinforcement or punishment itself.

Once skills are well learned, you only need to reinforce them occasionally.

Be careful, though, not to make the mistake of taking your athletes' positive behaviors for granted, forgetting to reinforce them for their accomplishments. Athletes have been known to intentionally perform poorly to get recognition from the coach.

When Should You Reward?

When athletes are first learning, reward as soon as possible after correct behaviors or their approximations occur.

Shouting "good" as a player executes a skill correctly is what reinforces, not a postpractice

debriefing an hour later. However, once skills have been learned and as athletes mature mentally, it is less important to give rewards immediately after appropriate behaviors occur—with one exception. Athletes low in self-confidence always need to be reinforced soon after making appropriate responses.

Reward athletes only when they have earned it.

When players have made repeated errors, cost the team a victory, or had an all-around miserable day, praising them for some insignificant behavior makes them feel misunderstood and subtly manipulated. When players have poor performances, communicate empathy (understanding) but not sympathy (feeling sorry for them). All athletes have bad days, and they will appreciate that you understand that.

What Type of Reward Should I Use?

The rewards that are reinforcing are unique to each athlete. Coaches commonly err by selecting rewards that *they* like rather than ones the athlete likes. Athletes will reveal what rewards they like if you observe them or ask them. In Table 5.1, I list in three categories some common rewards that athletes frequently like. Find out which of these rewards and others are reinforcing for each of your athletes.

Table 5.1 Extrinsic Rewards

Tangible rewards	People rewards	Activity rewards
Trophies	Praise	Playing a game rather than doing drills
Medals	Smiles	Being able to continue to play
Ribbons	Expressions of approval	Taking a trip to play another team
Decals	Pats on the back	Getting to take a rest
Money	Publicity	Changing positions with other players
T-shirts	Expressions of interest	

The rewards in Table 5.1 are called *extrinsic rewards* because they come from you or another external source. Most athletes respond positively to extrinsic rewards like praise and recognition for their accomplishments. These rewards are powerful reinforcers that you can skillfully use to shape and motivate behaviors.

Another group of rewards, though not directly available for you to use, also have powerful effects on athletes. These rewards are *intrinsic* to playing the sport. They include such things as feeling successful, having a sense of pride in accomplishment, and feeling competent. Although you cannot directly offer these rewards to your athletes, by belittling them or not recognizing their accomplishments you may deny them the opportunity to experience intrinsic rewards.

Successful coaches emphasize playing for intrinsic rewards over extrinsic ones. Intrinsic rewards are self-fueling, that is, self-satisfaction and pride lead to greater desire to succeed without any extrinsic rewards. Coaches who emphasize extrinsic rewards may find that athletes want ever-increasing amounts, until the demand exceeds the supply. The trophies can be only so big; the social recognition can be only so great.

Athletes who play only for extrinsic rewards seldom maintain the long-term motivation needed to succeed in sport. Athletes who most enjoy sports and who excel in them for an extended period of time are motivated primarily by intrinsic rewards.

Coaches can help athletes be more intrinsically than extrinsically motivated in two ways. By administering extrinsic rewards effectively through the principles of reinforcement, coaches can help athletes experience the intrinsic rewards of enjoyment, satisfaction, and feeling competent. Also, coaches should help athletes understand that while extrinsic rewards are nice to earn, the intrinsic rewards associated with participation are of greater value.

Shaping Behavior

How can you reward behavior if the appropriate behavior does not occur? How do you reward hitting the ball over the net if the ball never makes it over? Think small initially, and reward the first signs of behavior that approximate what you want. Then reward closer and closer approximations of the desired behavior. In short, use your reward power to shape the behavior you seek.

If you were teaching children who fear the water to swim, you wouldn't expect them to jump into the deep end and begin swimming. Instead, you would use a series of small steps—introducing them to the water in the shallow end, getting them to put their faces in the water, teaching them to float, to glide, to kick, and to breathe. Slowly, with your patience and their practice, the youngsters learn to swim. The same procedure works with many other sport and social skills.

In fact, among the fundamental skills of coaching is this very process of shaping behavior, which involves two aspects: (a) the sequence of steps used to develop the skill and (b) the principles of reinforcement for shaping the behavior. To become a good coach you must learn the steps for teaching the skills of your sport. This involves knowing how to break complex sport skills into smaller parts to optimize learning and then helping athletes combine these parts into complex skills.

In addition to knowing the steps for teaching sport skills, you must know the principles of shaping—the rules that govern the learning process. Too many coaches almost ignore these principles of learning in favor of studying the techniques for performing skills. Here are six additional guidelines to help you teach sport skills more effectively through shaping (adapted from Karen Pryor's *Don't Shoot the Dog*).

- Break skills into small steps with a high probability of being performed correctly so that success can be rewarded. Then gradually combine these steps into more complex skills. Or in a sport where speed, distance, or time is involved, raise the criteria for rewards in small enough increments that your athletes have a realistic chance for success. Continual progress, even in very small steps, is better than pushing too fast for perfect performance.

- Develop one component of a skill at a time; don't try to shape for two components simultaneously. For example, putting in golf requires accuracy in both distance and direction. You can learn to putt more accurately if you work first on one and then the other. When athletes fail to make progress in learning a skill after considerable practice, it often is because they are trying to improve two or more things at once. When you see this, look for a way to break the skill down further so you can isolate a single component.

- Always put the current level of performance onto a variable schedule of reinforcement before moving on to higher performance levels. This is an essential rule for shaping. Karen Pryor explains why:

  > Once a behavior is learned, you must start reinforcing it only occasionally rather than constantly to maintain it at the present level. . . . When you can afford to reinforce a given level of behavior only occasionally and still be sure of getting it, you will be free to use your reinforcements only on the best examples of the behavior. This selective reinforcement will "drive" the norm, or average behavior, in the direction of the improvement you're looking for. (p. 58)

- When teaching a new skill or combining simpler skills into complex ones, temporarily relax standards for achieving rewards. When athletes attempt to learn new skills that are to be integrated with existing ones, the old well-learned skills may temporarily fall apart.

- If one shaping procedure is not working, try another. I'm amazed at how some coaches stick with systems that clearly aren't working. Remember, athletes differ in how they learn, and there is no one correct way to learn any sport skill. No matter what the skill, there are many successful ways to shape the behavior you desire.

- If performance of a well-learned skill deteriorates, review the shaping. A skill may temporarily suffer for many reasons; the best way to restore it is to go back to the basics.

Dealing With Misbehavior

Principles of reinforcement can serve you in ways beyond skill development. As experienced coaches know, athletes will misbehave at times; it's only natural. You can respond with a positive or negative approach to this undesirable behavior.

Extinction

One technique of the positive approach is to ignore the misbehavior. That is, neither reward nor punish it. This is called *extinction*, which can be effective under certain circumstances. In some situations, punishing young people's misbehavior only encourages them to act up further because of the recognition they get. Ignoring misbehavior teaches youngsters that it is not worth your attention.

Sometimes, though, you cannot wait for a behavior to fizzle out. When athletes cause danger to themselves or others or disrupt the activities of others, immediate action is necessary. Tell the offending athlete that the behavior must cease and that punishment will follow if it does not. If the athlete does not stop misbehaving after the warning, punish.

Extinction also does not work well when a misbehavior is self-rewarding. For example, you may be able to keep from grimacing if a youngster kicks you in the shin, but he or she still knows you were hurt. Therein lies the reward. In these circumstances, it is also necessary to punish the undesirable behavior.

Extinction works best in situations where young people are seeking recognition through mischievous behaviors, clowning, or grandstanding. Usually if you are patient, their failure to get your attention will cause the behavior to disappear.

On the other hand, be alert that you don't extinguish desirable behavior. When youngsters do something well, they expect to be positively reinforced. Not rewarding them causes them either to discontinue the behavior or to interpret your silence as negative reinforcement.

Punishment

Some educators say we should never punish young people but should only reinforce their positive behaviors. They argue that punishment does not work, that it creates hostility and sometimes develops avoidance behaviors that may be more unwholesome than the original problem behavior. It is true that punishment does not always work and that it can create problems when used ineffectively, but when used appropriately, punishment is effective in eliminating undesirable behaviors without creating other undesirable consequences. Coaches must be able to use punishment effectively, because it is impossible to guide athletes through positive reinforcement and extinction alone. Punishment is part of the positive approach when these guidelines are followed:

- Use punishment in a corrective way designed to help athletes improve now and in the future. Do not use punishment to retaliate and make you feel better.
- When violations of team rules or other misbehaviors occur, impose the punishment in an impersonal way. Shouting or scolding athletes indicates your attitude is one of revenge.
- Once a good rule has been agreed upon, ensure that athletes who violate it experience the unpleasant consequences of their misbehavior. Don't wave punishment threateningly over their heads. Just do it.
- Give an athlete one warning before delivering punishment.
- Be consistent in administering punishment.
- Don't pick punishments that cause you guilt. If you cannot think of an appropriate consequence right away, tell the athlete you will talk with him or her after you think about it.
- Once the punishment is completed, don't make athletes feel they are in the doghouse. If you have dealt with them fairly and are comfortable with your decision, make them feel valued members of the team again.
- Be certain that what you think is a punishment is not perceived by the athlete as a positive reinforcement.
- Never punish athletes for making errors when they are playing.
- Never use physical activity—running laps or doing push-ups—as punishment. To do so only causes athletes to resent physical activity, something we want them to learn to enjoy throughout their lives.
- Punish sparingly. Constant punishment and criticism cause athletes to turn their interests elsewhere and to resent you as well.

One effective form of punishment is the time-out. Athletes usually want to participate, to be active. When misbehaviors occur, isolate offenders by having them sit well away from all other players. Instruct other players to completely ignore offenders during time-outs, which may last from 5 to 30 minutes.

Reinforce Yourself

You have learned much about the principles of reinforcement in this chapter, the emphasis throughout being on applying these principles in coaching your athletes. Yet you can apply these principles to yourself as well. It is easy when coaching to become so busy moving from task to task, looking ahead to the next contest, that you neglect to reflect on your accomplishments. You may not always get the rewards you deserve from others, so take time now and then to reward yourself.

Key Points to Remember

1. Learning to use the principles of reinforcement effectively is a valuable communication skill.
2. When the consequence of doing something results in a tendency to repeat the behavior, reinforcement is involved. When it results in a tendency not to repeat the behavior, the consequence can be seen as punishment.
3. Reward the performance, not the outcome.
4. Reward athletes more for their effort than for their actual success.
5. Reward little things on the way toward reaching larger goals.
6. Reward the learning and performance of emotional and social skills as well as sport skills.
7. Reward frequently when youngsters are first learning new skills. Reward occasionally once skills are well learned.
8. Reward as soon as possible after the correct behavior or its approximation occurs.
9. Give rewards only when athletes have earned them.
10. Use a variety of extrinsic rewards, being careful not to deny athletes the opportunity to experience the intrinsic rewards of playing.
11. Teach athletes that intrinsic rewards are of greater value than extrinsic ones.
12. Ignoring athletes' misbehavior when they are seeking attention (extinction) teaches them that unacceptable behavior is worthless.
13. You must learn to use punishment effectively because it is impossible to guide young athletes through the use of positive reinforcement and extinction alone.

Chapter 6

Understanding Motivation

When speaking with coaches, I am often asked two questions about motivation:

- Why are some athletes so motivated and others so unmotivated?
- How do we motivate our athletes to be the best they can be?

I often answer by asking a question of my own:

- How do I motivate you to be the best coach you can be?

I don't ask this question to beg the issue. Instead, I want coaches to examine their own motives in hopes of discovering a basic principle of motivation:

**People are motivated
to fulfill their needs.**

If you understand what your athletes' needs are, and you are able to help them fulfill these needs, you possess the key to their motivation.

You should meet with each of your athletes to learn specifically why he or she has decided to play the sport this season. The more you understand why your athletes are playing the sport, the easier it will be to understand their behavior throughout the season—and to deal effectively with any motivational problems.

Sport psychologists have learned that the two most important needs of young athletes are

- to have *fun*, which includes the need for stimulation and excitement, and
- to feel *worthy*, which includes the need to feel competent and successful.

In this chapter, you will learn how you can help your athletes satisfy these two needs.

Needs, Rewards, and Motivation

By helping athletes meet their needs through participation in sports, coaches can influence players' motivation. Different things are motivating, or rewarding, to different players at different times. Trophies, medals, money, praise, and trips to a tournament are examples of *extrinsic rewards*—i.e., they are provided to players by others. *Intrinsic rewards* are those things that are internally satisfying when players participate in sport. Having fun and feeling competent and successful are intrinsic rewards.

Extrinsic rewards such as recognition from others and trophies can be motivating, but over time, these rewards often become less and less valued while intrinsic rewards become more and more valued. Unlike extrinsic rewards, intrinsic rewards are self-fueling. You as the coach do not need to provide them. What you must do, however, is create the conditions in practice and games that provide each player the opportunity to attain their own intrinsic rewards. Coaches who are great motivators know that they do not motivate players. Instead they create the conditions or the climate where players motivate themselves. And they skillfully use extrinsic rewards to help build intrinsic motivation. When players fail to achieve the intrinsic rewards of having fun and feeling worthy, they will lose motivation to play and are likely candidates to quit. I'll discuss the specific use of rewards in more detail later in this chapter, but for now remember that intrinsic rewards are the best motivators for the long term. Now let's take a closer look at the two most important intrinsic rewards: having fun and feeling worthy.

Need for Fun

Why do people play—not only sports, but play at all types of things? This question has intrigued philosophers and scientists alike for centuries. Only recently have we begun to know why. Each of us is born with the need for a certain amount of stimulation and excitement—what is often called the need for arousal, and what I simply call fun.

Optimal Arousal

When our arousal level is too low, we become bored and seek stimulation. We call this "playing" when the primary purpose of the stimulation we seek is to have fun. Sometimes, however, we find ourselves in situations that are more arousing than we would like, and we become fearful or anxious. Then we try to decrease our arousal however we can.

In other words, people have a need for an optimal amount of arousal—not too little and not too much (see Figure 6.1). This optimal level of arousal differs from person to person. We all know individuals who seem to thrive on a great deal of stimulation and others who are quite content with only a little.

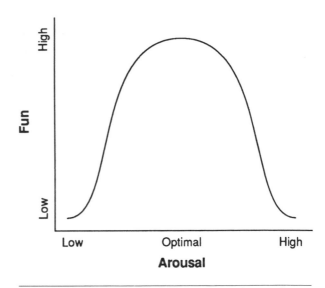

Figure 6.1 Relationship between fun and arousal.

Not only do optimal arousal levels differ from person to person, there are periods during the day when each of us prefers more or less arousal. If you normally hold practice in the late afternoon and switch to an early morning practice, you will see that this is true.

The Flow Experience

What makes optimal arousal so desirable? Why do we seek it out? The answer lies in how we feel when experiencing optimal arousal, what one scientist has called the "flow experience." *Flow* occurs when we are totally immersed in an activity; we lose our sense of time, feeling everything is going just right because we are neither bored nor anxious.

When experiencing flow, our attention is so intensely centered on the activity that concentration is automatic. When in flow we are not self-critical because our thoughts are totally focused on the activity. Because we are neither bored nor threatened, we feel in control of ourselves and our environment. One athlete explained it this way: "You are so involved in what you are doing you aren't thinking of yourself as separate from the game."

The flow experience is so pleasing that it is intrinsically rewarding. We will engage in activities for no other reason than to experience flow, because it is fun. Sports, of course, are popular with young people because they increase arousal to an optimal level, and therefore are fun.

But not always. For some young people, sports simply aren't fun—they don't increase arousal enough or they create too much. Coaches are greatly responsible for making sports either dull and monotonous or so threatening that athletes feel anxious. Here, then, are some ways you can help young athletes experience optimal arousal and thus flow.

- Fit the difficulty of the skills to be learned or performed to the ability of the athletes. The task must be difficult enough to be challenging, but not so difficult that they see no chance of success. This very important point is illustrated in Figure 6.2. If athletes' abilities are high but the challenge is low, they will be bored. If athletes' abilities are low and the challenge is high, they will experience anxiety. But if their abilities are reasonably close to the challenge at hand, athletes are more likely to experience flow and have fun.
- Keep practice stimulating by using a wide variety of drills and activities to work on

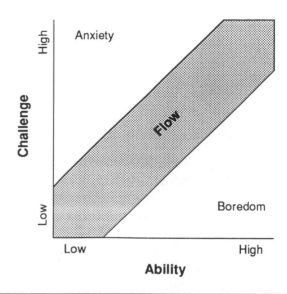

Figure 6.2 Increase the probability of experiencing flow by matching the challenge of the task to the ability of the athletes.

skills. Moreover, let the youngsters help design some of the activities that will help them learn new skills.

- Keep everyone active rather than standing around for long periods waiting their turns. By following the suggestions presented later in this chapter and in Part III, you can make practices nearly as much fun as games.
- Avoid constant instruction during practices and games. Give athletes time when they don't have to pay attention to you and can get absorbed in the activity. Your yelling instructions constantly from the sidelines during contests does not permit athletes to experience flow.
- Do not constantly evaluate your athletes (as we discussed in chapter 4). The flow experience cannot occur when young athletes are being continually evaluated or made to evaluate themselves—whether the evaluation is positive or negative. There is a time for evaluation, but it is not when the contest is in progress.

Other Sources of Fun

Besides seeking optimal arousal and flow as ways to have fun, athletes find fun in being with other young people who share their interest in sport. Coaches who fail to recognize this reason for participation may inadvertently create a team environment that denies athletes the opportunity to enjoy social interaction with teammates. This may happen by overregimenting practices and contests, which greatly reduces opportunities for players to socialize and to engage in spontaneous and frivolous activities, both enjoyable aspects of sport participation. Coaches may also create such a competitive environment on the team that the players come to feel they are playing *against* each other rather than *with* each other.

The results of several studies examining the reasons athletes quit sports reveal how important fun is to athletes. The most frequent reasons given for quitting were these:

- I found other activities more enjoyable.
- I lost interest.
- I didn't play enough.
- It was all work and no fun.
- I didn't like the coach.

Take the fun out of participating in sport and you'll take the athletes out of the sport. And if they don't quit entirely, their motivation will be seriously impaired.

So how do you motivate athletes? One key way is to help them meet their need for fun by making the sport experience challenging and exciting, not boring or threatening. Another is to help athletes meet their need to feel worthy.

Need to Feel Worthy

We all share basic needs to feel we are competent, to experience some success, to feel we are worthy persons. In our society we quickly learn that our worth depends largely on our ability to achieve. Children as young as 5 years old understand this, and with respect to sports, they translate it to mean

Winning = Success
Losing = Failure

Consequently, participation in sports is potentially threatening to athletes, because they equate their achievement with their self-worth. To win is to be successful, to be competent, to be a worthy person; to lose is to be a failure, to be incompetent, to be unworthy.

When athletes experience a reasonable amount of success it reinforces their sense of competency, which in turn reinforces their further pursuit of excellence. But if athletes fail to experience success, they may blame themselves for failure and attribute it to a lack of ability. With repeated failure, athletes may decide that if they cannot be certain of success, then at least they will protect their dignity by avoiding failure. Emerging then from early success and failure experiences are two very different types of athletes: one who is motivated to achieve success and another who is motivated to avoid failure.

How Winners Think

Success-oriented athletes engage in drastically different reasoning about winning and losing than do failure-oriented athletes. Wendy Winner, a model success-oriented athlete, sees winning as a consequence of her ability, which inspires her confidence in the ability to succeed again. When Wendy encounters an occasional failure, she is likely to blame it on insufficient effort; this robs failure of its threat to her self-worth because it doesn't reflect on her ability. To succeed, Wendy believes, she simply needs to try harder. Thus, failure increases her motivation rather than reduces it.

For Wendy, an occasional failure is inevitable to playing sports and is not a fault within herself. Thus she is willing to take reasonable risks of failure—risks that are necessary to achieve success. Wendy and athletes like her direct their energies to the challenges of the sport rather than to worry and self-doubt. They take credit for their success and accept responsibility for their failure. This is a healthy attitude, one you want to foster in your athletes.

How Losers Think

In contrast, meet Larry Loser, a failure-oriented athlete who is filled with self-doubts and anxiety. Larry tends to attribute his failures to a lack of ability and his infrequent successes to luck or to weak or incompetent opponents. Such thinking produces disaster; Larry blames himself for failure, yet takes little or no credit for his successes.

Athletes like Larry Loser come to believe they are powerless to change their plight because their early sport experiences have convinced them that no matter how hard they try, the outcome is always the same: failure. They conclude, "Well, trying didn't help, so my problem must be low ability. So why try?"

Because sport so clearly identifies winners and losers, failure-oriented athletes like Larry Loser have little choice in protecting their self-worth but to not participate or to maneuver to avoid failure. Although many such young people choose not to play sports, parental, coach, and peer pressure keep Larry playing, and he has learned to protect his threatened self-worth by playing the "token effort" game.

Rather than putting forth maximum effort, Larry almost unknowingly gives only token effort so that if he fails he can say he just didn't try hard enough. Why does he do this? Because if he gave maximum effort and failed, others would know he didn't have ability. Not to put forth maximum effort is less threatening, in Larry's thinking, than to have others discover that he lacks ability, which he equates with being unworthy. The tragedy of choosing not to put forth full effort, however, is that it increases the likelihood of failure in his desperate attempt to avoid it.

But the tragedy becomes even greater. Coaches usually reward effort because it seems fair—not everyone is skilled, but everyone can try. Yet for Larry Loser and failure-oriented athletes like him, to put forth full effort risks discovery that he lacks ability, so he doesn't. His failure to do so after encouragement from the coach leaves the coach puzzled or angry. The coach attributes it to a lack of motivation, but in reality Larry is far from unmotivated. Instead, he is highly motivated—to avoid the threat to his self-worth. It becomes a vicious circle.

Another common ploy of Larry Loser is to stay well-armed with excuses. "I was robbed by the ump." "My leg hurts." "I don't have the right shoes." "Something got in my eye." "I don't feel good." And on and on.

Coaches with Larry Losers on the team often try to solve the problem by arranging some successful experiences for them. But once athletes begin thinking like Larry, they tend to reject success, which mystifies and frustrates coaches even more. Although failure-oriented athletes want to accept success to enhance their self-worth, they reject it because they fear they will be expected to succeed again. They may so fear impending success that they purposely perform so as to avoid winning. Not until failure-oriented athletes can learn to accept their own successes is there hope of enhancing their confidence in their ability and thus self-worth.

You will find both Wendy Winners and Larry Losers on your team, as well as players with

I HOPE THE GAME DOESN'T DEPEND ON MY FOUL SHOTS... I'LL BLOW IT!

varying degrees of both athletes' characteristics. It's especially important that you recognize Larry Loser and those athletes who tend to be like him, so that you do not misdiagnose their motivational problems. Although the problems of Larry Loser may seem unsolvable, they are not. I will describe a solution shortly.

Self-Fulfilling Prophecy

Just as athletes assign reasons to their successes and failures, so do their coaches. These reasons—attributions—in turn lead coaches to have certain expectancies of their athletes, which if conveyed may affect their motivation to perform. Doug's case illustrates how this can occur.

Doug had played basketball satisfactorily last season under Coach Hanson, who encouraged him frequently in practices. This season, playing for a new coach, Mr. Johnson, Doug just couldn't get "on track." Never too confident, Doug began attributing his poor playing more and more to a lack of ability. He sensed that Coach Johnson didn't think very much of his ability because he spent little time helping him and encouraged him far less than Coach Hanson had. As Doug's self-doubts increased, he played even worse, and slowly began giving up. After a while, even an occasional good performance and encouragement from Coach Johnson were shrugged off as flukes.

When Doug failed to respond to his encouragement, Coach Johnson became discouraged with Doug's lack of effort, attributing it to laziness. Finally, in hopes of instilling the missing enthusiasm, Coach Johnson took Doug off the first team and sent him to the second. Now convinced more than ever that he was worthless, Doug quit the team.

Coach Johnson told Doug clearly that he had lowered his expectations by sending Doug to the second team. But coaches often communicate expectancies in more indirect ways. For example, they more often reward players for whom they have higher expectancies and spend less time with those for whom they hold low ones ("Why waste my time with this kid?"). Coaches may have closer relationships with their better players, permitting them to have more input about what the team is doing. Although these messages may be indirect, youngsters easily pick them up.

When these expectations are conveyed to athletes, they may become self-fulfilling prophecies; that is, athletes may act in ways to fulfill what coaches have prophesied for them. These expectancies-turned-prophecies may, of course, be either positive or negative.

As we would expect, failure-oriented athletes are most vulnerable to negative expectations. When such athletes, already full of self-doubt, perceive that the coach has low expectations of them, it only affirms what they suspected: "Coach thinks I'm no good, so why should I try?" When positive expectancies are communicated to failure-oriented athletes, they reject them for the same reasons they reject occasional success.

On the other hand, success-oriented athletes—whose self-confidence is strong—most often reject negative expectancies conveyed by coaches or others. Instead of fulfilling what has been prophesied for them, they work even harder to show that others are wrong. Positive expectations, of course, strengthen success-oriented athletes' beliefs in their own abilities.

By now you may be apprehensive as to whether you can do anything positive to influence the motivation of your athletes. The success-oriented athlete apparently doesn't need to be motivated by you, and it seems you can do little to help the failure-oriented youngster. But don't despair—read on!

naturally raise their goals a little to keep the activity challenging. So without adult intervention, young people tend to adjust their goals to compromise two opposing forces: setting goals low enough to avoid repeated failures yet high enough to be challenging. The result is that youngsters tend to keep their goals near the upper limits of their current abilities. Through this self-regulated learning, mistakes are seen not as failures, but as a natural part of the learning process.

How Athletes Learn to Fear Failure

Organized sports are very different from the backyard sports most children first learn to play. Some differences are obvious: uniforms and regulation playing surfaces, rules and officials to enforce them, spectators and scorekeepers, and you: their coach. But you should be aware of other subtler differences. These differences are root causes for athletes learning to fear failure, and understanding these causes will help you appreciate what I prescribe for overcoming motivation problems.

Emphasis on Performance, Not Learning

When young people are left to themselves to learn sport skills—without coaches, peer pressure, or spectators—they have an ingenious way of avoiding failure. Each time they do not obtain their goals, they simply lower them slightly, learn from their mistakes, and try again. A few practices and adjustments like these and success is virtually guaranteed. But they'll never achieve any difficult goals that way, you say? Wrong! When young people do succeed, they

But when young people begin playing organized sports, evaluation becomes public and official. The emphasis shifts from learning to performing. The mistakes and errors that are a natural part of the learning process may now be misinterpreted as failure to perform.

Unrealistic Goals

Something else happens when young people begin playing organized sports. They quickly observe that coaches prefer superior performance and tend to give greater recognition to the athletes who excel. Envious of their superior skills and desirous of similar recognition, less-skilled players attempt to be like the more-skilled ones. In doing so, these young athletes may set their goals too high for their present levels of skill.

And if athletes themselves don't set unrealistically high goals, coaches or parents sometimes do. Coaches, for example, may set the same performance goal for the entire team, but set it so that it is only within the grasp of the few best athletes. And parents who aspire to be stars vicariously through their children may also make the mistake of convincing their children to pursue goals that are beyond their reach.

Regardless of who is at fault, the result is the same—unrealistically high goals almost guarantee failure. They cause young people to play in order to attain the goals set for them by others, not to meet their own. Tragically, young athletes do not realize such goals are unrealistic; they believe their performance is out of kilter and mistakenly accuse themselves of not having ability and thus being unworthy.

Extrinsic Rewards and Intrinsic Motivation

Third, when young people begin playing organized sports, the sport skills that they have been trying to master for the sheer satisfaction of doing so (intrinsic reward) become subject to an elaborate system of extrinsic rewards. Trophies, medallions, ribbons, plaques, all-star team recognition, and so on may cause a change in why young people play sports—a

change that is not desirable. Rather than playing sports for self-satisfaction, athletes may begin to play primarily to earn these extrinsic rewards. The extrinsic rewards are given not for achieving personal goals, but for goals set by others. Once again, the result can be that athletes are influenced to pursue unrealistic goals and doom themselves to failure.

Overemphasis on extrinsic rewards has another negative consequence—it may result in an addiction. Hooked on the glitter of trophies and medals, such addicted athletes continually want more and bigger rewards to feed their growing habits. When the gold is no longer offered or within their capability to achieve, they see no value in continuing to participate.

How many athletic "junkies" are there? How often do trophies and medals (extrinsic rewards) undermine athletes' intrinsic motivation to play sports? We don't really know, but it need never happen if we help young athletes understand the meaning of these rewards.

Because extrinsic rewards can undermine intrinsic motivation does not mean that extrinsic rewards should never be given. As I noted in chapter 5, extrinsic rewards, when properly used, are excellent incentives for motivating

athletes who are struggling to learn sport skills. And, of course, we all like to be recognized for our achievements and to have mementos of past accomplishments.

Our concern is not with the extrinsic rewards as such, but the meaning athletes attach to the rewards. Coaches should continually let athletes know by word and deed that extrinsic rewards are only tokens of recognition for achieving the larger goal of acquiring and performing sport skills. These tokens do not make one person better than another, they do not guarantee future success, and they are not the primary reason for playing sports. Coaches should help athletes remember instead that the most important reason for participating in sport is the participation itself. When athletes understand this message, extrinsic rewards are unlikely to undermine their intrinsic motivation to play the game.

In summary, you now know three reasons why participation in organized sports may cause athletes to fear failure.

- The mistakes and errors that are a natural part of the learning process are misinterpreted as failures.
- Due to competitive pressures, athletes set unrealistically high goals that, when not attained, lead them to conclude that they are failures.
- Athletes begin to play for extrinsic rewards rather than to attain personal goals.

Enhancing Athletes' Motivation

Nearly everything I have suggested in previous chapters and discuss in chapters to come will be directly or indirectly helpful in enhancing the motivation of your athletes. Your decision to put the well-being of athletes first and winning second, along with adopting a cooperative rather than a command style, are essential prerequisites. The communication skills discussed in chapters 3 through 5 also are integral to successfully motivating athletes. And I have specified some ways that you can help athletes fulfill their need to have fun. What remains is to find a way to help each young athlete feel worthy. The goal is a difficult one; you must find a way for every athlete to experience suc-

cess in an environment where actual winners are few and losers are many.

The simplest solution is to eliminate losing; in that way, the vicious cycle that produces failure-oriented athletes could never begin. Of course, this is not realistic; besides, learning to lose has positive aspects. The solution lies in changing the way athletes (and coaches) learn to interpret their losing experiences.

Success Is Not Winning

The basic problem in this issue of worthiness is that athletes learn from parents, coaches, teammates, and the media to gauge their self-worth largely by whether they win or lose. The devastating result of this belief is that athletes can maintain their sense of self-worth only by making others feel unworthy. The most important thing you can do as a coach to enhance the motivation of your athletes is to change this yardstick of success.

Winning is important, but it must become secondary to striving to achieve personal goals. Success must be seen in terms of athletes exceeding their own goals rather than surpassing the performances of others.

This is the cardinal principle for understanding motivation in sport. Read it again: *Success must be seen in terms of athletes exceeding their own goals rather than surpassing the performances of others*. It is a principle easy to state, but oh so difficult to achieve. If your coaching helps athletes understand and implement this principle, you will do more to help them become excellent athletes—and successful adults—than by any other coaching action.

These personal goals are specific performance or behavioral milestones rather than goals concerning the outcome of winning or losing. The following are examples of personal goals that focus on performance and other behavioral objectives:

- My goal is to jump 6 inches further than I did last week.
- I want to improve my backhand so that I can hit it deep into the corner 75% of the time.
- I want to learn to relax more and enjoy playing.

Setting Realistic Personal Goals

By placing greater emphasis on achieving personal goals, athletes can gain control over an important part of their sport participation—their own success. The important thing here is to set realistic goals, for by doing so athletes ensure themselves a reasonable degree of success. With all the competitive pressures and parental and teammate influences, it is the coach who must help each athlete keep a realistic perspective in setting goals suitable for him or her alone.

Team goals should not be confused with these personal goals. In fact, team goals are hardly needed if one of the personal goals of each team member is to make the best contribution possible, given his or her current skill level. Setting team goals that state that we want to win so many games or this or that championship are not useful, and they actually undermine the type of personal goals I have just described. Team goals more appropriately deal with learning to play together as a unit, respecting each other, having fun, and playing with good sportsmanship. Accomplishing these team goals and each individual's personal goals is

more important than winning. Besides, when athletes achieve both individual and team goals, winning usually takes care of itself.

Consequence of Setting Personal Goals

When winning the game becomes secondary to achieving personal goals, athletes are much more motivated to practice. Practices provide athletes opportunities to work toward their personal goals with assistance from the coach. Contests are viewed not as the end-all, but as periodic tests along the way toward achieving personal goals. Athletes do not judge themselves as having succeeded or failed on the basis of whether they have won or lost, but in terms of achieving the specific performance and behavioral goals they have set.

Evidence from many sources indicates that not only outstanding athletes but also less successful ones who have most enjoyed and benefited from sport hold this viewpoint. They focus on personal goals, not the defeat of others. The consequence of this perspective is incredibly positive. When athletes are allowed to set their own goals, guided by the coach when necessary to make sure they are realistic, they become responsible for their own progress. They feel in control and take credit for their successes and responsibility for their failures. As I stated earlier, this is the first step toward helping motivate athletes.

Coaches need good judgment to help athletes set realistic goals, for they must be able to assess each athlete's skill level. And this brings up another crucial point, one you perhaps have thought about while reading this chapter.

Recognizing Athletes' Limitations

Athletes do not always perform poorly because they lack motivation. Poor performance may be a signal that personal limits have been reached, that athletes are performing up to their ability. Neither increased effort nor all the confidence in the world will improve their ability to perform.

Athletes must learn to gracefully accept their limitations without undermining their motiva-

tion to participate. No one is perfect, yet many athletes are threatened by imperfect performance, especially when coaches, parents, and teammates make them feel perfection is necessary to feel worthy.

Many athletes need help in learning to face their limitations without devaluing themselves. Coaches, rather than conveying the nonsense that every athlete can become a superstar or a professional, will help athletes mature more by encouraging them to seek out and discover for themselves their limits. Only in this way can athletes learn to maintain realistic goals. But if coaches make athletes believe that they have no limits, that to accept limits is loathsome, then athletes will be pushed to unrealistic goals, to eventual failure, and perhaps even to personal injury.

Experiencing Success

When coaches help athletes set realistic goals, athletes inevitably experience more success and feel more competent. By becoming more competent, they gain confidence and can tackle skills of moderate difficulty without fearing failure. They discover that their efforts do result in more favorable outcomes and that falling short is most likely caused by insufficient effort. Realistic goals rob failure of its threat. Rather than indicating that athletes are not worthy, failure indicates they should try harder.

De-emphasize winning and re-emphasize attaining personal goals. This principle is the key to meeting athletes' needs to feel worthy—not only to maintain their self-worth but to develop it further. It is this principle that is essential to enhancing the motivation of all young athletes.

From Motivation to Anxiety

My concern to this point has been exclusively with maintaining and increasing motivation, because we know being motivated is essential to performing well and enjoying participation. Some coaches wrongly believe the more motivation the better, but athletes can be too motivated or aroused.

Arousal-Performance Relationship

Just as there is an optimal level of arousal for having fun, there is an optimal level of arousal for performing well (see Figure 6.3). When athletes are aroused too little or too much, they do not perform as well as they might; but if they are aroused just the right amount, their performance can be the best.

This optimal arousal level varies for different sport skills. As shown in Figure 6.4, high precision sport skills requiring fine motor control,

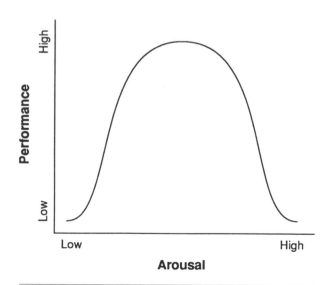

Figure 6.3 The inverted U relationship between arousal and performance.

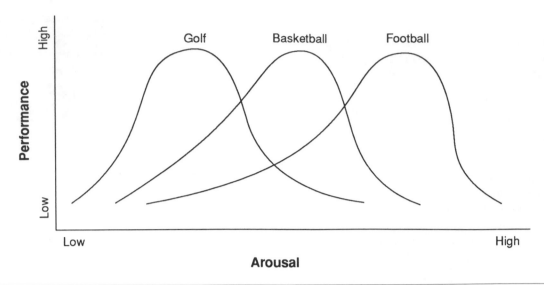

Figure 6.4 Optimal arousal levels for peak performance in different sports.

such as putting in golf or any skill in the shooting sports or bowling, are best performed with lower levels of arousal; sports such as basketball, baseball, and volleyball are played better at slightly higher levels of arousal; and skills requiring large muscle movements, like weight lifting or tackling and blocking in football, are best done with even higher levels of arousal. Optimal arousal levels also differ from athlete to athlete. One athlete may perform a sport skill better with considerably less arousal than another.

If some motivation is good, why isn't more better? When athletes are too motivated or aroused, they become anxious and worried about whether they will be able to succeed—especially failure-oriented athletes. Anxiety causes muscles to tense, so athletes' movements are not as smooth and easy as when their muscles are more relaxed. Players think about how they are doing rather than concentrating on just doing. Consequently, their attention is not well centered on the contest, and they may feel out of control.

As you probably recall, these conditions are precisely the opposite of those necessary for experiencing flow. Athletes perform their best—have their peak performances—when they are in the flow state, which by definition means they are optimally aroused.

Therefore, just as you must help your athletes increase their motivation to an optimal level, you must also help them decrease it when they are too anxious. To do so, you need to understand why they become anxious.

Causes of Anxiety

The fundamental cause of anxiety in sport is athletes' becoming uncertain about whether they can meet the demands of coaches, parents, peers, or themselves when meeting these demands is important to them. The more uncertainty athletes have and the more important an outcome is to them, the greater their anxiety.

Some coaches fail to understand this, and instead of helping athletes to feel less uncertain, they make them feel more so. Some coaches, for example, keep athletes uncertain about whether they will make the team or the starting lineup or get to play at all. Others continually remind their players about the uncertainty of winning and make them feel especially uncertain about their individual capabilities. The coach, along with parents and teammates, may also make athletes feel insecure about their social status or importance on the team. Coaches often create these feelings of uncertainty, intending not to make athletes feel anxious but to motivate them. Unfortunately, these coaches do not understand the motivation process discussed in this chapter.

Many factors make sport important to athletes. As we have already seen, winning itself has a great deal of importance because athletes link winning with their self-worth. In addition, publicizing the outcome of the game, adding pageantry to the game, and, of course, offering all types of extrinsic rewards increase the game's importance.

Some coaches seem particularly insensitive to the emotional states of athletes and thus do not recognize the need to reduce the anxiety of some athletes by decreasing the uncertainty and importance of the game. Instead, they give a traditional pregame pep talk that reminds athletes of the importance of the game and the uncertainties associated with competition. For insufficiently motivated athletes, a pep talk may increase arousal toward the optimal level. For athletes who are already optimally aroused, this additional hype may push them beyond their optimal arousal level, creating anxiety. And for already anxious athletes, it is petrifying!

Most coaches probably give pep talks out of tradition and to help alleviate their own anxiety. Unfortunately, they do more harm than good. Pep talks fail because they do not address the needs of individual athletes. Although one athlete may need a coach's oratorical inspiration, another may need reassurance.

You can help overly anxious athletes alleviate their anxiety by finding ways to reduce both the uncertainty about how their performance will be evaluated and the importance they attach to the game. We already have discovered one powerful way to do this. Helping athletes change the criterion for evaluating themselves from winning to achieving their realistic personal goals goes a long way toward removing the threat that causes anxiety. With an emphasis on personal goals, athletes are not attempting to defeat an opponent of uncertain ability, but only to achieve their own performance goals. When athletes do not link their self-worth to winning and losing, sports are defused of their threat and athletes do not fear failure.

Key Points to Remember

1. Athletes are motivated to play sports to fulfill their need for fun and to feel worthy.

2. People need optimal amounts of arousal.

3. When one is optimally aroused, the "flow experience" is more likely to occur.

4. You can help athletes experience optimal arousal and thus flow by matching the difficulty of the skill to the ability of the athlete, keeping practices varied and all players active, and avoiding continually instructing and evaluating your athletes.

5. Sports are potentially threatening to young athletes because athletes equate their achievement with their self-worth.

6. Success-oriented athletes see winning as a consequence of their ability, blaming failure on insufficient effort.

7. Failure-oriented athletes attribute losing to a lack of ability and infrequent wins to luck, thus blaming themselves for losing yet not taking credit for winning.

8. Failure-oriented athletes attempt to protect their self-worth by putting forth only token effort so others will not discover their feared lack of ability. Coaches often mistake this lack of effort as a lack of motivation, but in actuality, failure-oriented athletes are highly motivated to avoid the threat to their self-worth.

9. Coaches develop expectancies of athletes that, when conveyed, may become self-fulfilling prophecies.

10. Failure-oriented athletes are most vulnerable to coaches' negative expectancies.

11. Athletes learn to fear failure because

    • the mistakes and errors that are a natural part of the learning process are misinterpreted as failures;
    • competitive pressures result in youngsters' setting unrealistically high goals that assure failure; and
    • athletes begin playing for extrinsic rewards rather than to attain personal goals.

12. The most important way you can enhance your athletes' motivation is to teach them that success means achieving their personal performance goals rather than the goals of others.

13. You can play a vital role in helping athletes to set realistic goals, those that motivate athletes to achieve their finest but to recognize their limitations as well.

14. Athletes perform best when they are optimally aroused or motivated. Too little or too much arousal impairs performance.

15. Optimal arousal differs from skill to skill and from athlete to athlete.

16. Athletes become anxious when they are uncertain about whether they can meet the demands placed on them when meeting these demands is important to them. The greater the uncertainty and the more important the outcome, the greater the anxiety.

17. You can help alleviate athletes' anxiety by decreasing uncertainty and helping reduce the importance of the outcome.

Part III

Sport Pedagogy

Chapter 7
PLANNING FOR TEACHING

Chapter 8
HOW ATHLETES LEARN

Chapter 9
TEACHING SPORT SKILLS

Pedagogy means teaching, and *sport pedagogy* refers to the science and art of teaching sport skills—not specific skills such as dribbling, throwing, or tumbling, but the process that coaches use to teach all types of skills. From the study of sport pedagogy we know better how successful coaches organize for the season, select and sequence the specific skills they teach, provide verbal instructions, demonstrate skills, and give feedback. We can also learn about other actions that the most successful coaches use to help athletes learn and improve their skills.

Good coaching is good teaching. And what is good teaching? It involves all that you have learned in Parts I and II—the right philosophy, good communication skills, understanding athletes' motivation, and a knowledgeable, motivated, and empathic coach. These are all important, but to be a good teacher you need more.

First, you need to know your subject matter very well. There is no substitute for a thorough understanding of the techniques, tactics, and knowledge associated with your specific sport. But you need to know more than being able to apply these skills as an athlete. You need a deeper understanding. You need to be able to take apart and put back together the techniques and tactics—to see them from different angles, to apply, adapt, integrate, and critically evaluate them for each athlete.

Coaches who are master teachers do far more than just present the techniques and tactics; they provide their athletes with real understanding about them. They help them understand how each technique and tactic fits into the total picture of the sport. They strive to provide them with insight so they can make intelligent decisions about how to perform. With better understanding, athletes are able to take greater responsibility for their own learning.

In Part III you will learn what master coaches and sport scientists have learned about how to best organize and teach sport skills. In chapter 7, you will learn how to develop the instructional plans that are so essential to a successful season. In chapter 8, I will tell you what we know about how athletes learn, which if properly applied will help you be a more effective teacher. And in chapter 9, you'll learn the specific steps for teaching sport skills effectively, including how to help athletes correct errors with useful feedback.

Chapter 7

Planning for Teaching

Some coaches don't like to plan for the teaching part of their jobs; they are active people and prefer the hands-on coaching of their athletes and the competition. Yet failing to plan is planning for failure. Regardless of the competitive level at which you coach, your knowledge of the sport, or your years of experience, you need an instructional plan. Without a plan you won't know where you're going, and thus you might wind up where you don't want to be.

In this chapter you will learn how to develop two types of plans:

- a plan for the season
- plans for each practice

Coaches need to do additional planning, but you will learn about that in chapter 14, "Team Management." In this chapter the planning pertains entirely to teaching and practicing techniques, tactics, and other knowledge areas associated with the sport.

Benefits of Planning

If you're like most coaches, you already know that planning is a good idea. But who has time to plan! I hope *you* do, because the time you give to planning will save you time later—and it will make you a better coach.

A season plan helps to ensure that you will have time to teach the key skills and strategies for the season. It helps you to keep on track, as well as to keep in mind what's important and not so important to do. A season plan also pays off over the course of many seasons. It's a framework for evaluating the past seasons and developing a better plan for the next season.

Gathering Basic Information for Developing a Season Plan

✔ How many practices will you have over the entire season?

✔ How many contests will you have over the entire season?

✔ What special events (team meetings, parent orientation sessions, banquets, tournaments, etc.) will you have and when?

✔ How many athletes will you be coaching?

✔ What is the age range of your players?

✔ What are the skill levels and experience of your players at the beginning of the season?

✔ What facilities will be available for practice?

✔ What equipment will be available for practice?

✔ What instructional resources (films, videos, charts, books, etc.) will be available?

✔ How many assistant coaches will you have?

✔ What other support personnel will be available?

✔ What other factors may affect your season planning?

Situation Analysis

In preparation for developing a season plan you need to analyze your situation. To help you do so answer the questions above as completely as you can. You may need to do a little investigative work to answer some questions.

Daily Planner

Also in preparation for developing your season plan, you need a daily planner, with pages similar to the ones shown in Figure 7.1. Review the many varieties available in office supply stores and select one that will work for you. Now go through the daily planner and identify each day you plan to practice and each day you will be competing. It may also be helpful to note any holidays that may interfere with your planning. Record the following information:

1. Write "Practice 1" on the day of your first practice and number all remaining practices sequentially.
2. Record practice locations if they will vary and you know them now.
3. Record the game number, opponent, and location for each contest on the appropriate day.
4. Record any special events, such as the preseason team meeting, parent orien-

tation program, postseason organization meeting, and award banquet.

I'll ask you to do more work with your daily planner later. Now I will take you through the steps for developing a season plan, explaining each and providing examples for you.

Season Plan

Many coaches fail to make functional season plans because they don't know how to develop them or they think the planning process will be overly time-consuming and complex. This chapter removes these obstacles to planning. I will show you a straightforward, highly practical way to develop a season plan. It will take some work, but the time you invest in planning will pay big dividends; your athletes will learn more, your practices will be more enjoyable, and you will save considerable time in the long run.

The steps to develop a season plan are these:

1. Establish your instructional goals.
2. Select the subject matter to be taught to achieve each goal.
3. Organize this subject matter for instruction.

Armed with this plan for the season, you put it to use by completing two more steps.

4. Evaluate athletes' preseason skills and knowledge.
5. Plan practices.

November

Notes: _____
_____
_____

Sunday	Monday	Tuesday	Wednesday	Thursday	Friday	Saturday
			1 305/060	2 306/059	3 307/058	4 308/057
5 309/056	6 310/055	7 311/054 Election Day	8 312/053	9 313/052	10 314/051	11 315/050 Veterans Day
12 316/049	13 317/048	14 318/047	15 319/046	16 320/045	17 321/044	18 322/043
19 323/042	20 324/041	21 325/040	22 326/039	23 327/038 Thanksgiving	24 328/037	25 329/036
26 330/035	27 331/034	28 332/033	29 333/032	30 334/031		

Figure 7.1 Sample daily planner.

Step 1. Establish Your Instructional Goals

What are instructional goals? They are general statements of what you hope your athletes will know and be able to do at the end of a season. You can have many seasonal goals, but the major ones fall into the following categories:

- Technique—goals about learning and performing motor skills for playing the sport
- Tactical—goals about knowing when and how to use the various techniques
- Legal—goals about knowing the rules and basic officiating procedures

- Physical—goals about teaching and training athletes so they are physically prepared for practices and contests
- Mental—goals about teaching and training athletes so they are psychologically prepared for practices and contests
- Moral—goals about teaching athletes sportsmanship and their responsibilities to others

Usually we are told that goals are to be specific and measurable, but let's violate that rule and simply state that your goal is this: Accomplish as much as possible in each category, given the opportunities and limitations you face.

I have listed a sample set of instructional

goals for a soccer team of 14- to 17-year-olds. You'll notice I've written a goal for each category.

Instructional Goals for Soccer

The players will be able to demonstrate the following:

1. Mastery of individual skills necessary to participate in games at this level (technique)

2. Knowledge of the offensive and defensive patterns of team play needed to successfully participate in games at this level (tactical)

3. Comprehensive knowledge of the rules and the ability to quickly apply this knowledge during competition (legal)

4. Knowledge and practice of good nutrition and health, improved strength through safe training methods, and the endurance necessary to play hard throughout practices and competition (physical)

5. The ability to psychologically prepare for competition and to evaluate themselves based on performance rather than outcome (mental)

6. The ability to enhance the self-worth of teammates, opponents, coaches, and officials (moral)

Using these goals as examples, write down your goals for these six categories, modifying them for your situation or using them exactly as stated here. If your daily planner has a blank page, use it to record your goals so that they will be readily available. If you are taking the ASEP/NFICEP Coaching Principles Course, worksheets for preparing the season plan are provided in the *Study Guide*.

Step 2. Select the Subject Matter for Each Goal

Now here's where you'll earn your big money for coaching. The hard work in developing a season plan is selecting the specific subject matter to be taught for each of the six goals. In the coming pages you will see examples of the subject matter I have selected for two of the six goals for soccer. I encourage you to use these examples as a starting point. Be as thorough as you can in developing your lists; if you don't plan for it here, you are not likely to remember to teach it later.

When you begin selecting your subject matter for the technique and tactical goals, start by answering the most important question: What is essential for your athletes to know to play the game or compete in a contest successfully? For most sports, it is quite easy to identify the major essential techniques and tactics. List those first. Then break these major items down into smaller components. Depending on the level at which you coach, you may need to break these components down even further.

Finding Help

You can find help in selecting skills to teach from a number of sources:

- Observe the sport being played at various skill levels, keeping in mind the skill level of your team.
- Review the many books and videos available on teaching your sport. (The ASEP books titled *Coaching [Your Sport] Effectively* or *Coaching [Your Sport] Successfully* are excellent resources for teaching the basics in your sport. Most also contain sample practice plans for three different age groups.)
- Consult with more experienced coaches.
- Consult with your assistant coaches, if you have any.
- Seek advice from your athletes if they are sufficiently mature and experienced. Don't underestimate their knowledge and abilities.

Reality Check

After listing the subject matter you want to teach for each of the six goals, give each item a quick reality check. For the technique and tactical goals, evaluate the appropriateness of each

Goal 1—Technique
The soccer players will demonstrate the following skills necessary to participate effectively in games.

Individual Soccer Skills

Offensive:

Dribbling

1. With inside of the foot
2. With outside of the foot
3. Speed dribble
4. Change of speed
5. Change of direction

Passing

1. Chip passes
2. Curved passes
3. Short, low passes
4. Long, lofted passes

Receiving and controlling

1. With inside of foot
2. With outside of foot
3. With instep
4. With laces
5. With sole of foot

Faking

1. Side-step fake
2. Step-over fake
3. Pass fake
4. To get open without the ball

Shooting

1. With inside of foot
2. With instep
3. With laces
4. With sole of foot
5. With outside of foot
6. Following shots

Heading (passing and shooting)

1. Forward
2. Backward
3. Sideways

Defensive:

1. Block tackle
2. Slide tackle
3. Marking opponent with the ball
4. Marking opponent without the ball

Goal 6—Moral
The soccer players will demonstrate that they have developed positive moral attributes in practices and games.

Respect for others

1. Courtesy
2. Empathy

Sportsmanship

1. Self-discipline
2. Fair play

Teamwork

1. Unselfishness
2. Cooperation
3. Social support

Trust

1. Honesty
2. Loyalty

item to be taught by asking the following questions:

- Do the athletes have the physical strength or endurance to perform the task?
- Do the athletes have sufficient motor coordination to begin learning the task?
- Is the task reasonably safe for athletes who are properly trained?

For all goals, review the appropriateness of the subject matter to be taught by asking the following questions:

- Does the subject matter contribute to the instructional goal more effectively than other choices?
- Are the athletes interested in learning the subject matter? If not, can enthusiasm for learning it be generated at this age level?
- Do the athletes have sufficient emotional and cognitive maturity to begin learning the subject matter?

If the answer to any of these questions is *no*, replace or eliminate the item from the list or teach the prerequisites that will prepare athletes to learn the subject matter you've selected.

Now review all the items again, keeping in mind the following conditions, which will determine how much you can teach:

- The amount of practice time available
- The ratio of athletes to coaches
- Your athletes' level of physical and mental development
- The facilities, equipment, and money available for the season

It's a good idea to have a little more on the list than you think you'll be able to teach during the season, but keep the season plan realistic.

Step 3. Organize the Subject Matter for Instruction

Once you have selected the subject matter to achieve your instructional goals, you need to organize it into the best sequence for teaching and practicing. Begin by ordering the skills for each instructional goal by applying two criteria.

1. Teach the more basic skills first, of course.
2. Teach those skills essential for athletes to be able to compete in the first contest.

I ordered the subject matter the way I think it is best to teach soccer. My sequence of instruction for the technique and moral goals is shown below. (The numbers in parentheses are how many minutes I think I'll need to teach each item—more about that later.) Because I have neither played nor coached soccer before, it was difficult for me to develop an instructional sequence for this sport. Thus, I consulted with more experienced coaches and studied several soccer books to develop my season plan.

Sequence of Instruction for Goal 1—Technique

1. Dribbling with inside and outside of feet (10)
2. Speed dribbling (10)
3. Change of speed dribbling (10)
4. Change of direction dribbling (10)
5. Short, low passes (15)
6. Receiving and controlling with inside and outside of feet (10)
7. Receiving with laces and sole of foot (10)
8. Long, lofted passes (10)
9. Chip passes (10)
10. Pass fakes (10)
11. Side-step fakes (10)
12. Step-over fakes (10)
13. Curved passes (10)
14. Shooting with inside of foot and instep (25)
15. Shooting with laces, sole of foot, and outside of foot (10)
16. Heading forward, backward, and sideways—shot or pass (15)
17. Following shots (10)
18. Marking opponents with and without the ball (25)
19. Faking to get open without the ball (10)
20. Block tackling (10)
21. Slide tackling (10)

Sequence of Instruction for Goal 6—Moral

1. Courtesy and empathy (15)
2. Self-discipline (10)
3. Fair play (10)
4. Unselfishness (5)
5. Cooperation (10)
6. Social support (10)
7. Honesty and loyalty (15)

Notice that I do not plan to teach all the skills in a category at the same time. For example,

I would first teach dribbling and then a passing technique. Then I would teach two ways to receive the ball followed by other passing techniques, and so on. Later I would teach how to fake when dribbling, passing, or moving to get open without the ball.

Go on now to estimate the number of minutes you think it will take to initially teach this subject matter. Your estimate should be for the time allotted to initially present the subject matter and practice it in that session. It is *not* the practice time needed in later practices to master the skill. Without knowing more about my athletes, I can't plan precisely how much practice time they will need to achieve the goal set.

Now that I have sequenced and set aside time for the subject in each goal, I must plan when during the season I will present the material. To do this I must look at my sequence of subject matter for each goal, then decide what my players need to know first, second, third, and so on. Below I show how I sequenced the subject matter for my soccer team. Notice that I initially emphasize rules and conditioning, move on to teaching individual skills, and then introduce team concepts. This, then, is my general blueprint for teaching over the course of the soccer season—my season plan.

Sequence of Instruction for a Soccer Season

1. Perspective on success and handling failure
2. Intrinsic motivation
3. Illness and injury prevention and care
4. Basic principles of training
5. Dribbling
6. Receiving and controlling
7. Passing
8. Field dimensions and marking
9. Position names and roles
10. Fakes
11. Elements of the game
12. Heading the ball
13. Shooting (including headers)
14. Major and minor fouls
15. Sportsmanship
16. Respect
17. Marking an opponent with and without the ball
18. Getting open without the ball
19. Elements of a balanced diet
20. Water intake and pre- and postgame meals
21. Block and slide tackles
22. Goal setting
23. Offensive attack strategies
24. Teamwork
25. Offensive formations
26. Components of muscular fitness
27. Energy balance, sleep, and rest
28. Types of defenses
29. Defenses against certain offensive formations
30. Trust
31. Body composition and weight
32. Offensive set plays
33. Aerobic fitness concepts
34. Anaerobic fitness concepts
35. Physical stress management methods
36. Mental stress management methods
37. Drugs and their effects on health and performance

Remember, the list you just prepared reflects the order in which you will initially introduce and teach each concept or skill. Each will be addressed repeatedly throughout the season. Keep in mind that athletes learn skills and improve performance through repetition, not only in a single practice, but in practices throughout the season. Furthermore, one item may constitute only a small part of a day's practice, or it may be the sole emphasis of a practice. That depends on your planning. Finally, try to balance physical activity with mental activity. Although your athletes need to learn about several concepts, avoid the temptation to simply lecture. Athletes are active people. Keep your practices full of variety and activity!

Follow the three steps—establishing instructional goals, selecting subject matter, and sequencing the material—and you'll have a good season plan. Although it takes some time, you can see that it's not that difficult, and you'll more than recover that time when you are planning practices later. If this is your first season plan, and especially if it's your first season coaching, the plan is not likely to be perfect. Yet it provides you with an organized approach and a systematic way to refine the plan as you progress during the season and in future seasons. Now I'll explain the two final steps to instructional planning so you'll be ready for your first few practices.

Step 4. Evaluate Athletes' Preseason Skills and Knowledge

Good teaching requires that you individualize instruction. To do so you need to know the skills and knowledge of your athletes as you begin the season. Then you can develop the appropriate practice plans. Also, you may be coaching in a situation where you cannot keep everyone who would like to play on the team. Initial evaluation is a way to select those players you wish to keep. Evaluation is also useful if you are responsible for organizing team or individual competitions and you want to match players or teams by their skills and knowledge to achieve safe and equitable competition.

Many coaches avoid preseason evaluation. They either don't want to take the time or they don't know how to evaluate. Moreover, without a season plan they really don't know what to evaluate. By completing the first three steps of your season plan you now know *what* to evaluate—the initial skills you will teach or the prerequisites needed for these initial skills. And I will show you *how* to evaluate using a simple table. I created a sample evaluation table using the technique goal of our soccer example (see Table 7.1). You can readily adapt this example to the other goals and to your sport. I suggest the rating scale below for evaluating each component.

What to Evaluate?

It's not practical to evaluate all the subject matter you listed for each instructional goal. In fact, some subject matter is likely to be so advanced (to be learned by athletes later in the season) that in some sports it would be dangerous to have athletes attempt to perform these skills.

Rating Scale

5 = Very good
4 = Above average
3 = Average
2 = Below average
1 = Very weak/unable to perform
NA = Not Applicable

Table 7.1 Rating of Skills Selected for Goal 1—Technique

Players' names

Subject matter									Team total	Team average
Dribbling										
Passing										
Receiving and control										
Faking										
Shooting										
Heading (pass/shoot)										
Marking										
Tackling										
Total score										

Thus, what I have done in the examples, and what you need to do, is to select the basic skills and most essential subject matter that can be safely evaluated in order to determine the level of competency for each athlete.

If you are coaching at a more advanced level, you may need to identify prerequisite skills that must be mastered before a person can participate at this advanced level because you won't be teaching those prerequisite skills. This is common in sports like gymnastics, diving, and figure skating.

How to Evaluate?

You can conduct this preseason evaluation in one of two ways. First, you can conduct a formal testing program where you organize the athletes to perform each of the skills and have them complete written or oral examinations. Or you can evaluate more informally by observing and talking with the athletes to provide you with enough insight to make a reasonably accurate rating. You should select the method that best suits your situation.

If this is the first time you are using a season plan, I recommend you use the informal method. It is not the most accurate, but it is reasonably good and practical. It certainly is better than no evaluation at all. After coaching a season or two you can try more advanced methods of evaluation.

Step 5. Plan Practices

The preseason evaluation will tell you much about how to plan your practices. You will know more about what your athletes know and don't know, the variability of skills and knowledge among the team, and what you need to emphasize in early practices. In fact, as you analyze the results of your evaluation, you may want to modify some of the subject matter and the order you had planned to teach it in your season plan.

Now get out your daily planner. For each goal, take each item and select a practice day that you will teach it. Write this in your planner, as shown in Figure 7.2. Do this for every item you definitely want to teach, working from the top of the list down.

Now you will be ready to develop practice plans for each of those days. I suggest you plan only one or two practices ahead because you will need to take into account the events of the previous practice—what you observed and what your athletes and assistant coaches told you.

The basic elements of a practice plan are these:

- Date
- Practice objective
- Equipment needed
- Practice activities
- Warm-up
- Practice of previously taught skills
- Teaching and practice of new skills
- Practice under competitive conditions
- Cool-down
- Coach's comments
- Evaluation of the practice

Date

Record the date so you know when you taught and practiced certain skills. This will help after the season is over, when you are evaluating and revising your season plan.

Practice Objective

State succinctly what you want the athletes to know or be able to do as a result of this session.

Monday	Tuesday	Wednesday	Thursday	Friday

29
Practice 6
 	
Legal
— minor and major
   fouls
Moral
— sportsmanship
— respect
	30
	Practice 7
	
	Physical
	— elements of a
	   balanced diet
	— water intake
	— pre-/postgame
	   meals
		1
		Practice 8
		
		Technique
		— block and
		   slide tackling
			2
			Practice 9
			
			Mental
			— goal setting
			   (types of goals
			   and guidelines)
				3
				Practice 10
				
				Tactical
				— offensive attack
				   strategies
				   (spacing of
				   players with
				   an advantage)

Figure 7.2 Sample daily planner for one week of a season.

Equipment

List the equipment (e.g., mats, balls, bats) you need to conduct the practice. Before practice, check the equipment you plan to use to be certain it is safe, clean, and operational. Also make any special arrangements required for the facility.

Practice Activities

The common activities of a practice session and the order in which they typically occur are explained below. Use the list as a guideline. On occasion, however, you may not use all of these parts or follow the order shown.

You should develop a time schedule for each part of the practice to help you use time efficiently and achieve your practice objective. But don't be afraid to adjust the schedule as practice proceeds. Athletes may need more practice time than you allocated to master a difficult skill. Or everybody may seem stale, and you have to inject something new to motivate them.

Warm-Up

Every practice should begin with a warm-up that takes 10 to 15 minutes. Its physiological purpose and function in injury prevention are discussed in chapter 11.

Practice Previously Taught Skills

Skills that were taught previously, especially those that your athletes need to improve on,

should be practiced during this period, which typically lasts for 20 to 40 minutes. This practice will often take the form of drills you have designed or obtained from other sources. Drills should be effective for learning the skill, fun, and safe (see chapter 9).

It is a good idea to let your team help design drills occasionally; they'll practice harder when they share in the ownership of a drill. Be as creative as you can to keep drills from becoming monotonous. Athletes learn little by simply going through the motions of a drill with their minds turned off to what they are doing.

It is a good idea to set aside some time in this period for athletes to individualize their practice. Simply have them practice those skills on which they need more work. Allow them to practice the skills any way they like, provided it is safe and effective for learning.

Teach and Practice New Skills

This part of the practice typically lasts 20 to 30 minutes. Usually only one major skill is taught in any one practice. The steps for teaching a new skill are presented in chapter 9.

Practice Under Competitive Conditions

This part of the practice session should finish on a high note and be devoted to practicing skills in simulated contest conditions. Early in the season you may spend only 20 minutes on this phase of practice, but as the season progresses plan to devote as much as 40 minutes to it. This phase of practice is *not* a time to just let athletes play. You should direct and control their play to accomplish specific objectives. Such direction and control, however, should not be overbearing, and you should occasionally grant some time to letting them play without interruption.

Cool-Down

Just as every practice begins with a warm-up, the activity portion of practice should conclude with a cool-down. (See chapter 11 for more information about how to cool down properly.)

Coach's Comments

Use this closing 5 to 15 minutes for one or more of the following purposes.

- Review how the team practiced, directing your comments to the whole team rather than to particular athletes. Tell them what they still need to improve upon. Compliment them for their efforts and for what they performed well.
- Informally teach a mental or moral lesson by recalling and commenting on an incident that occurred during practice. You might point out an act of good or poor sportsmanship and how it fits in with your moral instructional goals. Usually you will

find athletes more receptive to this type of information if you avoid preaching and instead encourage discussion by asking good questions.
- Inform the team of the time and place of the next practice session, and tell them briefly what you plan to do. You may even ask for suggestions from the team.

Evaluation of the Practice Session

Evaluate each practice as soon after its conclusion as possible. Indicate whether or not the performance objectives were achieved. Consider suggestions from your athletes, and ask your assistant coaches to give their input to this evaluation. Then file each practice plan in a three-ring notebook. You'll find these plans very helpful when planning for the next season.

A practice plan format that is popular with many coaches is shown at the bottom of page 70. The sample contains all the elements just reviewed plus columns for the key teaching points and drills.

Planning Checklist

Analyze situation

_____ Assistant coaches: number, background, philosophy

_____ Other support personnel: team doctor, trainer, etc.

_____ Players: number, eligibility, age, physical development

_____ Instructional resources: books, videos, etc.

_____ Facilities: location, availability, maintenance

_____ Equipment: condition, amount, uniforms, etc.

Select daily planner

_____ Pick style best suited to situation

_____ Note practice dates

_____ Note game dates

_____ Note any holidays that interfere with the schedule

Establish instructional goals

_____ Technique

_____ Tactical

YES!

COACH GETS REAL EXCITED WHEN WE HAVE A GOOD PRACTICE.

_____ Legal
_____ Physical
_____ Mental
_____ Moral

Select subject matter for goals
_____ Skills
_____ Skill subcomponents
_____ Reality check

Organize subject matter for instruction
_____ Basic skills
_____ Skills necessary for games
_____ Amount of time to initially teach
_____ Sequence

Evaluate athletes' preseason skills and knowledge
_____ Rating scale
_____ Method of assessment
_____ Results

Enter season plan on daily planner

Develop practice plans
_____ Record date
_____ Note performance objective

_____ Identify and check equipment needed
_____ Considerations for practice planning
    Maximum use of facilities and equipment
    Contributions of assistant coaches
    Athletes' input
    Experience of some success for each athlete
    Athletes' weaknesses
    Physical demand upon athletes
    Creating gamelike conditions
    Fun for athletes
_____ Prepare time schedule
    Warm-up
    Practice previously taught skills
    Teach and practice new skills
    Practice under competitive conditions
    Cool-down
    Coach's comments
    Evaluation
_____ Meet and discuss plan with assistant coaches

Practice Plan

Date: April 24

Practice objective: Tactical—offensive spacing of players and attack with an advantage

Equipment: balls, scrimmage jerseys, cones

Practice activities:

Time	Activity	Key teaching points	Drills
10 min	Warm-up	Check attendance; preview today's practice	Stretching and dribbling
30 min	Review and practice tackling	Proper position; tackle the ball, not the player; when to contain and when to commit	Partner tackle practice; block tackle
35 min	Teach and practice offensive attack with an advantage	Dribbler awareness of field and recognition of situations; getting the defender to commit; proper spacing (spread/depth); support from trailers	Give-and-go; 2 on 1; 3 on 2
20 min	Competitive practice scrimmage	Emphasize skills reviewed and taught today; have all players participate	
10 min	Conditioning	Emphasize speed and control	Speed dribble
10 min	Cool-down and coaching comments	Check player injury status; get feedback	Stretching and jogging

Evaluation:

Chapter 8

How Athletes Learn

Coaching is teaching, and teaching is helping your athletes learn. You will be able to help them learn more by understanding more about how they learn. And that's the purpose of this chapter.

What Is Learning?

To prepare you for our journey into the athlete's mind, I need to explain two words used often in this book—*skill* and *performance*. Then I'll define *learning*.

Skill has two meanings. It may mean a task. For example, I could say, "The *skill* of rifle shooting is underappreciated in the sport world." You could easily substitute the word *task* for skill in this sentence. Skill also may mean the quality of a person's motor performance. When I say, "She demonstrates excellent shooting *skill*," I use skill to mean the *quality* of the shooter's performance. If the two meanings could be confused here, I'll use *task* for the first meaning.

Performance is observable behavior that demonstrates a skill (quality of performance), such as throwing, kicking, sliding, catching, and so on.

Learning is a relatively permanent improvement in performance capability arising from practice. Because learning is not directly observable (it's an internal change), it must be inferred from changes in performance over time. Because other things besides learning can cause changes in performance, it is not always easy to know whether an athlete has actually *learned* a skill (task). Sometimes an athlete may perform exceptionally well due mostly to luck or poorly due to a loss of concentration. The key to knowing whether learning has occurred is that the improvement in performance is relatively permanent.

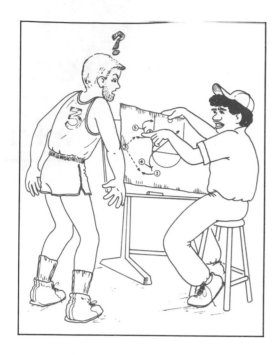

From Blueprints to Motor Programs

Just what happens in athletes' brains when they learn complex sport skills? It used to be thought that athletes learned skills by developing mental blueprints that were created through repeated practice of the task. This explanation worked well for very simple skills, but as scientists studied highly complex skills like shooting in basketball, pitching in baseball, and volleying in tennis they realized that these tasks actually consist of many different responses of a similar type.

Because each mental blueprint would be useful only when the conditions in which a skill is performed are identical, you would need thousands, maybe even millions, of blueprints to perform skills well when competing. Even if your brain could accommodate so many blueprints, it could not constantly select the right blueprints to fit the changing situation as a contest was played.

Abstracting Rules

Today scientists believe athletes learn complex motor skills in quite a different way. They abstract key pieces of information from each performance to create rules about how to perform in the future. This is a far more efficient

way to deal with the many variations that are possible for complex sport skills.

This process of abstracting information from specific experiences to create rules for guiding future behavior is the way we humans learn many things. It is a unique ability of our brain. For example, when learning language so that you can read this book, you don't learn every possible combination of words to understand their meaning (the blueprint approach). Instead you learn language by coming to understand a set of rules that permits you to use words in a far more functional and creative way.

Each time athletes perform complex skills, their brains will seek to abstract four types of information about the movement. These are the following:

- The condition of the environment and the position from which performance is initiated
- The demands of the movement being performed, such as speed, direction, and force
- The consequences as perceived by the senses during and after the movement
- A comparison of the actual outcome with the intended outcome based on available feedback (information that tells them how well they are doing the task)

Motor Program

As athletes continue to practice, using feedback to adjust their movements, these abstracted pieces of information are synthesized to mold the general rules into what is called a *motor program*. A motor program is a complex set of rules that, when called into action, permits athletes to produce a movement. Once the movement is initiated the *basic* pattern of action is carried out, even though the wrong movement may have been selected. Minor adjustments can be made in the basic movement pattern, but the pattern itself cannot be changed.

For example, if you attempt to hit a pitched baseball, once you initiate the swing you will complete the basic action, even if you later see the ball is outside the strike zone. We used to think that once the motor program was initiated, minor adjustments in the movement in response to sensory feedback could not be made. Evidence now shows that minor responses are possible. Thus as you see the ball is going to be outside of the strike zone, you can adjust your swing to reach out for it.

This motor program, remember, is only a generalized plan of a movement; it enables athletes to make skillful movements. To actually make the correct movement, you must add the details of the particular situation. In the baseball example, your motor program enables you to swing skillfully at a rapidly thrown ball, but to hit a specific pitch you must determine its exact speed and location.

One of your major responsibilities, then, as a coach is to help athletes develop good motor programs. Many factors affect the learning of motor programs: the characteristics of the athletes you coach (such as their maturation level and experience), their motor and cognitive intelligence, their attention capacity, and their motivation. Your athletes' learning will also be influenced greatly by what you do—how you teach, how you organize practice, and how you give feedback. In chapter 9 you will learn many practical things to enhance athletes' learning and improve your teaching.

Learning to Juggle

Now you have a good basic understanding of how athletes learn motor skills. When was the last time you learned a new skill? Perhaps it's been a long time, and you've forgotten what it's like to learn. Let's have you be an athlete again, and I'll be your coach. I'm going to teach you how to juggle.

I will assume you have never juggled and have never even seen anyone juggle. What do you need me to do to help you learn this skill? The answer is obvious, of course. The first thing you need is for me to explain or demonstrate the act of juggling so you know what you must learn.

As you begin to practice juggling, you also will need sensory feedback—sensory information that tells you how well you are doing the task. For example, you can see that you are repeatedly dropping balls or that you don't have the feel for how high to throw them. You don't need me yelling in your ear, "Hey, dumb klutz, you're screwing up."

This is an important coaching point. You need not give athletes feedback when their senses already tell them they are making errors. On the other hand, it is useful to provide positive reinforcement when their senses tell them they are performing correctly.

In the early stages of learning, sensory feedback often is not enough information to optimize learning. Thus, as your coach, I can provide you with useful feedback to help you learn faster. For example, I can point out that you should not try to watch any one ball, but maintain an overview of all three balls. (I should also point out that many people learn to juggle without a coach, but with good coaching they learn to juggle better, faster.)

Three Stages of Learning

As you practice, and of course with my coaching, you will move from beginner to expert juggler (we hope). As you do so you will move through three stages of learning: mental, practice, and automatic. These three stages are illustrated in Figure 8.1 as a learning continuum. It is important that you understand

Figure 8.1 Stages of learning.

these three stages of learning because each requires different instructional strategies.

Mental Stage

When you are first learning to juggle, your objective is to understand what is required to perform the skill correctly. To do so requires a great deal of mental activity as you search for a mental plan of the correct technique and strategy. That's why this beginning stage of learning is called the mental stage.

To help you learn the skill of juggling I must find a way for you to understand the sequence of the components of juggling. I can do this best through demonstration and explanation. From my experience in coaching juggling, I have learned that some people can get the basics in only a few minutes and others take quite a bit longer. (For those who learn it quickly, I like to take the credit for their success by recognizing my superior teaching ability. For those who learn slowly, I am inclined to attribute it to their inferior learning ability.)

Actually, I know that I am more successful when I am careful not to teach too much during this mental stage, for it is easy to overload your learning circuits. Nevertheless, I'm often tempted to do so, because I know juggling so well and it gives me a chance to show what I know. Also, sometimes I'm impatient and try to go faster than you are able to learn.

You may need to remind me to go slowly with you and be patient. My goal when you are practicing during this mental stage should be to help you develop a good plan for what you need to do.

Practice Stage

The next stage of learning is called the practice stage. It doesn't mean that you didn't practice during the mental stage, for you did, but now the emphasis is on quality practice to refine the skill. You will spend much more time in this stage than you did in the mental stage.

During this stage the mental energy required will be less, and your mental activity will shift from an emphasis on learning the sequence of movements to refining the timing and coordi-nation of each phase of the juggling sequence. As you learn the basic fundamentals or mechanics, not only do your errors decrease but your performance becomes more consistent (a good sign that learning is happening).

Sensory feedback and useful feedback from me are also very important during this practice stage, but as you practice more you become increasingly able to detect your own errors. This important ability enables you to make your own adjustments as you practice.

As I coach you during this phase, I know that it is not just the quantity of practice but the quality that will increase your rate of learning. Thus, I need to make good judgments about how often you will practice, how long each practice should be, how to drill the component parts of juggling, and when to move on to more advanced juggling skills. I have learned that to do so it is best if I work *with* you rather than dictate *to* you, for I need to consider your capacity to learn, your motivation, and your fatigue. I can make all these judgments better with your input than without it.

Automatic Stage

As you continue to practice juggling, the skill becomes more and more automated. Consequently you free up more mental capacity—which you can use to focus on the more critical elements of juggling in order to achieve superior performance or to add flair or style.

In the automatic stage, your juggling performance is very reliable, and when you do make an error you frequently know what to do to correct the problem. In fact, in the automatic stage, thinking about your juggling by overanalyzing it is likely to hurt your performance. The skill is now so automated that when you begin analyzing it during execution you disrupt your own performance. That's why at times I may tell you to stop thinking and just let it happen.

My Changing Coaching Role

As you enter the automatic stage of learning a skill, my coaching role becomes far different from my role in earlier stages. Instead of my continuing to decide how you should best practice, you take increasing responsibility because you frequently know when you err and probably why. Although most complex sport skills are never totally mastered, and although I may be able to continue to help you learn the finer points of juggling, my coaching role shifts substantially from coaching-to-learn to coaching-to-perform. This is a crucial distinction, and one many coaches fail to recognize.

When I *coach-to-learn*, I'm concerned with the problems associated with your learning how to do something new. When I *coach-to-perform*, I'm concerned with the problems associated with your doing something you already know how to do but for some reason aren't doing. If you are having a learning problem and I coach-to-learn, or you are having a performance problem and I coach-to-perform, I'll be able to help you. But if I get my roles mixed up, and I coach-to-perform when you need help learning or I coach-to-learn when you need help performing, I'll be little help.

Let's consider two scenarios. You enter a juggling contest and you perform poorly. I incorrectly assume that you performed poorly because you didn't try hard rather than because you didn't know how to perform the skill. (Perhaps I'm not inclined to admit a learning problem because this would reflect poorly on me as a teacher.) The consequence of my misjudgment is that I don't spend time trying to teach you the skill or correcting your errors through

constructive feedback. Instead I merely work at encouraging you to put out more effort. I'm coaching for the wrong thing.

Or consider the opposite mistake. When you perform poorly in the contest, I assume you haven't mastered the skill as well as I thought. Consequently I set up an intensive practice schedule to thoroughly ingrain the skill (perhaps to the point that you become totally bored with juggling). Actually your problem was that you were extremely anxious in your first competition. I don't do anything, of course, to help you manage your anxiety in the future because I don't recognize the problem. Again, I've coached for the wrong purpose and didn't help you solve your problem.

Keep in mind that an athlete who is in the automatic stage for one skill may be at an earlier stage in another skill. To be a successful coach, you must be able to assess when the problem at hand requires you to coach-to-learn or coach-to-perform. When athletes are in the early stages of learning, you will usually coach-to-learn, but not always. When athletes' skills are well into the automatic stage, most often you should coach-to-perform, but that's not absolute either. When athletes are in the practice stage of learning, it is most difficult to determine the correct role.

I don't have any easy answers to help you know which coaching role to use when. Deciding requires good judgment and cooperative relationships with athletes so they'll let you know the type of help they need.

Checking Your Learning

It is appropriate that this chapter end with a test to help you evaluate what you've learned about learning. Answer the following questions true or false:

1. The term *skill* may refer either to *task* or to *quality of performance*.
2. Learning may be inferred from observing an athlete perform a skill one time.
3. Abstract informational rules in the brain, not mental blueprints, allow athletes to perform complex motor skills.

4. One type of movement information abstracted by athletes results from their comparing actual versus intended outcomes.
5. A generalized motor program is used by athletes to respond correctly to each particular event.
6. It is impossible to give an athlete too much information during the mental stage of learning.
7. The emphasis should be on quality, not quantity, during the practice stage of learning.

8. Athletes in the automatic stage of learning execute skills better when they closely analyze each aspect of their performances.
9. Coaches' roles change depending upon what stage of learning their athletes have achieved.
10. The coach-to-perform approach is usually best for athletes in the mental stage of skill learning.

Answers: 1 = True; 2 = False; 3 = True; 4 = True; 5 = False; 6 = False; 7 = True; 8 = False; 9 = True; 10 = False

Chapter 9

Teaching Sport Skills

In chapter 7 you developed a season plan that will be your guide in knowing what to teach and when you will teach it. You've learned how to develop a practice plan so that you can be as efficient as possible when you teach. In chapter 8 you gained an understanding for how athletes learn, knowledge essential to helping you coach more successfully by teaching more effectively. Now you're ready to hold your first practice and to teach the first skill.

This chapter will help you be an effective coach by explaining the four steps to teaching sport skills. Although this chapter focuses on teaching technique, the major principles of instruction are equally applicable to teaching other subject matter. These are the four steps to teaching sport skills:

Step 1: Introduce the skill.
Step 2: Demonstrate and briefly explain the skill.
Step 3: Practice the skill.
Step 4: Provide feedback to correct errors.

The chapter closes with a summary in the form of an evaluation to help you assess your teaching effectiveness.

Step 1: Introduce the Skill

Introduce the skill with enthusiasm expressed in actions and words. Speak clearly and use language your athletes can understand; the younger the athletes the simpler your words need to be. Be brief too. Say what you have to say in less than 3 minutes. Avoid sarcasm, annoying mannerisms, and abusive language; they create a negative learning environment.

Three events make up a good introduction.

1. Get the team's attention.
2. Arrange the team so all can see and hear.
3. Name the skill and give a reason for learning it.

Get the Team's Attention

Develop a regular routine in practice for starting each teaching session. Go to your usual place to begin the session and give a signal, such as blowing a whistle, to get athletes' attention. Position yourself to face the team when you speak to them.

If a few athletes are inattentive, look directly at them, move closer to them, and politely but firmly address them by name and ask for their attention. If this fails, have them move to where they cannot disrupt the session. Speak with these athletes either at an opportune time later during the practice or afterward. (See chapter 5 for procedures on how to punish athletes.)

Arrange the Team So All Can See and Hear

When you speak to your athletes, be sure to organize them so they can see and hear you. If they are milling around or crowding together, it will be much harder for you to keep their attention. Figure 9.1 shows two good team formations for teaching. Be certain that the background behind you is free of visual distractions and that athletes are not facing the sun. Try also to select a practice area with minimum noise so that athletes can hear you.

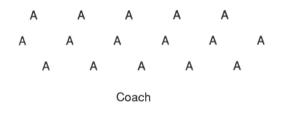

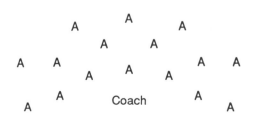

Figure 9.1 Team formations to use during demonstrations.

Name the Skill and Give a Reason for Learning It

Naming skills is important so that you can make quick reference to them. If a skill is widely known by a certain name, use that one. If not, select a short, descriptive title that is easy to remember.

Sometimes the reason for learning a skill is not obvious, especially to athletes with little experience. The more athletes understand why they are learning a particular skill and how it fits into the total plan for playing the sport, the easier it is for them to develop a mental plan for learning it. It also increases their motivation to learn because they know why they are being asked to learn.

Step 2: Demonstrate and Explain the Skill

Recall from chapter 8 that demonstration and explanation are the primary ways to help your athletes acquire a mental plan for a skill. The skill should be demonstrated by someone who can perform it proficiently and whom the athletes respect for being good in the sport. If you cannot demonstrate a particular skill, you have several alternatives.

- Practice the skill until you are able to demonstrate it correctly.
- Ask someone who is skilled to demonstrate, perhaps a more able player on the team, an assistant coach, or a friend.
- Use a film or video to demonstrate the skill.

If none of these alternatives is possible and you cannot give an adequate demonstration, seriously reconsider teaching the skill. If there is any risk of injury in learning the skill, you definitely should not teach it.

An effective demonstration and explanation consists of a sequence of four steps.

1. Get athletes' attention.
2. Demonstrate and explain.
3. Relate to previously learned skills.
4. Check for understanding.

Get Athletes' Attention

Prepare athletes for the demonstration by getting their attention. Tell them how the demonstration will be given and what to look for.

Demonstrate and Explain

Follow these guidelines for giving demonstrations:

- Demonstrate the whole skill just as it would be performed in a competitive situation.
- Demonstrate several times, showing how to do the skill from different angles.
- If the skill is performed from a dominant side, demonstrate it for "lefties" and "righties."
- If the skill is complex, demonstrate the major parts separately.
- If the skill is performed rapidly, demonstrate it at a slower speed so athletes can clearly see the sequence of movements.

During the demonstration you should also explain the skill. Remember that it is harder for most athletes to convert words into a mental plan for performing the skill than it is to make use of the demonstration. Follow these guidelines for your explanations.

- Before the demonstration, point out one or two important things to which the athletes should attend.

- Keep your explanations simple and brief.
- Make certain that the explanation agrees with what is being demonstrated.
- Time the explanation to either prepare the athletes for what they will see or to reinforce what they just saw.

Relate to Previously Learned Skills

After the skill is initially demonstrated, relate it to any previously learned skills. Why is this important? As you learned in chapter 8, the motor programs for a skill are generalized rules. Thus it is possible to transfer some of these rules for movement to the new skill being learned. For example, if you are teaching the tennis serve, tell and show your athletes how these movements are similar to throwing a ball.

Check for Understanding

Now check to see if your athletes understand how to perform the skill by inviting or asking questions. When a question is asked, repeat it if necessary so everyone can hear. Keep your answers short and relevant. Don't begin explaining all the nuances of the skill at this point.

Step 3: Practice the Skill

Athletes should begin practicing the skill as soon as possible following the demonstration and

explanation. This brings you to a critical decision. Will the players practice the skill as a whole or break it into parts? (You'll obviously make this decision when you develop your practice plan, but I introduce the issue here because it is particularly relevant.)

Whole Versus Part Practice

The whole method of practice is obvious. The whole skill is practiced intact. The part method is actually the whole-part-whole method. You teach the whole method as just outlined, practice it in parts, and then recombine the parts back into the whole through practice.

What's the best method to use? When possible, it is best to practice the whole skill to avoid spending time to combine the parts back into the whole. However, if the skill is so complex that athletes cannot develop a good mental plan (the first stage of learning), then it is better to break the skill into parts.

When to Break Skills Into Parts. To decide if you should break a skill into parts you need to evaluate the task on two dimensions—its complexity and the interdependence of parts. Two questions will help you determine task complexity, or how difficult it may be for athletes to develop a good mental plan.

- How many parts are there to the task?
- How mentally demanding is the task?

Next you need to evaluate how interdependent or independent the parts of the task are. That is, how closely is one part of the skill related to the next? For example, in the tennis serve, you can fairly easily separate the ball toss

from the swing of the racquet. But it's quite difficult to separate the racquet swing and contact with the ball from the follow-through.

So here is how you decide whether you should break a skill into parts when practicing: When the task is low in complexity and high in interdependence, it is best to practice the whole skill. By contrast, part practice is better when the task is high in complexity and low in interdependence. I've illustrated this in Figure 9.2, indicating how I would apply these rules for certain sport skills.

You might notice I've listed only one skill in the part method category. That is because few sport skills are low in interdependence. However, a great many skills can be taught by using a combination of part and whole methods.

Where to Break. Now you have some guidance for when to break a skill into parts.

High	Interdependence of task parts		Low
Whole method	Whole and part methods combined	Part method	
Weight lifting Archery Shooting Heading a soccer ball Cycling	Tennis serve Floor exercise routine Swimming strokes Golf swing Pitching a baseball Basketball lay-up	Dance sequences	

Low	Complexity of tasks	High

Figure 9.2 Complexity and interdependence determine whether skills should be taught in parts or as a whole.

But how do you know where to make the breaks in the sequence of movements? This is another judgment you must learn to make, perhaps with help from more experienced coaches. In general, the more interdependent the movement, the more it should be left intact. When you analyze a skill, look for those points in the movement where there is less interdependency, where there is a transition from one type of movement to another. Most skills have a preparation phase, an action phase, and a follow-through phase. Often you can break between the preparation and action phases; it's usually not easy to break between the action phase and the follow-through.

Integrating Parts Back to the Whole

You have several options from which to select the specific way you will teach a given skill. These options are limited only by your creativity. Let's start by taking a look at a way to integrate parts back to the whole.

Progressive-Part. Just because you are breaking a skill into parts doesn't mean you must teach each part independently. If an athlete has mastered a few parts of a skill, but still needs work on others, or if an athlete needs work on putting parts together, you might select this approach. To use the progressive-part method, start by having an athlete practice the first part of a skill. Then, move on to the next part by having the athlete practice it together with the first part. Progress through each part of the skill until the athlete is finally practicing the entire skill.

Additional Ways to Teach Skills

Sometimes your athletes will not have mastered enough parts of a skill to make the progressive-part approach effective. In these instances, you may want them to practice the entire skill. Simplification and attention focus can be effective ways to teach skills to these athletes.

Simplification. An effective approach to teaching is to simplify the skill to be learned. The athlete practices the entire skill, but you simplify it. For example, baseball coaches frequently select this approach when helping their players improve their swing. Instead of swinging at a live pitch, players hit off a tee. This approach simplifies the process of practicing the swing by removing the variable of the pitch, allowing an athlete to focus more closely on the mechanics of swinging the bat. Once the mechanics of the swing are performed better, then the player practices hitting pitched balls.

Attention Focus. This approach again involves practicing the entire skill, but players are instructed to concentrate only on one aspect of the skill. You might instruct discus throwers, for example, to practice the entire throw, but to focus only on keeping the discus as far as possible from the body as they pull. It's worth mentioning that this method tends to work best with more skilled athletes. Athletes who are still trying to learn fundamentals of a skill may have difficulty focusing only on one aspect.

Principles for Better Practice

Once you have decided on whether you will practice using the whole or the whole-part-whole method, you will need to determine the appropriate methods of practice. For many sports, drills are used to teach the parts of the skill and to recombine them into the whole skill. The following principles are important for making practice most productive.

Practice Principles

Principle 1: Practice the right skill.

Principle 2: Practice the skill in contestlike conditions as soon as athletes can do so.

Principle 3: Keep practices short and frequent when teaching new skills.

Principle 4: Use practice time efficiently.

Principle 5: Make optimal use of facilities and equipment.

Principle 6: Make sure athletes experience a reasonable amount of success at each practice.

Principle 7: Make practice fun.

Let's look at each of the principles in greater depth.

Practice the Right Skill. Suppose you saw me practicing a volleyball serve and said, "Hi there. What are you doing?" And suppose I replied, "Why I'm learning how to play tennis." What would you think? Suppose I then said, "You know, I've been working hard at this, but my tennis just isn't getting any better. Got any suggestions?" I think your reply would be obvious: "If you want to learn how to play tennis, you need to practice tennis!" you proclaim. And of course you would be right—and I'd thank you for not calling me an idiot.

I use this example to overstate the principle. One of the most common mistakes in designing practice experiences is having athletes perform drills that do not help them learn the skill at hand. Instead the drill requires learning a skill unique to that drill. What does running through a series of tires or ropes teach a football player? My answer is, how to run through tires and ropes—but I've never seen tires or ropes on the playing field during a football game.

Many coaches teach particular drills merely because their own coaches used them. Carefully analyze the drills you use. Select only those that you are confident will help your athletes learn the target skill. Otherwise you may spend time and effort having your athletes get better at the wrong thing.

Practice the Skill in Contestlike Conditions. This principle is closely related to Principle 1. The purpose of many drills is to limit the variety of choices to be made and responses to be performed. That's useful when athletes are initially learning complex skills. But when such drills are overused and competitive simulations are few, athletes are not prepared to make choices and responses in the rapidly changing conditions of a game. Thus, as you learned from Principle 1, the more your drills simulate the competitive situation in which the skill will be used, the more likely it is your athletes will be learning the right things.

To apply Principle 2, it's also important to practice the skill at the speed it is to be performed in competition, provided it can be executed safely and with a reasonable degree of accuracy. This produces more rapid and effective learning than does emphasizing slow, accurate movements and gradually increasing the speed. On the other hand, if the skill requires both speed and accuracy, practice should give equal emphasis to both.

To practice in contestlike conditions, you should simulate three different aspects of the contest:

1. practicing the skills and strategies in game-like conditions,
2. simulating the heightened emotional state of competition so that athletes get used to dealing with their emotions, and
3. preparing to face differences in the environment, including changes in weather, different competition times, varying noise levels and visual distractions, and in some cases changes in altitude.

Keep Practices Short and Frequent When Teaching New Skills. When first learning a skill, athletes are likely to make many mistakes and tire quickly. Therefore, the skill should be practiced frequently, but not for too long. In other words, when athletes must use considerable mental and physical effort to perform a skill, practice should be interspersed with either rest intervals or practice of another skill that uses different muscle groups and demands less effort.

Use Practice Time Efficiently. Here are some big practice time wasters and a suggestion or two for improving your use of time.

Time Wasters	Time Savers
Drills where most of the athletes' time is spent waiting	Reorganize the drill so athletes are more active.
The coach's talking too much	Keep demonstrations, explanations, and feedback concise.
Moving between activities in the practice schedule	Be sure you have a practice plan so you know what you'll do

(continued)

Time Wasters (continued)	Time Savers (continued)
	next, and develop routines for athletes to follow when changing activities.
Practicing things that don't help athletes play the sport better; selecting useless drills	Don't spend too much time on skills athletes already know well; work on those that need the most improvement.

Make Optimal Use of Facilities and Equipment. Design drills, practice formations, and so on to make efficient use of your facilities and equipment. Consider not only maximum use, but best use as well.

Make Sure Athletes Experience a Reasonable Amount of Success at Each Practice. If you have set realistic instructional goals, as discussed in chapter 7, and you have helped your athletes set realistic personal goals, as discussed in chapter 6, they will be no strangers to success. An important way to build success into every practice is to select the right progressions for learning skills. If you make the steps too difficult, then few athletes can experience success. If athletes are having difficulty performing a skill correctly, it may be best to take a break or practice some other aspect of the sport. You may even want to back off from a new skill entirely and approach it afresh another day. Forcing the learning process is likely to produce failure and frustration.

Make Practice Fun. Avoid repetitious and boring practice sessions. You can make practices fun by using a variety of drills and gimmicks, changing your practice schedule occasionally, being enthusiastic, letting the team help plan practices, and "playing" the sport during practice.

Step 4: Correct Errors

Practice alone is not enough to learn a skill correctly. For practice to be productive, you must provide your athletes with two types of infor-

mation to correct errors: (a) how the completed performance compared with the desired performance, and (b) how to change an incorrect performance to more closely approximate the desired performance. Both types of information are called *feedback*.

Understanding Errors

Errors can be of two types: learning errors and performance errors. *Learning errors* are ones that occur because athletes don't know how to perform a skill; that is, they have not yet developed the correct motor program. *Performance errors* are made not because athletes don't know how to do the skill, but because they made a mistake in executing what they do know. This mistake may be caused by lack of attention or motivation or by a psychological problem of some type. As you will recall from chapter 8, you must be able to distinguish learning errors from performance errors in order to know whether your role is to coach-to-learn or coach-to-perform.

Observe and Evaluate Performance

The process of helping your athletes correct errors begins with your observing and evaluating their performances to determine if the mistakes are learning or performance errors. For performance errors, you need to look for the reasons that your athletes are not performing as well as they know how. If the mistakes are learning errors, then you need to help them learn the skill, which is the focus of this section.

There is no substitute for knowing skills well in correcting learning errors. The better you understand a skill—not only how it is done correctly but what causes learning errors—the more helpful you will be in correcting mistakes. Experience is the most common way to learn to correct errors, but you can expedite the slow process of learning by experience through the study of sport biomechanics and motor learning, as well as detailed study of your sport. The use of videotapes to help you observe your athletes more carefully can also be of great help.

One of the most common coaching mistakes is to provide inaccurate feedback and advice

on how to correct errors. Don't rush into error correction; wrong feedback or poor advice will hurt the learning process more than no feedback or advice. If you are uncertain about the cause of the problem or how to correct it, continue to observe and analyze until you are more sure. As a rule, you should look to see the error repeated several times before attempting to correct it.

Providing Feedback

Take this short true-false test to check your common sense about giving feedback.

1. Save feedback until the end of practice so as not to disrupt practice time.

False.   The sooner feedback is given, the less likely that athletes will forget what the feedback pertains to and continue to practice incorrectly, making later correction more difficult.

2. More frequent feedback is better than less frequent.

True, within reason.   The more often athletes get useful feedback, the more they will try to correct their performance, and thus, the faster their learning. As athletes' skills increase, they need to learn to rely more on their own feedback and less on feedback from the coach.

3. When an athlete is making several mistakes, it is best to correct only one error at a time.

True.   Learning is more effective when an athlete attempts to correct only one error at a time, which means you must decide which error should be corrected first. To do so, begin by determining whether or not one error is causing another. If it is, have the athlete try to correct it first, because this will eliminate the other error(s). However, if the errors seem to be unrelated, have the athlete correct the error that you think will bring the greatest improvement when remedied. Improvement will likely motivate the athlete to correct the other errors.

4. You and your assistant coaches should be the only people providing feedback in practice.

False.   Especially with athletes who are a little older, you can have them give feedback to each other. A word of caution, though: If athletes are going to give feedback and suggestions for correcting errors, they must be able to offer accurate information. This is most likely to be true with less advanced skills.

5. When giving feedback, you don't need to tell the athlete what was done incorrectly; just provide feedback about how to do the skill right.

False.   In fact, feedback means to *feed back* exactly what was done. If the athletes performed incorrectly, you should feed back what they did wrong. Then explain how to do the skill correctly.

6. Give simple and precise information about how performance can be improved.

True.   Tell as well as show your athletes what they must do to correct errors. Be careful not to go overboard; give just enough information so that they can concentrate on correcting one error at a time.

7. Provide frequent positive feedback (like "Nice job!").

False. Positive feedback is good. However, specific positive feedback is much more valuable. Such feedback specifies what was correct and reinforces those aspects for all the athletes in a group. An example of specific positive feedback would be "Nice follow-through on that shot."

The same principle holds for negative feedback. If a player performs incorrectly, simply saying "You shoot terribly" is not very effective. The player already knows he or she didn't shoot well. What is important is how to improve. A more effective approach might be, "Your shot was off the mark because you allowed your elbow to swing to the outside. Try keeping the elbow tucked in to your side."

8. Use sight and sound in providing feedback.

True. Because people learn in different ways, some gain most from explanations of how to improve, whereas others need demonstrations. Both explanations and demonstrations should incorporate specific feedback. For example, you might demonstrate how a player per-

formed a skill, explain what was good and what you believe needs more attention for improved performance, and demonstrate the refinement you would like to see. Show *and* tell your players how they can improve, using specific positive and negative feedback.

A Positive Approach to Correcting Errors

Throughout this book I have encouraged you to use the positive approach in coaching your athletes. That is especially applicable when correcting errors. It is a real challenge to stay positive when your athletes repeatedly perform a skill incorrectly or lack enthusiasm for learning. It can certainly be frustrating to see athletes who seemingly don't heed your advice and continue to make the same mistake. And when an athlete doesn't seem to care, you may wonder why you should.

Please know that it is normal to get frustrated at times when teaching skills. Nevertheless, part of successful coaching is controlling this frustration.

A positive approach to coaching-to-learn views practice as the opportunity for athletes to make mistakes. Remember, a mistake undetected is a mistake uncorrected. Mistakes tell you the progress your athletes are making in the learning process. Root out errors with patience and enthusiastically help your athletes correct them.

It is sometimes easier to envision implementing a positive approach to correcting errors in an individual sport than it is in a team sport. After all, you can focus on individuals more easily in such sports as wrestling, tennis, riflery, or skating. Furthermore, your comments are usually more private, so the performer is not embarrassed by them.

Team sports provide unique challenges. How do you provide individual feedback in a group setting using a positive, ego-protecting approach? Instead of yelling across the court or field to correct an error (and embarrassing the player), consider substituting for the player who erred. Then you can make the correction individually. This procedure offers three benefits:

- Players are more receptive to the feedback because they are not being corrected in front of an audience.
- The other team members remain active, so they don't pay attention to the discussion between player and coach. Furthermore, they are continuing to practice the skills themselves, fostering additional skill development.
- Because the rest of the team continues to play, the coach must make corrective comments simple and concise. This saves both coach and athlete from long, drawn-out explanations that lack value because of their complexity.

In a team setting you can also use specific positive feedback to emphasize correct group and individual performances. These performances and the accompanying feedback will serve to reinforce the kinds of behavior and play you want to see. Use this approach *only* for positive statements. Keep your specific negative feedback for individual discussions.

Teaching Evaluation Scale

The scale on pages 87 and 88 is designed to help you evaluate how well you apply what you have read in this chapter. One way to use it is to sit down immediately after practice and fill it out yourself. Even better is to have another person who is familiar with the information in this chapter complete it after observing you in a practice situation. Discuss the results with your evaluator and use them as a guide to improve your teaching.

Look at your scores. Ideally you would like to have mostly *1*s and a few *2*s. Realistically, you probably have a few *3*s and *4*s. Work to improve your skills in those areas in which you achieved a rating of *3*. Think about those areas marked with a *4*. If that behavior didn't apply to your particular practice session, should it have? Spend time now making an effort to become the best teacher—and coach—that you can be!

Teaching Evaluation Scale

Directions: Place a checkmark in the appropriate column at the right to indicate how frequently you use the principle in your practices.

Rating Scale: 1 = Usually or always; 2 = Occasionally or sometimes; 3 = Seldom or never; 4 = Not applicable to this practice

Introducing the skill	1	2	3	4
Is enthusiastic in actions and words	___	___	___	___
Avoids sarcasm, annoying mannerisms, and abusive language	___	___	___	___
Uses terminology athletes can understand	___	___	___	___
Speaks clearly	___	___	___	___
Has a routine for starting practice	___	___	___	___
Gets attention quickly	___	___	___	___
Faces the team when speaking to them	___	___	___	___
Makes good eye contact	___	___	___	___
Controls temper	___	___	___	___
Models poise when dealing with inattentive athletes	___	___	___	___
Uses a formation from which all can see the demonstration	___	___	___	___
Uses a formation from which all can hear the explanation	___	___	___	___
Sets formation in a location free of distractions	___	___	___	___
Identifies the skill to be taught	___	___	___	___
Indicates why the skill is important to learn	___	___	___	___
Introduces the skill in less than 3 minutes	___	___	___	___

Demonstrating and explaining the skill				
Directs the team's attention to the demonstration	___	___	___	___
Explains how the demonstration will proceed	___	___	___	___
Demonstrates the whole skill as it would be performed in competition	___	___	___	___
Demonstrates skillfully	___	___	___	___
Demonstrates for left and right dominance	___	___	___	___
Demonstrates the skill several times	___	___	___	___
Demonstrates the skill so that it can be viewed from different angles	___	___	___	___
Demonstrates the skill slower if necessary	___	___	___	___
Explains the major sequence of actions that comprise the skill when it is demonstrated slowly	___	___	___	___
Points out the most relevant cues	___	___	___	___
Keeps explanation simple and brief	___	___	___	___
Demonstrates parts of the skill when appropriate	___	___	___	___
Briefly demonstrates and/or explains the similarities between skills	___	___	___	___
Repeats and answers relevant questions so all can hear	___	___	___	___

(continued)

Teaching Evaluation Scale (continued)

Rating Scale: 1 = Usually or always; 2 = Occasionally or sometimes; 3 = Seldom or never; 4 = Not applicable to this practice

Practicing the skill	1	2	3	4
Begins skill practice as soon as possible after the demonstration	___	___	___	___
Uses a formation that allows the most athletes to practice safely and effectively	___	___	___	___
Uses drills that allow the most athletes to practice safely and effectively	___	___	___	___
Uses drills that emphasize the skill being taught	___	___	___	___
Demonstrates and explains how drills work	___	___	___	___
Checks to be certain the team understands how drills work	___	___	___	___
Eliminates or minimizes any danger involved in performing the skill	___	___	___	___
Creates an atmosphere to minimize fear of failure	___	___	___	___
Is in control of the team during practice	___	___	___	___
Checks to be certain all are proceeding through the drill correctly	___	___	___	___
Repeats the demonstration and explanation if the team cannot perform the skill effectively	___	___	___	___
Uses key terms step-by-step if the team cannot perform the skill effectively	___	___	___	___
Checks after each step to be sure that everyone is performing correctly when initial teaching has been unsuccessful	___	___	___	___
Repeats and answers relevant questions so all can hear	___	___	___	___
Divides the skill into parts when athletes have difficulty mastering the whole skill	___	___	___	___
Stops practice and corrects common errors when necessary	___	___	___	___
Presents brief explanations and demonstrations of errors and their corrections when confronted with common errors	___	___	___	___

Providing feedback to correct errors

	1	2	3	4
Observes and evaluates performance	___	___	___	___
Compliments efforts and parts of the skill that were performed correctly	___	___	___	___
Corrects one error at a time	___	___	___	___
Gives specific positive feedback	___	___	___	___
Gives specific negative feedback	___	___	___	___
Uses visual feedback of errors and corrections	___	___	___	___
Makes certain athletes understand the information given	___	___	___	___
Shows patience with athletes	___	___	___	___
Encourages athletes to continue to practice and improve	___	___	___	___

Part IV

Sport Physiology

Chapter 10
PRINCIPLES OF TRAINING

Chapter 11
FITNESS FOR SPORT

Chapter 12
*DEVELOPING YOUR
TRAINING PROGRAM*

Chapter 13
NUTRITION FOR ATHLETES

Sport physiology is the study of the immediate and long-term effects of exercise and training on the body; it provides guidelines for conducting safe and healthy practices and training programs. The ultimate goal of the sport physiologist is the same as yours—to enhance the performance of the athlete. Like you, the physiologist wonders how heredity and training affect performance; how bodies, systems, and tissues respond to exercise and training; and how training can best be conducted to optimize performance.

How much do you, the coach, need to know about sport physiology? Like the physiologist, the dedicated coach never knows enough or stops learning. The following chapters provide a foundation of knowledge for you to build on. As an athlete and coach you already know a lot about sport and performance. You've ex-

perienced the effects of exercise and training, and you have learned from your own coaches. But in this fast-developing field there is always new, important information, and you'll need up-to-date knowledge to remain successful.

You need to be able to teach your athletes and answer their questions. They want to know why they should do warm-ups and cool-downs, how interval training improves performance, what to eat and when, and why junk food is bad for them. You'll have to provide information about individual responses to training and the concept of overtraining. The chapters in Part IV provide some of the answers and, more important, help you fulfill your coaching-to-perform role by guiding your athletes to better performances with sound training and nutritional programs.

Chapter 10

Principles of Training

Brian J. Sharkey, PhD
University of Montana

This chapter introduces important physiological principles that must be followed if your athletes are to make steady progress in practices and training programs and avoid illness and injury. We begin with the 10 principles of training upon which successful programs are constructed:

Principle 1: Readiness
Principle 2: Individual response
Principle 3: Adaptation
Principle 4: Overload
Principle 5: Progression
Principle 6: Specificity
Principle 7: Variation
Principle 8: Warm-up and cool-down
Principle 9: Long-term training
Principle 10: Reversibility

Several of the principles explain why athletes must be treated as individuals, some point out how and why training influences the body, a few describe important elements of daily programs, and several explain the long-term effects of training or detraining. All are important.

Study the principles carefully, keeping in mind the responsibility you accept when you become a coach. Remember that the adolescent is not a small adult, that the body is not fully mature until the bones have stopped growing (between ages 18 and 21), that the demands of growth require considerable energy and rest, and that sport should be developmental, not destructive. Successful coaches understand and practice the principles of training. Those who don't may harm athletes more than they help them.

Principle 1: Readiness

The value of training depends on the physiological readiness of individual athletes. Readiness comes with maturation. As a result, before puberty athletes simply aren't physiologically ready to respond fully to training.

In prepubescent athletes, aerobic training is less effective than in adolescents or young adults. Improvements in performance may actually be due to increased stature and improved skill and efficiency. Anaerobic training of young athletes is ineffective because anaerobic capabilities depend on strength and maturation. Strength training in prepubescent athletes improves strength via neuromuscular changes (improved fiber recruitment, reduced inhibitions), but shows little evidence of the changes in muscle size that occur after puberty.

Neuromuscular skill, on the other hand, is a function of practice, not age or maturation. Therefore, training for young athletes should focus on skill development and fun. More serious training should await development of the physiological capacity to respond. See Figure 10.1 for an illustration of what goals you should emphasize with athletes of various ages.

Because immature athletes are less able to benefit from training, and because differences in maturation can mean enormous differences in muscle mass and power, immature athletes are often disadvantaged when they compete with mature youths in contact sports. Weight categories reduce this advantage but do not eliminate it. Look for additional information on readiness in chapter 11.

Principle 2: Individual Response

Athletes respond differently to the same training for many reasons. Among them are differences in heredity, maturity, nutrition, rest and sleep, level of fitness, environment, illness, injury, and motivation. Successful coaches are aware of individual differences and how they affect athletes' responses to training. And they

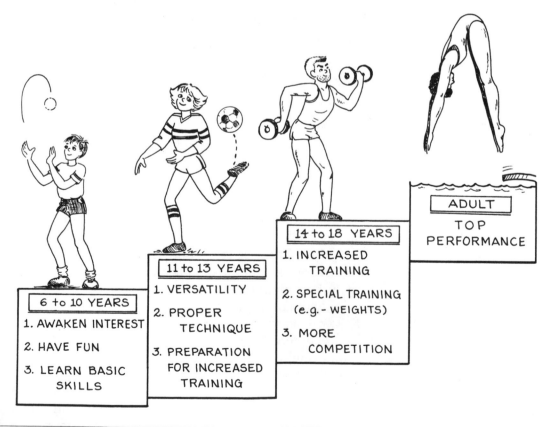

Figure 10.1 Stages of training.

are sensitive to changes in performance that may signal poor nutrition, lack of rest, illness, or injury. Let's examine each of the factors that affect athletes' responses to training.

Heredity

Physique, muscle fiber characteristics, heart and lung size, and other factors affecting sport activity are inherited. But even for inherited characteristics, the eventual expression of those characteristics is also influenced by environmental factors, such as diet and training. So although factors associated with aerobic fitness and endurance may be approximately 35% genetically determined, the remainder is subject to change.

Maturity

Bodies that are more mature can handle more training. Less-mature athletes need more energy for growth and development, and they don't respond as well to training (see Principle 1). Maturation leads to stronger muscles, bones, ligaments, and tendons, greater cardiovascular and anaerobic capacities, improved thermoregulation, and the hormones to support growth and training.

Nutrition

Training involves changes in tissues and organs—changes that require protein and other nutrients. Without proper nutrition, even the best training program will fail. One coach took on the challenge of coaching a big city high school basketball team that had been a perennial cellar-dweller. He soon learned that these listless, low-income athletes usually missed breakfast and often had soda and cream-filled cupcakes for lunch. The coach instituted a nutrition program, taught defense, and was runner-up his first year. The next year his team won the league championship and he was named Coach of the Year! This coach certainly learned the importance of nutrition. You can, too. See chapter 13 to learn more.

Rest and Sleep

Although many high school athletes will prosper with 8 hours of sleep, others need more rest, especially when they are involved in vigorous training. Watch for fatigue and staleness in your athletes and be ready to recommend additional rest or a day off from practice. Be particularly alert if you coach younger athletes; developing bodies need more rest.

Level of Fitness

Training improvements are most dramatic when the initial fitness level is low. As fitness improves, long hours of effort are needed to achieve small changes. Realize that unfit athletes fatigue easily and that fatigued athletes are more prone to illness and injury.

Environmental Influences

Factors in the physical and psychological environments influence athletes' responses to training. On the psychological side, an athlete who is facing emotional stress at home or school doesn't need a coach adding to the burden. Be sensitive to your athletes' stress. How you handle them may determine their future sport participation. It will certainly influence their responses to training.

Heat, cold, altitude, and air pollution are influential environmental factors. The coach must recognize differences in athletes' abilities to tolerate such stressors and provide relief when conditions are severe. For example, a runner with allergies may experience breathing problems during exercise when pollen or pollution is high. Or a football player may suffer heat stress on a humid summer day. In both cases the athletes need relief, not more effort. Failure to provide that relief and proper treatment could result in serious consequences.

Illness or Injury

Of course, illness or injury will influence an athlete's response to training. Your challenge is to spot the problem before it becomes serious.

Many physical infirmities surface during hard effort, so you may be the first to detect an impending problem. Be certain ill or injured athletes have recovered before they return to practice. Illness could be a sign of reduced resistance brought on by overtraining.

Motivation

Athletes work harder and progress farther when they are motivated—when they see the relationship between their hard work and the attainment of personal goals. Athletes who participate to satisfy their parents' goals are usually easy to spot. They may need help setting their *own* goals, even if defining those goals means dropping out of the sport.

Principle 3: Adaptation

Training induces subtle, progressive changes as the body adapts to added demands. Dr. Ned Fredrick, a noted sport scientist, describes proper training for sport as "a gentle pastime in which we coax subtle changes from the body." The day-to-day changes from training are so small as to be unmeasurable. It takes weeks and sometimes months of patient progress to achieve measurable adaptations. By trying to rush the process you risk illness, injury,

or both. Typical adaptations to training include these:

- Improved respiration, heart function, circulation, and blood volume
- Improved muscular endurance, strength, and power
- Tougher bones, ligaments, tendons, and connective tissue

Youth sport and school coaches don't have months of time to devote to training. With only a few weeks of practice before the first competition, you need to know how to get the most from your athletes. The principle of adaptation tells us that training can't be rushed. The best you can do is to design a *sensible* program and be satisfied with the results. Don't try to do it all in one season, or you are likely to cause more harm than good. Principle 9 offers suggestions on how to get the most from training.

Principle 4: Overload

The legendary tale of Milo, a warrior in ancient Greece, illustrates the overload principle. Milo built his strength by lifting a young calf every day. As the calf got bigger, Milo got stronger. Eventually, according to the legend, he was able to lift the full-grown animal. Milo's training was effective because it placed a progressive demand on his body, and the desired adaptations took place.

Initial training must exceed the typical daily demand. As the body adapts to the increased load, more load should be added. The rate of improvement is related to three factors, which you can remember with the acronym FIT.

F—Frequency
I—Intensity
T—Time (duration)

The overload principle is evident in all kinds of training. You gradually add weight to a barbell to build strength. Endurance athletes increase training time and intensity to improve race performances. The overload stimulates changes designed to help the body cope with growing demands on the muscles and other

systems. These changes involve the nervous system, which learns to recruit muscle fibers more effectively; the circulation system, which becomes better able to send more blood to the working muscles; and the muscles themselves, where the overload stimulates the production of new protein to help meet future exercise demands.

Principle 5: Progression

To achieve adaptations using the overload principle, training must follow the principle of progression. When the training load is increased too quickly, the body cannot adapt, and instead it breaks down. Progression must be observed

in FIT terms, daily, weekly, monthly, and yearly:

- Frequency—More sessions
- Intensity—More load
- Time—Greater duration

But progression does not mean making continual increases without time for recovery. The body requires periods of rest in which adaptations take place. Figure 10.2 shows the progression principle properly applied for a runner. Notice that every fourth week provides relative rest or relief from the previous increases in training load. We'll say more about 4-week training cycles in chapter 12.

When an enthusiastic coach allows or encourages athletes to progress too quickly, the best that can happen is that they peak too early. But illness or injury is the more likely result. Excessive fatigue can suppress the immune system, leading to illness. And the most common cause of injuries in endurance sports is increasing training load (distance or intensity) too quickly. The best advice for using the progression principle is this: Make haste slowly!

The principle of progression has additional implications for coaches. Training should also progress from

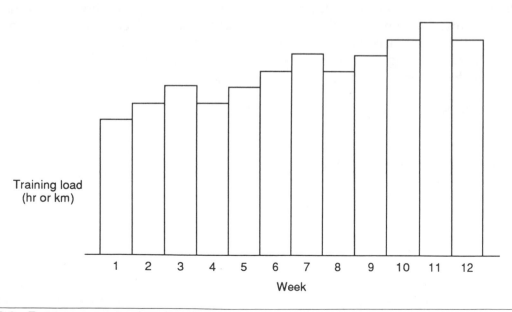

Figure 10.2 Training progression for a runner.

- the general to the specific,
- the parts to the whole, and
- quantity to quality.

In chapter 11, I give detailed advice on how to make steady progress toward training goals.

Principle 6: Specificity

Exercise is specific. Every time you jog you recruit the same muscle fibers, energy pathways, and energy sources. If you jog every day you train, adaptations will take place in the muscle fibers used during the exercise. The adaptations to endurance training are different than those that occur as the result of strength training. Endurance training brings improvements in oxidative enzymes and the muscle's ability to burn fat and carbohydrate in the presence of oxygen. Strength training leads to increases in the contractile proteins, actin and myosin, but only in the muscles exercised.

What this means is that specific training brings specific results. You won't get much stronger with endurance training, and you won't improve endurance with strength training. Furthermore, cycling is not the best preparation for running, or vice versa. Performance improves most when training is specific to the activity.

Of course, every rule or principle can be taken to the extreme. Specificity does *not* mean you should avoid training opposite or adjacent muscles. Other muscles should be trained to avoid creating imbalances that could predispose the athlete to injury. Training adjacent muscles also helps the athlete adapt to changes in conditions and provides a back-up when the primary muscle fibers become fatigued. So some cycling may be good for a runner to provide muscle balance, to train adjacent fibers, and to provide relief from the pounding of running. However, these changes cannot compensate for the specific training mode of running.

Principle 7: Variation

Training programs need to vary to avoid boredom and maintain athletes' interest. The principle of variation embraces several important concepts:

- Work versus rest
- Hard versus easy
- Training cycles
- Cross-training

Adaptation comes when work is followed by rest. Neglecting variation leads to boredom, staleness, and poor performance. Successive sessions of hard work without adequate time for rest and recovery are certain to hinder training progress.

You can achieve variation by changing your training routine and drills. Conduct workouts in different places or under different conditions. Follow a long workout with a short one, an intense session with a relaxed one, high speed activity with easy distance exercise. When workouts become dull, do something different. Use variety to diminish monotony and lighten the physical and psychological burdens of heavy training. You might also find games and relays valuable to liven practices, especially with younger athletes.

Another form of variation involves the use of training cycles (for example, 4-week cycles). Change training activities every four weeks to avoid stagnation and to maintain interest. Finally, let's consider the popular concept of cross-training. Runners swim or cycle for variety and to avoid overuse injuries. Cross-training allows maintenance of fitness while muscles and bones recover from hard training. Properly selected cross-training activities can contribute to performance. For example, riding a mountain bike up steep hills in the standing position can build stamina on hills for a cross-country runner. But cross-training on a bicycle will not replace specific training for a runner.

Principle 8: Warm-Up and Cool-Down

A warm-up should always precede strenuous activity to

- increase body temperature,
- increase respiration and heart rate, and
- guard against muscle, tendon, and ligament strains.

The warm-up should consist of stretching exercises, calisthenics, and sport-specific activities with gradually increasing intensity. Many athletes find it more effective to stretch after warming the muscles with calisthenics or sport-specific exercise (for example, basketball drills).

The cool-down is just as important as the warm-up. Abruptly halting vigorous activity causes pooling of the blood, sluggish circulation, and slow removal of waste products. It may also contribute to cramping, soreness, or more serious problems, such as fainting. Light activity and stretching after exercise continue the pumping action of muscles on veins, promoting both circulation and removal of metabolic wastes. It is your responsibility to teach the warm-up and cool-down and to include them in each practice or training session (see chapter 11 for more information).

Principle 9: Long-Term Training

The gradual overload of body systems leads to impressive improvements in performance, but it takes years of effort to approach high-level performance capability. Long-term training allows for gradual progress, growth and develop-ment, skill acquisition, learning strategies, and a fuller understanding of the sport.

Long-term training does not mean that an athlete must give up everything else to specialize in one sport. Young people should be encouraged to participate in a variety of activities. As coach you should neither expect nor demand exclusive control over athletes' time. The need for specialization comes soon enough. Don't rush an athlete toward specialization just to bolster your ego.

In time, as athletes grow and develop, they will begin to specialize in one or two sports. An athlete with the desire to reach the top will eventually choose a single sport and give it undivided attention—for years. It takes 5 to 10 years of development to become an elite athlete. Keep that in mind when you work with dedicated athletes. Increasing training intensity too rapidly could precipitate a career-ending injury. Never risk sacrificing an athlete's long-term personal or career goals just to achieve short-term success.

So don't rush the process; too much training too soon may lead to mental and physical burnout and early retirement from the sport. Excellence rewards those who persist with well-planned, long-term training programs.

Principle 10: Reversibility

Most training adaptations are all too easily reversible. It usually takes longer to gain endurance than to lose it. With complete bed rest, fitness can decline at a rate of almost 10% per week! Strength declines more slowly, but disuse eventually causes atrophy of even the best-trained muscles. Smart coaches understand the principle of reversibility and provide their teams with off-season maintenance programs.

Fallacies of Training

Before I close this chapter on principles, let me address some popular fallacies or misconceptions concerning training. These oft-quoted "principles" have no basis in medical or scientific research.

Training Myths

- No pain, no gain.
- You must break down muscle to improve.
- Go for the burn.
- Lactic acid causes muscle soreness.
- Muscle turns to fat (or vice versa).
- Running out of wind.

No Pain, No Gain

Although serious training is often difficult and sometimes unpleasant, it shouldn't hurt. In fact, well-prepared athletes can perform difficult events in a state of euphoria, free of pain and oblivious to discomfort. Marathon winners sometimes seem to finish full of vitality, whereas the losers appear near collapse.

Pain is not a natural consequence of exercise or training. It is a sign of a problem that shouldn't be ignored. During exercise the body produces natural opiates, called endorphins, that can mask discomfort during exercise. But an athlete who experiences real pain during training should back off. If the pain persists the problem should be evaluated.

Discomfort, on the other hand, can accompany difficult aspects of training, such as heavy lifting, intense interval training, or long distance effort. Discomfort is a natural consequence of the anaerobic effort associated with lifting or intervals and of the muscle fatigue, microtrauma (tissue damage), and soreness that follow long distance training.

Overload sometimes requires working at the upper limit of strength, intensity, or endurance, and that can be temporarily uncomfortable. If it results in pain it is probably excessive. Perhaps a more accurate motto would be, No discomfort, no excellence!

You Must Break Down Muscle to Improve

Microtrauma sometimes occurs in muscles during vigorous training and competition, but it isn't a necessary or even desirable outcome of training. Significant trauma has been observed at the end of marathons with long downhill stretches requiring eccentric muscular contractions (contractions of a lengthening muscle). Eccentric contractions are a major cause of muscle soreness, which has been associated with muscle trauma, reduced force output, and prolonged (4- to 6-week) recovery. It should be obvious, then, that excessive trauma doesn't help training, it stops it.

Weight lifters may traumatize muscle with excess weight or repetitions, but that is not necessary to develop strength. The most authoritative book on resistance training, with over 350 references to the scientific literature, makes no mention of tearing muscle down to achieve development (Fleck & Kraemer, 1997). Neither pain nor injury are normal consequences of training. Both should be avoided.

Go for the Burn

This popular statement is often heard among bodybuilders who do numerous repetitions and sets to build, shape, and define muscles. The burn they describe is probably due to the increased acidity associated with elevated levels of lactic acid in the muscle. Although this sensation isn't dangerous, it isn't a necessary part of a strength program designed to improve performance in sport. Chapter 12 describes resistance training programs designed to improve performance without athletes' experiencing the "burning" sensation.

Lactic Acid Causes Muscle Soreness

This fallacy has been around for years, with no facts to support it. Although it is true that lactic acid may be produced in contractions that lead to soreness, the lactic acid isn't the cause of the soreness. Lactic acid is cleared from muscles and blood within an hour of exercise. Soreness comes 24 hours or more after the effort—long after the lactic acid has been metabolized. Soreness comes after unfamiliar exertion or after a long layoff. It is probably associated with microtrauma to muscle and connective tissue and the swelling that results thereafter. Stretching can help reduce soreness. After recovery from the soreness, additional exposure to the activity will not cause as much discomfort.

Muscle Turns to Fat (or Vice Versa)

Another common misconception is that when an athlete stops training, muscle can turn to fat. This idea is also a fallacy. Although a cessation of training will lead to a reversal of exercise gains, muscle will no more turn to fat than fat will turn to muscle. Both are highly specialized tissues with specific functions. Muscles are composed of long, spaghetti-like fibers with contractile proteins designed to exert force; fat cells are round receptacles designed to store fat. Training increases the size of muscle fibers (hypertrophy) and detraining reduces it (atrophy). Eating too many calories causes fat cells to grow in size as they store more fat. The cells shrink when you burn more calories than you eat. But long, thin muscle fibers never change into spherical fat cells, or vice versa.

IT'S NOT DIFFICULT TO SEE WHO IS DEVELOPING MUSCLE AND WHO IS DEVELOPING FAT!

Running Out of Wind

Athletes often have the sensation of being out of air when they run too fast for their level of training. The sensation comes from the lungs and reflects another discomfort of exertion. However, it is more likely to be due to an excess of carbon dioxide than a lack of oxygen or air. Carbon dioxide, which is produced during exercise, is the primary stimulus for respiration. So when levels are high, as during vigorous effort, they cause distress signals in the lungs. The respiratory system thinks it is more important to get rid of excess carbon dioxide than to bring in more oxygen. Excess carbon dioxide is a sign that you are working above your level of training. Become familiar with the sensation and what it is telling you—keep it up and you will soon become exhausted.

Checking Your Principles

You will want to remember the 10 principles of training as you develop your own training program. A simple matching exercise to check your learning appears on page 100. Match the principle with the correct description.

Principle	Description
1. _____ Individual response	A. Maturation of athletes
2. _____ Adaptation	B. Not beginning, or ending, vigorous exercise abruptly
3. _____ Overload	C. Putting greater demand on the body
4. _____ Progression	D. The loss of training gains
5. _____ Specificity	E. Uniqueness of the athlete
6. _____ Variation	F. Adjustment to overload
7. _____ Warm-up/cool-down	G. Years of performance effort
8. _____ Long-term training	H. Changing activities to avoid monotony
9. _____ Reversibility	I. Training to meet particular demands
10. _____ Readiness	J. Pacing the overload

Answers: 1 = E; 2 = F; 3 = C; 4 = J; 5 = I; 6 = H; 7 = B; 8 = G; 9 = D; 10 = A

Chapter 11

Fitness for Sport

Brian J. Sharkey, PhD
University of Montana

Athletes must be fit to play well and to avoid injury. I tell people, "Don't play sports to get in shape, get in shape to play sports!" One of your major coaching responsibilities is to help your athletes achieve the levels of energy fitness and muscular fitness demanded by your sport.

Energy fitness involves storing and using fuels to power muscle contractions. It also involves the development of important supply and support systems, including the respiratory, cardiovascular, and endocrine (hormonal) systems. While others speak of aerobic or cardiovascular training, I use the term *energy fitness* to describe the training of specific aerobic and anaerobic energy systems and to focus on how such training enhances the muscles' ability to use the body's available energy.

Muscular fitness encompasses flexibility, strength, muscle endurance, power, and speed. It also involves the nervous system, which controls muscle contractions, and so cannot be separated from neuromuscular (nerve and muscle) or training for skill, strength, muscular endurance, and power. Properly designed training programs follow the principle of specificity: Energy and muscular fitness activities should support the skills involved in the sport.

I will begin this chapter by examining the warm-up, go on to energy and then muscular fitness, and conclude with a discussion of the cool-down. It is impossible to tell you all there is to know about those topics in one short chapter, but we'll cover the basics. Chapter 12 uses examples to teach you how to develop training programs for specific types of sports and discusses the problem of overtraining. As you proceed, remember how the principle of readiness influences each individual's response to training.

Warm-Up

You should begin each training session with a warm-up designed specifically for your sport. In low-energy, high-skill sports such as archery or pistol shooting, the warm-up should include stretching and skill rehearsal. In high-energy sports such as swimming, the warm-up should raise the respiratory and heart rates and body temperature and involve stretching and technique rehearsal. Adequate warm-up is an essential part of injury prevention because it decreases the incidence of strains and sprains. And before competition, warm-up is a good time for athletes to review and practice important psychological skills (imagery, relaxation, concentration) and to review their strategies for the event.

The stretching part of a warm-up reduces soreness and the risk of injury and increases the range of motion around joints. Try to begin the warm-up on a comfortable surface and have athletes slowly stretch the lower back, hamstrings, and other muscles susceptible to soreness or injury. Don't use old-fashioned bobbing and bouncing movements to stretch—they cause a reflex muscle contraction that makes stretching difficult and risky. Athletes should

reach until they feel slight discomfort, hold the position for five counts, then relax. Another effective approach is the *contract-relax* technique: Athletes stretch, hold, and relax, then they contract the muscle for several counts and immediately stretch it again.

Five minutes of easy stretching is usually adequate. Players should stretch any muscles that get sore or are more easily injured when stiff and cold. Warm muscles are easier to stretch, so if you want to stress improved flexibility (as in gymnastics, wrestling, or even running), do additional stretching after some warm-up. See Figure 11.1 for examples of popular stretches.

After stretching go on to calisthenics, beginning with slower movements before doing vigorous ones like jumping jacks to increase respiration, circulation, and body temperature. After 5 minutes your athletes should be warmed up enough to practice skills. Start out easy; don't begin contact drills or violent moves until players are well warmed up.

Energy Fitness

Energy fitness is the body's ability to store and use fuels efficiently to power particular muscle contractions. It also includes important adaptations in the supply and support systems (respiration, cardiovascular, and hormonal) that deliver oxygen and fuels to muscles and carry off carbon dioxide and other wastes. As a coach you should know the major energy sources and pathways used in your sport and how to help athletes achieve the energy fitness they need to compete successfully. You should understand how muscles use the energy available to them and how inefficient energy use hastens fatigue. This is important, as you will see, because the demands of different sports cause muscles to use energy differently. By matching training regimens to the energy demands of your sport, you will help your athletes meet these differing demands most effectively.

Energy Pathways

The energy that muscles use to contract comes from two systems. One is called *aerobic* (meaning "with oxygen") and the other

WHILE STANDING, GRASP FOOT OF FLEXED LEG AND FIRMLY PULL TOWARDS YOUR BODY TO STRETCH YOUR LEG. REPEAT A COUPLE OF TIMES AND SWITCH LEGS.

WITH ARMS OUTSTRETCHED, KEEPING EYES FORWARD, TWIST TRUNK SLOWLY FROM SIDE TO SIDE

SLOWLY SLIDE INTO STRIDE POSITION WITH FRONT FOOT FLAT ON FLOOR, KNEE AT 90° ANGLE, AND REAR FOOT ON TOES. CHANGE EVERY 5 SECONDS.

SIT WITH LEGS OUTSTRETCHED AND SLOWLY STRETCH TO TOUCH YOUR TOES – REPEAT SEVERAL TIMES.

PULL KNEES TO CHEST AND ROCK BACK AND FORTH ON YOUR BACK.

STAND 3 FEET FROM WALL WITH HEELS ON GROUND, LEAN FORWARD SLOWLY, HOLD FOR 15 TO 20 SECONDS....

USE JUMPING JACKS IN YOUR WARM UPS TOO...

Figure 11.1 Stretching exercises.

anaerobic ("without oxygen"). Which system the body uses depends on several factors, including the availability of oxygen and the intensity and duration of activity. The anaerobic energy system has two parts:

- short term (under 30 seconds), and
- the lactate energy system (30 to 90 seconds).

Anaerobic energy sources are used at the beginning of exercise, before respiration and circulation adjust to the physical effort and begin supplying oxygen to the muscles, and when energy demands exceed the body's ability to generate aerobic energy. During the short-term anaerobic phase, energy comes from limited energy supplies stored in the muscles. In the lactate system, energy comes from stored muscle glycogen. Aerobic energy sources are used during longer, steady-paced activities, such as running. Aerobic energy comes from the oxidation (burning) of fat and carbohydrate. If the activity becomes so intense that the energy demands exceed the aerobic or oxidative system's ability to provide oxygen, additional energy for muscle contractions then comes from the anaerobic or nonoxidative breakdown of muscle glycogen. The product of glycogen use is lactic acid.

Fueling muscle anaerobically is far less efficient than fueling it aerobically. For example, when muscle glycogen is burned aerobically it produces 38 units of energy; used anaerobically it produces only 2 units. The anaerobic pathway also produces more lactic acid, and excess lactic acid interferes with the muscle's ability to contract and hinders energy production, causing fatigue and poor performance.

When athletes exercise at a level of intensity that demands anaerobic energy production, they quickly reduce muscle energy stores, produce excess lactic acid and hasten fatigue. If they continue too long, the inefficient anaerobic energy pathway depletes muscle glycogen and sours the muscle with acidic by-products. The athlete then must slow down or stop the activity in order to replenish energy stores, remove acidic by-products, and allow the muscle to recover. Fortunately, muscles can be trained, even at higher intensities, to work much more efficiently.

Energy Training

It may be helpful to think of energy training like building a pyramid (see Figure 11.2). As you can see, the training pyramid is constructed on a solid aerobic foundation.

Aerobic Foundation. Aerobic fitness—the ability to take in, transport, and use oxygen—is necessary for athletes in every sport. Training

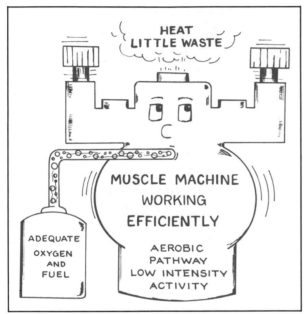

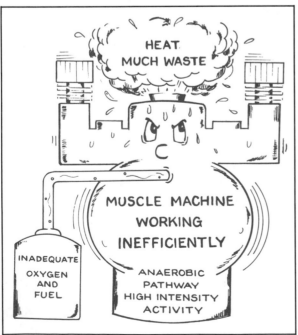

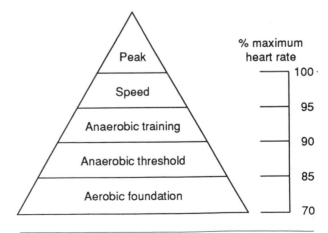

Figure 11.2 The training pyramid. *Note*. From *Training for Cross-Country Ski Racing* (p. 88) by B.J. Sharkey, 1984, Champaign, IL: Human Kinetics. Copyright 1984 by Brian J. Sharkey. Reprinted by permission.

for aerobic fitness helps toughen ligaments, tendons, and connective tissue and reduces the risk of injury, while developing the toughness and endurance needed for more intense training. It lays the foundation upon which all future practices and performances are built. Even in football (predominantly an anaerobic sport because the average play lasts but a few seconds), aerobic fitness helps athletes recover faster between plays and practice longer before fatigue sets in.

Good aerobic training includes these components:

- Low-intensity, long-duration activity (such as distance running, swimming, or cycling)
- Natural intervals (medium distance with occasional periods of increased intensity)
- Resistance effort (such as hills in running) once a week

As endurance grows, you can increase the aerobic overload with greater distance or intensity of effort. Remember, though, that intensity should not be so demanding that the muscles need to use the anaerobic energy pathway. It is far more efficient for muscles to use oxygen, so get all you can from the aerobic pathway before moving on to more intense training. Follow the principles of training outlined in chapter 10. Start slowly, use gradual progression, and then overload the system, first with distance and then intensity. Alternate hard and easy workouts and permit adequate rest and sleep. Provide variation, but don't forget about the principle of specificity.

In working to improve your athletes' aerobic foundation, remember that prepubescent athletes differ from young adults in several respects. Whether or not their aerobic fitness is low, they are less efficient and less able to withstand high temperatures. Therefore, intense aerobic training can be more difficult and risky, especially in hot weather. And while training of aerobic energy pathways is less effective before puberty, aerobic training provides neuromuscular benefits, helping athletes relax and become more efficient, using less energy to cover the distance. So conduct aerobic training but hold back on hard training until athletes reach puberty. You want to avoid the burnout that can result from excessive training.

Anaerobic Threshold. As shown in our training pyramid, the second stage of training is designed to raise the *anaerobic threshold*. The anaerobic (or lactate) threshold marks the level of exertion at which an athlete begins to produce excess lactic acid. It designates the upper limit of efficient aerobic energy production. Exercise that exceeds the anaerobic threshold demands work by less efficient muscle fibers and anaerobic energy pathways. Fortunately, you can help athletes raise their anaerobic thresholds with specific training:

- 4 to 6 work intervals of at least 2 minutes just below threshold
- Fartlek training (varying speed) over natural terrain
- pace training (e.g., 1 kilometer at race pace)

How does an athlete know when he or she is at or near the threshold? The most accurate (but expensive) ways to find out are laboratory treadmill and field lactate tests. But with practice the athlete can learn what the threshold *feels* like. When breathing becomes difficult and sustained effort doubtful, it is a good sign that the threshold is near.

Some coaches like to determine anaerobic thresholds by measuring heart rates. The anaerobic threshold is usually 85% to 95% of the maximum heart rate. The maximum heart rate is calculated using this formula:

Maximum heart rate = 220 − Age in years

(*Note:* Some prefer to use the rating of perceived exertion to guide threshold training. When the exercise feels very hard, you are close to the threshold. See Table 11.1.)

Once athletes have learned to identify their thresholds, they should back off from the threshold slightly while maintaining pace and completing one of the training tasks previously described. A month with twice-a-week bouts of this training will raise athletes' thresholds, presumably by helping muscle fibers work better aerobically.

Table 11.1 Borg's RPE scale

6	No exertion at all
7	Extremely light
8	
9	Very light
10	
11	Light
12	
13	Somewhat hard
14	
15	Hard
16	
17	Very hard
18	
19	Extremely hard
20	Maximal exertion

Reprinted, by permission, from G. Borg, 1985, *An Introduction to Borg's RPE Scale* (Ithaca, NY: Mouvement Publications), 7.

Anaerobic threshold training is difficult for athletes of all ages and should be used only once or twice a week during the preseason. In particular, prepubescent athletes are less able to utilize muscle glycogen and to produce lactic acid, so threshold training is of limited value for them. You may want to use a little threshold training to help young athletes achieve relaxation and efficiency at this level of exertion, but sustained threshold workouts are only likely to cause fatigue, burnout, or loss of interest.

Anaerobic Training. The lactate pathway is trained when it is overloaded in short, intense bouts of exercise. Anaerobic training is achieved by progressively increasing speed while decreasing distance or duration of effort. This method

of intermittent training, also called *interval training*, consists of an exercise interval followed by a period of active rest, such as easy jogging. The active rest maintains circulation and uses muscle contractions at low intensity to remove waste products and hasten recovery.

I have outlined basic interval training suggestions in Table 11.2 as a guide for designing your anaerobic training program. According to the principle of specificity, some part of the training should mimic the intensity of your sport, so identify intervals in the table that most closely approximate that intensity. The intermittent nature of interval training allows athletes to train longer at high intensity before they become fatigued. To avoid overworking your athletes, follow the guidelines provided in the columns "% of maximum speed" and "% of maximum heart rate." You'll notice that the more intense the interval, the greater the rest suggested. In interval training, rest is just as important as work. If your timing is right, your athletes will peak for the big competition. But be careful—too much anaerobic training can lead to chronic fatigue, staleness, illness, or injury.

Following these guidelines will enhance the quality of your interval training sessions:

- Be sure the athlete's heart rate has recovered to less than 125 beats per minute before beginning the next interval.
- Stop intervals when athletes can no longer maintain good form.
- Never schedule more than two high-intensity workouts per week (games or competitions are high-intensity workouts).
- Plan no more than 4 to 6 weeks of anaerobic training, then taper off before the season's most important competition.

For adult athletes the effects of anaerobic training are subtle at best. And before puberty the energy benefits, if any, are too small to measure. Anaerobic capabilities, glycogen stores, anaerobic enzymes, and lactic acid levels are lower for children than for young adults. Because development of anaerobic capacity seems to be related more to maturity than to training, the value of extensive anaerobic training for prepubescent athletes is questionable. Anaerobic training does help develop neuro-

Table 11.2 Interval Training Suggestions

Interval	Use	Work duration	Rest duration	Work/rest ratio	Reps	% of maximum speed	% of maximum heart rate
Long	Anaerobic threshold training	2-5 min	2-5 min	1:1	4-6	70-80	85-90
Medium	Anaerobic training	60-90 sec	120-180 sec	1:2	8-12	80-90	95
Short	High energy training (anaerobic)	30-60 sec	90-180 sec	1:3	15-20	95	100
Sprint	Speed (anaerobic)	10-30 sec	30-90 sec	1:3	25 +	100	100

muscular skill, mechanical efficiency, and psychological toughness. But wait until athletes are 13 to 15 years of age before instituting the more demanding interval training programs.

Speed. When athletes are new to a sport they should follow the training pyramid (Figure 11.2, p. 104) to prepare for high speed training and peak performances. Experienced athletes can do speed training throughout the season.

Speed is partially inherited and partially acquired. The inherited factor involves one's muscle fiber makeup and biomechanical characteristics. But even athletes who didn't inherit a preponderance of fast fibers or a biomechanical advantage can learn to run, swim, or cycle faster. Some speed improvement comes as athletes learn to relax and become more efficient; more comes when they do speed drills supplemented by weight training.

Speed training usually involves sprints. If your sport requires speed, try some of these:

- acceleration sprints (safest kind)—start easy, then speed up
- hollow sprints—start and end fast, go easier in the middle
- starts—if needed for track, swimming, or football

For skill sports like basketball, specific speed work must be done on the court, as in running line drills. And be sure to use a ball to increase specificity of the drill. Can you think of specific speed drills in your sport? I'll say more about speed training later in this chapter.

Peaking. The training pyramid shows you how the levels of training build toward a competitive peak. If you skip stages of training, the result will be less successful and may lead to injury. As the season progresses, so should training intensity. Don't attempt to achieve peak performances early in the season. Use your initial contests to build training, sharpen skills, and improve speed. By midseason athletes should be at a competitive level that can be maintained through the last game of the season. If athletes reach this peak too soon they may slump before the season ends.

In Figure 11.3 you can see how the different forms of training fit into an overall program. If possible, schedule *at least* one month each for aerobic, anaerobic threshold, and anaerobic training. If athletes train in the off-season, they should spend at least a month on aerobic training before regular practices begin. Young athletes may start the season without a solid aerobic foundation specific to your sport; if so, you should develop it before moving on to more intense anaerobic threshold training. Chapter 12 includes specific suggestions for developing training programs.

Tapering. The taper is a period of reduced training before an important competition. Tapering fosters recovery from the rigors of training, allows for optimal energy storage, and provides time to heal minor injuries. Some coaches train right up to early competitions, then provide a taper before the conference championship. The approximate length of taper differs according to the sport, the event (e.g., sprint vs. distance), and the difficulty of the training buildup. Some coaches taper for a few days (e.g., team sports, sprinters), others for

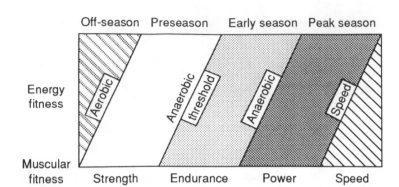

Figure 11.3 Seasonal training goals. *Note.* From *Physiology of Fitness* (2nd ed., p. 209) by B.J. Sharkey, 1984, Champaign, IL: Human Kinetics. Copyright 1984 by Brian J. Sharkey. Modified by permission.

a week or more (e.g., swimmers, long distance runners). The length probably depends on the volume of training, with a longer taper allowed for greater volumes of training. Experiment with tapering periods to see what works best for your athletes.

Muscular Fitness

Muscular fitness includes strength, endurance, power, and speed, along with flexibility. In Figure 11.3 you can see how all these components of athletic performance can be woven into the training program. However, young athletes and newcomers are best started on endurance training alone, with less resistance and more repetitions to avoid injury. Experienced athletes usually do off-season strength training to build muscle size and force, then proceed to add endurance, power, and strength. They can begin the preseason with strength training and then add endurance, power, and speed.

Each component of muscular fitness can be enhanced by resistance training, in which a body part is moved against a counterforce. High resistance with few repetitions builds strength, whereas low resistance with many repetitions builds endurance. Resistance can be applied with free weights, machines that use stack weights, hydraulic and electronic apparatus, or from a partner (counterforce). Weight machines may provide constant or variable resistance. (For more complete coverage of this expanding area, read *Designing Resistance Training Programs,* 2nd edition [Fleck & Kraemer, 1997].)

Strength

As you consider the issue of strength training, the first question to ask is, How much strength is required in my sport? If your sport demands more strength than your athletes have, then they need training. But if they don't need more strength, move on to endurance, power, or speed work.

How do you know whether your sport demands more strength or if certain athletes need more? In some cases it is obvious. Football players, especially linemen, need all the strength they can get, but distance runners do not. Strength is defined as the maximum amount that can be lifted *one time.* Sports such as swimming, basketball, and cross-country skiing that involve many repetitions of less-than-maximum (submaximal) contractions require endurance more than strength.

How do you know if an athlete has enough strength for an endurance sport? Experience shows that the strength of a muscle group should be at least 2.5 times the resistance encountered. More strength won't contribute to improved performance. But an athlete with less than 2.5 times the load needs more strength to overcome the resistance.

For example, consider a young swimmer who exerts 15 pounds of force in a simulation of the effort involved in the arm pull. If her maximal strength measured using a spring scale or pulley weight in that muscle group exceeds 37.5 (2.5 × 15) pounds, she probably has sufficient strength. If not, she needs a sport-specific strength training program.

Now consider a high school swimmer who can exert 55 pounds in a maximal arm pull.

Does he have enough strength for his sport? Use a spring scale or pulley weight to determine the force exerted in a typical pull. He exerts 25 pounds in the average pull—is that enough strength? The answer is no, because his maximal arm pull is less than 2.5 times his typical arm pull in swimming (25 × 2.5 = 62.5).

Strength improves when a muscle is overloaded. A weight heavy enough to be lifted only a few times is sufficient to overload the muscle and cause adaptation. Adaptations to strength training include increased contractile proteins, thickened connective tissue, increased ability to recruit muscle fibers, and, of course, increased strength. Male athletes show more increased muscle size (hypertrophy) than do females as they get stronger. Gradual progression using free weights, weight machines, or even resisted calisthenics will improve strength when you follow these basic guidelines:

- Set the amount of weight so the maximum number of repetitions the athlete can do is 7, 8, or 9.
- Do 3 sets of 8 to 10 repetitions for each muscle group.
- Increase the resistance when the athlete can do more than 10 repetitions in each set.
- Lift every other day, 3 times per week.

Calisthenics (such as push-ups) are another way to build strength if you add resistance (counterforce) and keep the repetitions under 10. Some calisthenic exercises, like the chin-up, are self-limiting—you can only do so many. Others, like the push-up, need added resistance, such as a partner's hand on the back. If free weights or weight machines are not available, have athletes work in pairs to accomplish strength goals with an inexpensive form of variable resistance training. For example, while one athlete does a push-up a partner can apply a resistance (counterforce) that matches the force of the contraction. For best results, have athletes go through the movement in 1 to 2 seconds and repeat each exercise for 3 sets of 10 repetitions. See Figure 11.4 for more suggestions, or use your imagination to devise your own "counterforce" exercises.

Follow the strength guidelines and your athletes will improve their strength at the rate of 1% to 3% per week. When they have achieved adequate strength for your sport, move on to the next stage of muscular fitness training. But remember to include at least one set of high resistance training each week to maintain strength.

Although young athletes gain strength from resistance training, they gain little muscle size before puberty. This suggests that the increases in strength are due to neuromuscular changes,

RESISTED PUSH-UP

LEG FLEXION

LEG EXTENSION

ARM FLEXION

ARM EXTENSION

Figure 11.4 Counterforce exercises.

including recruitment of more fibers, learning to exert force more effectively, and reduced inhibitions. Following the guidelines here will increase strength with little risk of injury. However, be sure that athletes warm up and lift properly, with proper spotting and supervision. Avoid using heavy free weights and oversized training apparatus with prepubescent athletes. Because strength and muscle development re-

quires maturation and hormonal support, it may be possible to achieve the neuromuscular benefits of resistance training with light weights or few sets, thereby minimizing the risk of injury to the immature skeleton.

Muscular Endurance

In many sports, having sufficient muscular endurance is more important than great muscular strength. There are several types of muscular endurance. In Table 11.3 you can see how training repetitions relate to strength and endurance—from short-term (anaerobic) endurance to long-term (aerobic) endurance developed with hundreds of repetitions.

Use the prescriptions to achieve the type of endurance suitable for your sport; if short-term endurance is required for 1 to 2 minutes of effort, use that prescription. If long-term endurance is the name of your game, follow that plan. For sports that involve both, combine several types of muscular endurance training.

Like strength training, endurance training should be specific to the way the muscles will be used in a sport. Try to imitate the movements used in competition. Use free weights, weight machines, calisthenics, or other methods or equipment (e.g., rubber tubing) to achieve the desired results. Endurance is extremely trainable, and improvements in capabilities of the energy pathways can increase endurance greatly. In time, an athlete could progress from doing 20 push-ups to completing 200 or more! Often such dramatic improvements in endurance are associated with improved performance and success in sport.

Power

Power is the rate of doing work, described by this equation:

$$Power = \frac{Force \times Distance}{Time}$$

Power involves both strength (force) and speed (distance divided by time). It is essential to many sports, including football, baseball, and ice hockey. Training for power usually involves strength training. To improve jumping ability in basketball or volleyball, for example, coaches may prescribe squats to build strength in thigh muscles. But squats are slow and somewhat nonspecific for the neuromuscular skill of jumping. Therefore, training must progress to power exercises that combine force and speed in a sport-specific movement. The following guidelines lead to successful power development.

- Use a weight 30% to 60% of the athlete's maximum single lift.
- Instruct the athlete to lift the weight as fast as possible.
- Prescribe three sets of 15 to 25 repetitions, three times per week.

Table 11.3 The Strength-Endurance Continuum

	Strength	Short-term endurance	Intermediate endurance	Long-term endurance
Goal	Maximum force	Persistence with heavy load	Persistence with intermediate load	Persistence with light load
Prescription	7-10 RM[1] 3 sets 3 times/week	15-25 RM 3 sets 3 times/week	30-50 RM 2 sets 3 times/week	Over 100 reps 1 set 3 times/week
Improves	Contractile protein (actin and myosin) Connective tissue	Some strength and anaerobic metabolism (glycolysis)	Some endurance and anaerobic metabolism Slight strength improvement	Aerobic enzymes Mitochondria Oxygen and fat utilization
Doesn't improve	Oxygen intake Endurance	Oxygen intake		Strength

Note. From *Physiology of Fitness* (2nd ed., p. 79) by B.J. Sharkey, 1984, Champaign, IL: Human Kinetics. Copyright 1984 by Brian J. Sharkey. Modified with permission.

[1]RM = Repetitions maximum

• Increase the resistance when the athlete can perform 25 repetitions in each set.

Weights. Free weights are not well suited for power training. Certain weight machines are acceptable, but the best equipment is isokinetic or variable resistance devices that allow some control of resistance and speed of contraction (e.g., Leaper, Nautilus, Cybex). With these devices you can use the resistance and speed you need and maintain a safe program. Another plus with this type of equipment is that muscles don't get sore as easily. Soreness is caused by working too hard early in the season or by lowering a heavy weight (contracting a lengthening muscle). Avoid soreness by starting with lower resistance and slower contractions; then work up to the recommended prescription during a 2-week adjustment period.

Plyometrics. Plyometrics are calisthenic-like exercises used to develop power. Used in conjunction with strength training, these explosive movements build strength and the elastic recoil that provides more power for jumping and other activities. Because body weight is generally about 33% of maximum leg strength, plyometrics fit the power prescription outlined earlier.

Athletes should start plyometrics gradually to avoid injury and should stop if their legs get sore. Do all training on a soft surface like grass or dirt. Work up to 3 sets of 25 exercises, then increase resistance by adding a more difficult exercise (e.g., working uphill or wearing a weighted vest). Plyometrics will increase strength 8% to 10% and improve elastic recoil. They also help athletes learn to use force more effectively.

Coaches have devised plyometric exercises for the upper body, using medicine balls or combinations of movements (e.g., push up fast, clap hands, and do another push-up). Consult a good reference (like Radcliffe & Farentinos, 1985) for more about this new method of power training.

Although power doesn't develop rapidly in young athletes, some power training will help develop the neuromuscular skill of moving quickly against resistance. But power training, especially plyometrics, can be hard on young knees, so use it sparingly with immature athletes.

Speed

You may have heard that sprinters are born and not made, which is essentially true because fast muscle fibers are inherited. But all athletes can use practice and specific training to improve the components of speed—reaction time and movement time. Reaction time is how long it takes to initiate a movement, and movement time is the interval from the start to the end of the movement.

Reaction time is enhanced by practice drills. The knowledgeable coach speeds reactions by narrowing the choices athletes must make and then drilling the proper reaction (e.g., if the defensive end comes at the option quarterback, the quarterback pitches the ball, if not he runs). In track and swimming there is but one choice—when the gun goes, so does the athlete. The fewer the choices, the faster the reaction.

Movement time can be enhanced by a program of stretching, strength and power training, form training, and specific speed training. *Sportspeed* by George Dintiman and Robert Ward (1988) suggests the program outlined in Table 11.4.

Table 11.4 Speed Training Program

Training component	Description
Basic training	Aerobic and muscular fitness
Functional strength/ power	Explosive movements with 55% to 85% resistance
Ballistics	Explosive movements
Plyometrics	Explosive jumping/throwing movements
Sprint loading	Resisted sprinting
Sport speed/speed endurance	Participation and extended sprints
Overspeed	Exceeding maximum speed

Adapted from Dintiman and Ward (1988).

Overspeed or assisted speed training involves getting athletes to move 10% to 20% faster than maximum speed, for example, by being pulled by an elastic cord or by running downhill. In time athletes relax and become skilled and efficient at higher speeds. Be sure you know the necessary safety measures before you use this training approach. To build speed endurance, gradually increase sprint length while decreasing the rest between sprints. A wise coach once said, "Speed is an environment, and one must become acclimated to it." Use sport-specific training to acclimatize your athletes to the speed they need.

Cool-Down

Whatever the type or level of training you are using, be sure athletes cool down after a vigorous workout. Light activity such as jogging, walking, or stretching helps the circulation clear metabolic by-products from muscles and reduces the likelihood of stiffness and soreness. It may look good to follow wind sprints with a spirited dash to the showers, but it is a bad choice physiologically. Plan a 5-minute cool-down after every practice. After easy jogging, walking, or light calisthenics, do stretching exercises to reduce the chance of delayed muscle soreness.

Key Points to Remember

1. Each training session should start with a warm-up designed specifically for your sport.
2. Muscles depend on two major sources of fuel for energy, carbohydrate and fat.
3. As exercise intensity increases, the energy pathway and fuel change:
   - Fat and some carbohydrate are used during low intensity
   - Carbohydrate and some fat are used during moderate intensity
   - Carbohydrate is used during high intensity
4. Of the two major pathways that deliver energy for muscular contractions, the aerobic pathway uses energy efficiently, whereas the anaerobic pathway is far less efficient.
5. Slow, easy distance training is used to develop the aerobic foundation.
6. Training just below the anaerobic (or lactate) threshold raises the threshold and increases the intensity at which an athlete's aerobic energy pathway is able to deliver energy.
7. Training that exceeds the lactate threshold improves anaerobic energy pathways.
8. Muscular fitness consists of flexibility, strength, endurance, power, and speed.
9. Strength improves when a muscle is overloaded. Coaches must help athletes decide how much strength is needed for the sport, how to achieve that strength, and when to move on to other forms of training.
10. Short-term (anaerobic) and intermediate endurance are improved with training using more repetitions and less resistance than is used in strength and training.
11. Power, or the rate of doing work, is the product of strength (force) and speed (distance/time). Power can be increased by improving strength, speed, or both. Fast contractions at 30% to 60% of maximum force build power.
12. Speed can be improved by practicing a movement faster than it is usually performed.
13. Each vigorous practice or contest should end with a cool-down of light activity and stretching.

Chapter 12

Developing Your Training Program

Brian J. Sharkey, PhD
University of Montana

The activities you plan for athletes during training sessions will depend on a number of factors, including your sport and athletes' ages, experiences, and goals. Programs for young athletes should emphasize fun, basic skills, and variety. With maturity and experience, some athletes will concentrate on one or two sports, and training will become more intense and specialized.

This chapter offers an overview and guidelines for training program development. The information here, along with the tips you pick up from coaching clinics, experience, and sport-specific books, will get you started in your quest for the ideal training program.

Energy Program Development

Developing a training program begins with setting goals, such as how many hours of what kind of training you want to do each day, week, and month of the season. Training can be scheduled around the sporting seasons—off-season, pre-season, and competitive season—each lasting one to several months. Modern training programs also use *training periods* or *cycles*, in which training is systematically rotated from lower to higher intensity and duration. A typical 4-week cycle incorporates progressive muscle overload with rest and recovery (see Figure 12.1). Each week within a cycle and each session in a week needs its own plan of activity.

Say the annual goal for an athlete calls for 150 hours of training (an average of 1 hour a day, 6 days a week for 25 weeks); you must break that down and decide how much time to spend in each season. Because the off-season is designed for aerobic training, you might plan for relatively long sessions and average

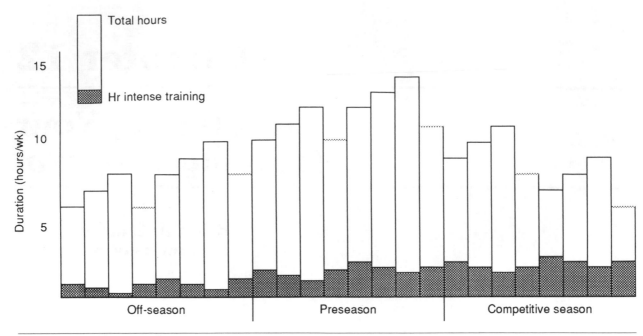

Figure 12.1 Training cycles.

10 hours a week for 12 weeks (10 hours × 12 weeks = 120 hours). You might further decide to achieve that 10-hour average by averaging 8, 10, and 12 hours a week for the three 4-week cycles of that season. So weeks within your first 4-week cycle might include 6, 8, 10, and 8 hours of training, for an average of 8 hours a week. Similar decisions must be made for other training parameters, such as training intensity, bringing all the elements together in a logical daily plan. If all these numbers sound confusing, don't despair—I'll provide specific guidelines to help you progress through the seasons, cycles, weeks, and sessions of training.

Training Guidelines

Follow these guidelines to ensure safe and effective training for your athletes.

- Base each training program on the maturity and experience of the athlete. Don't start a newcomer on a program designed for a veteran.
- Establish training goals (e.g., hours or distance per period of training, race pace, race distance).
- Increase hours or distance of training by no more than 10% to 20% per year,

season, or week (10% for newcomers and less mature athletes; up to 20% for experienced athletes).
- Limit intense training (anaerobic threshold, anaerobic, speed, and competitions) to 5% to 10% of total hours (5% for newcomers, 7% for trained athletes, 10% for elite athletes).
- Reduce the intensity of training as distance increases, and vice versa.
- Include at least three seasons (off-season, preseason, and competitive season) in your planning.
- Include at least two 4-week cycles in each season (three is preferable). (See the example in Figure 12.1.) Don't feel tied to the names of the seasons. It might be necessary to have your athletes begin a preseason cycle prior to formal team practices.

Weekly Plan

The goals and guidelines give general advice, but they don't translate into daily training activities. I have found that a *training menu* is a great help in developing weekly and daily plans. A menu includes the essential activities for each week of training. Table 12.1 is a

Table 12.1 Runner's Seasonal Training Menu of Activities

Training goal and season		
Aerobic base (off-season)	Anaerobic threshold (preseason)	Anaerobic and speed (competitive season)
Slow distance	Long intervals	Medium intervals
Hills	Fartlek	Short intervals
Fartlek[1]	Pace training	Sprints
Medium distance	Fast distance	Maintain aerobic base
Maintain speed	Maintain aerobic base	Maintain anaerobic threshold
Natural intervals[2]	Maintain speed	

[1]Fartlek is speed play, usually with a partner, of intervals of faster and slower running. Athletes choose the speed to suit the terrain and their level of training.

[2]Natural intervals utilize the changes in terrain to dictate pace.

speed work, and several twice-daily sessions. As training moves to the preseason, it is important to maintain aerobic fitness gains while working on increasing the anaerobic threshold. And as training approaches the competitive season, it is essential to maintain both aerobic and anaerobic threshold improvements with appropriate training.

Training hours depend on age, experience, and level of fitness. Table 12.3 provides guidelines for energy training hours in each season in an endurance sport. Because energy training requirements also depend on the sport, your athletes may get by with fewer hours of training.

Table 12.2 Sample Weekly Training Program for the Off-Season

Day	Activity
Monday	Natural intervals with some hills
Tuesday	Medium distance
Wednesday	Hills
Thursday	Fartlek
Friday	Easy day with light speed work
Saturday	Slow distance
Sunday	Rest or variety

Note: All training except speed training is to be done below the anaerobic threshold.

sample training menu for a middle-distance runner.

You develop your weekly plan from the menu, selecting one or more activities from the appropriate category for each day. Total distance or duration should meet your goals for that season and cycle. As you enter the preseason, you may need to plan two sessions a day to accommodate all the menu activities. Table 12.2 shows a typical weekly plan for the off-season.

More mature or experienced athletes should do more distance, more intense training and

Table 12.3 Hours of Energy Training Required Weekly for Endurance Sports

Age or level	Off-season	Preseason	Competitive season	Hours[1] per year
Under 15	5-6	6-7	4-5	200-300
15-17	8-9	9-10	7-8	300-400
17-21	9-12	12-14	8-9	400-600
Elite	10-13	13-16	10-11	500-700

[1]Based on an annual program.

These guidelines are based on the requirements for endurance sports. For team sports, sprints, or short-term activities, you can reduce the hours of energy training. Table 12.4 outlines aerobic foundation goals according to the amount of continuous effort required in your sport. If your sport is football, with an average play time of about 4 seconds, the off-season aerobic training required to meet the training goal is 1 to 2 hours, or 10 to 15 miles per week. The goal could be achieved in 3 to 5 days by running 3 miles each day.

Table 12.4 Training Goals for Building Aerobic Foundation

Continuous effort required	Training goals[1]
Under 10 seconds	10-15 miles/week or 1-2 hours
10 seconds-2 minutes	15-20 miles/week or 2-3 hours
2-15 minutes	20-30 miles/week or 3-5 hours
5-30 minutes	30-40 miles/week or 5-7 hours
Over 30 minutes	Over 40 miles/week or 7 hours

[1]Runners and others who train and compete on foot use miles per week; swimmers, cross-country skiers, and other nonrunners use hours per week.

Energy Needs

You may have wondered how to determine the energy demands for the sport you coach. Table 12.5 lists the energy needs and training emphases for some popular sports (if yours isn't listed, find one with similar requirements).

Sample Program

Now I'll put together a sample training program so you can see how the system works in an actual sport. Table 12.6 provides a seasonal program for basketball, a sport of medium energy requirements.

Although I would prefer to provide guidelines for a year-round training program, I realize that many coaches cannot work with athletes

Table 12.5 Energy Needs and Training Emphases for Popular Sports

Sport	Energy needs	Training emphases[1]
Baseball, football, hockey, sprinting	Short, intense (under 1 minute)	Anaerobic and speed
Basketball, tennis, wrestling	Intense (1-2 minutes)	Anaerobic threshold and anaerobic
Soccer, lacrosse, middle-distance swimming and track, skating	2-10 minutes	Aerobic, anaerobic threshold, and anaerobic
Cross-country running and skiing	Over 10 minutes	Aerobic and anaerobic threshold

[1]Remember to always develop the aerobic foundation before you begin intense training.

Table 12.6 Sample Energy Training Program for Basketball

Season: Off-season

Training emphasis: Aerobic foundation (20-30 miles or 3-5 hours/week)

Activities:

    Slow distance—1 time/week, 6-8 miles or 1 hour

    Fartlek—1 time/week (vary slow and fast), 3-4 miles or 30 minutes

    Medium distance—1 time/week, 4-6 miles or 30 minutes

    Hills—1 time/week, 3 miles or 30 minutes

    Pick-up games (full court)—2-3 times/week for 1 hour

    Other activities (e.g., cycling) for aerobic fitness, leg endurance, and variety

Coaching notes:

    Provide training goals and programs for the off-season.

Season: Preseason

Training emphasis: Anaerobic threshold and anaerobic

Activities:

    Fartlek—1 time/week (increasing intensity)

    Medium intervals—1 time/week, 8-12 reps of 90-second intervals

    Fast break drills—2 times/week (full court)

    Line drills and sprints—1 time/week

    Long intervals—1 time/week, 4 reps just below anaerobic threshold

Coaching notes:

    Include slow distance and hills when possible to maintain aerobic foundation.

Season: Competitive season

Training emphasis: Anaerobic and speed

Activities:

    Short intervals—1 time/week, 15-25 reps of 30- to 60-second intervals

    Speed drills—1-2 times/week (with ball)

    Medium intervals—1 time/week, 12 reps of 90-second intervals with reduced recovery time

Coaching notes:

    Do intense training several days before competition to allow recovery.

    Remember that competition substitutes for training during the busy part of the season.

    Continue doing some aerobic and anaerobic threshold maintenance work.

all year. You should understand, though, that serious athletes usually adhere to year-round programs. Olympic-level athletes follow 4-year plans designed to bring them to a peak for the Olympics. So don't try to squeeze too much out of an athlete in a single season. Remember the description of training I shared in chapter 10—that training is a gentle pastime, when you coax subtle changes from the body. This chapter should help you devise programs to maximize the fitness of your athletes in the time you have available.

Muscular Fitness Programs

Most muscular fitness programs involve weight training (review chapter 11). Whereas athletes once followed the same weight training regimen for months, cycling of training has become popular in resistance training. In one program, each cycle consists of four phases, with training progressing from high to low volume and from low to high resistance and intensity. The idea behind cycling in resistance training is to continually change the stimulus to achieve continual adaptation. The first phase increases muscle mass, the second and third phases are for strength, and the final phase is designed to bring strength to a peak. Each phase may last from 2 to 6 weeks, with 4 weeks being the typical length. So, for example, a complete cycle might involve 4 phases of 4 weeks each, totaling 16 weeks. See Table 12.7 for recommended training cycles for a strength and power sport like football.

Table 12.7 Training Cycles for a Strength/Power Sport

	Muscle growth	Strength (phase 1)	Strength (phase 2)	Peaking
Sets	3-5	3-5	3-5	1-3
Reps	8-20	2-6	2-3	1-3
Intensity	Low	High	High	Very high

Although more data are needed to determine the ideal program, cycling does seem effective and it is certainly more interesting for athletes. If yours is an endurance sport, adjust the cycles in Table 12.7 to fit the demands of the sport. For instance, cross-country skiing is a power and endurance sport, with many repetitions of explosive arm and leg strokes. Training cycles for this sport could include strength (if needed), short-term endurance, intermediate endurance, and power (15 to 25 reps with 30% to 60% of maximum, as fast as possible). You may want to review these categories of activities back in Table 11.3 (p. 111). With some experimentation and good record keeping, you'll soon know what you need to include to make a good muscular fitness program for your sport.

Exercise Selection

Muscular fitness demands differ among sports, and so do the muscle groups used. As coach you must know both the demands of your sport and the muscles it uses to design a program to train the proper muscles to meet those demands. For example, jumping is important in basketball, so a basketball coach should plan exercises that improve leg strength and power. Of course basketball players also need endurance to keep jumping and running the court throughout a game. Squats, hamstring exercises, and plyometrics will improve jumping, and many repetitions will improve endurance. Basketball also demands upper body strength and power for rebounding and shooting range, so exercises that develop arm muscles used in rebounding (flexors) and shooting (extensors) are important. You'd also want to develop trunk muscles that aid in pulling rebounds away from opponents.

Select a circuit of 8 to 10 important exercises and have your athletes do them for at least 4 weeks in the preseason. I suggest three sets of each exercise for important muscle groups. When progress plateaus, shift to another exercise for the same muscle. As the season approaches, use more sport-specific exercises and drills. Also, reduce the use of weights and weight machines as the competitive season gets underway.

Be sure to schedule strength maintenance sessions several days before competition to allow complete recovery. In most sports one day a week will maintain off-season strength gains (two days are necessary for high-strength sports).

Weight Training Guidelines

Follow these guidelines to ensure safe and effective weight training for your athletes:

- Teach proper lifting and training techniques.
- Always have a spotter when using free weights (two for heavy weights).
- Insist that athletes warm up and stretch before lifting and use a light weight to warm up for each lift.
- Require athletes to check weight collars before lifting—slipping weights can be hazardous. Check the safety features of other training devices.
- Teach athletes to *never* hold their breath during the lift. Athletes should exhale during exertion (lifting) and inhale during recovery (lowering).
- Select 8 to 10 exercises suited to your sport.
- Develop 4-week training cycles for the components of muscular fitness your athletes need.
- Alternate muscle groups during sessions, and allow recovery between sets of the same exercise.
- Keep accurate records, including reps, sets, strength, weight, and so on. It is best for athletes to keep detailed training logs.
- Cut back on training when the competitive season begins.

These are additional guidelines to be followed for advanced weight training (for football linemen, weight lifters, throwers, and other athletes who perform high-strength activities).

- Increase the number of sets (e.g., 5-6).
- Use a split program—upper body, M-W-F; lower body, Tu-Th-S.
- Instruct athletes to eat adequate protein, especially if they are losing weight.
- Cut back on calorie-burning endurance exercises.
- Change the program (lifts, mode of training) when progress stalls or every 8 weeks, whichever comes first.

The Total Program

During the off-season and preseason, you should schedule muscular fitness training 3 days a week. Energy training requires 5 or 6 sessions a week, so it will be necessary to do both types of training on some days. (If you cannot hold formal off-season practices, consider outlining a training program and making athletes responsible for their conditioning.)

Many coaches hold two training sessions on some days to achieve training goals. For example, they conduct energy training Monday through Saturday mornings and (if needed) Tuesday and Thursday afternoons; muscular fitness training is scheduled on Monday, Wednesday, and Friday afternoons. Athletes soon adjust to double sessions, and they appreciate the variety of training cycles for energy and muscular fitness.

When the competitive season begins, both types of training should be reduced. Cut back on the volume of energy training, and reduce muscular training to one or two sessions per week, especially before important contests. Just remember to maintain the energy and muscular fitness improvements you and your athletes worked so hard to develop.

Overtraining

It is your job as coach to conduct an *effective* training program. To do so, remember the principles of training. *Train, don't strain.* Overtraining is far worse than undertraining. Overtraining leads to injury or illness, while undertraining at worst delays reaching the competitive peak. Be alert to the signs of overtraining:

- Chronic fatigue
- Irritability
- Mood shifts
- Decreased interest in sport
- Weight loss
- Slower reflexes
- Reduced speed, strength, or endurance
- Poor performance in sport, school, or work

When you suspect overtraining or impending illness, talk with the athlete. If you develop good, honest relationships with your players, they will not hesitate to tell you when they feel run-down or stale. When they do, lighten the training load or give them the day off. Trust your athletes, and they will not consciously try to deceive you. If you make practice fun, athletes will want to be there.

Some coaches teach athletes to monitor training stress with measurements such as these:

- *Wake-up heart rate*—If the one-minute rate is 10% above the athlete's average you should suspect overtraining. The heart rate can be taken on the palm side of the wrist below the thumb or on the neck to the side of the Adam's apple.

- *Body temperature*—If the heart rate is elevated, check the oral temperature. An elevated temperature could mean an infection. Have the athlete take the day off.

- *Body weight*—Have athletes weigh themselves regularly, always at the same time (e.g., after using the toilet but before eating breakfast). A rapid or persistent weight loss could indicate dehydration, inadequate diet, or impending illness. Reduce that athlete's training until the weight stabilizes.

Have athletes record these measurements in their training logs and evaluate them periodically—they will learn a lot about their bodies in the process. The best protection against overtraining is a well-developed sensitivity to one's body and how it responds to training. Help athletes develop this awareness by teaching them how to sense exertion (through respiration, heart rate, and perceived exertion) and fatigue, valid signals that should not be ignored. You can reinforce this awareness by listening to your athletes and working to understand their concerns.

Key Points to Remember

1. Develop annual training goals suitable to the age, experience, and maturity of athletes.
2. Outline separate plans for the off-season, preseason, and competitive season.
3. Utilize training cycles within seasons.
4. Develop a training menu to guide each week's training.
5. Schedule sessions twice a day when necessary to accomplish energy and muscular training.
6. Cut back on training as the competitive season progresses.
7. Maintain fitness developed in the previous season.
8. Be alert to the signs of overtraining.
9. Teach athletes to use training logs.
10. Help athletes learn to listen to their bodies
11. Listen to your athletes.

Chapter 13

Nutrition for Athletes

Brian J. Sharkey, PhD
University of Montana

Most coaches recognize the importance of good nutrition but find it difficult to influence their athletes' eating habits. Junk food is so popular and available that it is hard to keep athletes from eating too much of it. Furthermore, helping athletes eat properly requires cooperation from parents, school cafeterias, and others responsible for selecting and preparing foods. Finally, many myths develop about nutrition and performance in sport, and it is difficult to stay accurately informed.

This chapter describes the basics of good nutrition for athletes. You will learn about sources of energy; nutrients; a balanced diet; the pregame meal; losing and gaining weight; and fluids and hydration.

Energy

Athletes will find it hard to train and perform if their diets lack adequate energy. The average female (15-24 years) needs 2,000 to 2,400 calories of energy daily; the average male, 2,500 to 3,000. Daily energy needs also depend on age and body size—young athletes require energy for growth and development, and a larger body takes more energy to move, regardless of age. And for every hour of practice, athletes may need 500 or more additional calories of energy.

When the daily diet fails to meet energy needs, the body may burn its own protein—muscle tissue—for energy. So athletes must realize the importance of eating enough calories—if they don't, they are wiping out the effects of their training.

High-Performance Diet

Most Americans eat more fat and protein than they need. For athletic performance and for good health, sport scientists

recommend a diet that includes more carbohydrate and less fat—the *high-performance diet*. In Table 13.1 you can compare the typical teenage diet with the high-performance diet.

Table 13.1 Components of Typical Teenage and High-Performance Diets

Component	Typical teenage diet (% of total calories)	High-performance diet (% of total calories)
Fat	40	20
Protein	15	15
Carbohydrate	45	65

Fat

While some fat is essential in a healthy diet, athletes don't need large amounts; in fact, 20% of calories is probably enough. Fat does enhance the taste of food and helps fill us up. An athlete's fat intake should stay at recommended levels not only for health reasons, but because fat does little good for athletic performance. Fats have more calories per gram than any other food source (see "Calories in Foods"). Eating too much fat is the easiest way to increase one's percent body fat, and excess body fat can interfere with performance in many sports. Too much fat in the pregame meal can also cause nausea.

Calories in Foods

Nutrient type	Calories (per gram)
Fat	9.3
Protein	4.3
Carbohydrate	4.1

Protein

The protein level recommended in high-performance diets is 15% (see Table 13.1). Regularly active adults can get by with 10% of their calories from good quality protein, so many Americans actually get more protein than they need. Athletes, however, need the additional protein for the development of muscle tissue in strength training, for the stimulation of aerobic enzymes during endurance training, and for tissue repair. And young athletes need extra protein to provide for normal growth and development.

Quality protein contains a good supply of essential amino acids, protein building blocks that cannot be manufactured in the body. Although animal protein is a better source of essential amino acids, proper combinations of plant protein can meet athletes' protein needs. The best dietary approach is to eat a variety of foods to meet protein and other nutrient needs. Table 13.2 lists the amounts of protein supplied by a number of high-protein foods. Encourage athletes to make selections from low fat sources (for example, skim milk versus whole, soft versus hard cheeses).

Protein isn't a major source of energy at rest or during exercise. But when an athlete trains hard and diets to lose weight, the body fears starvation and turns to tissue protein for energy. To avoid muscle tissue loss and to achieve the benefits of training, dieting athletes should ensure adequate protein intake. Athletes who continually lose weight during training should know that they risk the loss of muscle tissue, which could weaken them and hurt their performance. Also, hard training while dieting can

Table 13.2   High-Protein Foods

Food	Amount	Protein (grams)
Beans		
• and pork	1/2 cup	8.0
• lima	1/2 cup	6.0
• red	1/2 cup	8.0
• soy	1/2 cup	10.0
Beef		
• corned	3-1/2 ounces	21.5
• roast	3-1/2 ounces	24.0
• steak	3-1/2 ounces	25.0
Cheese (low fat)		
• American	1 ounce	7.5
• cottage	1/4 cup	7.5
• Swiss	1 ounce	8.5
Chicken	3-1/2 ounces	25.0
Chili with beans	1 cup	19.0
Clams	1/2 cup	8.0
Crab	5/8 cup	17.5
Egg	1 large	6.5
Fish	4 ounces	25.0
Flour		
• white	1 cup	11.5
• whole-grain	1 cup	16.5
Ham	3-1/2 ounces	21.0
Lamb	3-1/2 ounces	22.0
Lobster	2/3 cup meat	18.5
Macaroni and cheese	1 cup	19.0
Milk (low fat or skim)	1 cup	10.0
Peas (split)	1/2 cup	10.0
Pork		
• chop	1 medium	15.0
• loin	3-1/2 ounces	20.0
Pizza (cheese)	1/6 of 14 inch	12.0

affect the growth of a developing athlete. (I'll say more about weight control later in this chapter.)

Carbohydrate

You may be surprised to see carbohydrate as the leading source of energy in the high-performance diet—many people mistakenly think of all carbohydrates as "fattening." But carbohydrates such as potatoes, corn, beans, rice, and whole-grained cereals, breads, and pastas are nutritious and healthy. Carbohydrate is the major source of energy throughout the world. People in some less-developed countries get as much as 80% of their calories from carbohydrates, and they suffer far less heart disease than Americans.

Corn, beans, and other *complex carbohydrates* also contain protein, vitamins, minerals, and fiber, thereby providing more balanced nutrition along with energy. Concentrated or refined carbohydrates, such as table sugar, are less desirable because they are packed with "empty calories"—energy without nutrition. Honey is a natural but still concentrated source of sugar that is similar nutritionally to table sugar, providing energy but with minimal nutrient value. Fresh fruits, on the other hand, provide both carbohydrate energy and nutrition. Figure 13.1 shows the food guide pyramid.

Energy Summary

The best diet for the athlete, regardless of age, is low in fat and high in carbohydrate. Vigorous activity normally draws energy from carbohydrate stored in muscle (muscle glycogen). The high-carbohydrate diet refills the muscles so they are ready to go the next day. Athletes who eat low-carbohydrate diets will run out of gas during a hard practice because they won't have enough muscle glycogen.

As I discussed in chapter 11, the body burns both fat and carbohydrate during activity, but during intense effort it turns to carbohydrate (muscle glycogen). If muscles lack glycogen, they cannot sustain vigorous contractions in practice or competition.

Athletes will probably need help learning to choose appropriate foods for the high-performance diet. Potatoes are good, but potato chips are loaded with fat. Cookies sound appealing, but the typical chocolate chip cookie contains over 50% fat. Athletes and others interested in good health should eat lean meat, fish, poultry, complex carbohydrates (corn, rice, beans, potatoes, whole-grained cereals, breads, and pasta), lots of fruits and vegetables, and low-fat dairy products. They should mini-

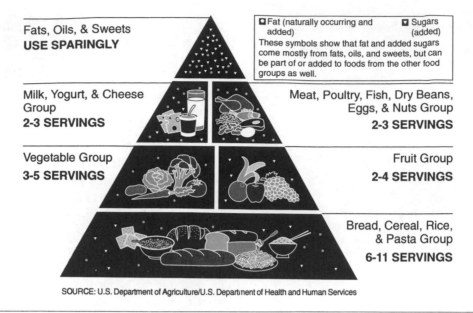

Fats, Oils, & Sweets
USE SPARINGLY

☐ Fat (naturally occurring and added) ▽ Sugars (added)
These symbols show that fat and added sugars come mostly from fats, oils, and sweets, but can be part of or added to foods from the other food groups as well.

Milk, Yogurt, & Cheese Group
2-3 SERVINGS

Meat, Poultry, Fish, Dry Beans, Eggs, & Nuts Group
2-3 SERVINGS

Vegetable Group
3-5 SERVINGS

Fruit Group
2-4 SERVINGS

Bread, Cereal, Rice, & Pasta Group
6-11 SERVINGS

SOURCE: U.S. Department of Agriculture/U.S. Department of Health and Human Services

Figure 13.1 The food guide pyramid.

mize fats (always read food labels to look for "hidden fats"), including sauces and dressings, and go light on desserts. One good way to ensure good nutrition is to eat a variety of foods.

Other Nutrients

The body needs more than energy alone to function—vitamins, minerals, and water are critical to help regulate the body's chemistry. Some coaches and athletes believe that vitamin and mineral supplementation enhance performance, but that is seldom true—you'll learn why in the following discussion.

Vitamins

Vitamins come in two general categories, fat soluble (A, D, and E) and water soluble (B and C). Excess water-soluble vitamins are washed away in the urine, whereas extra fat-soluble vitamins are stored in the body's fat. Vitamins help facilitate chemical reactions in the body's energy production system—they are essential because they help convert food into energy. When athletes don't get enough vitamins they are unable to convert food to energy efficiently. But huge doses of vitamins do not mean more energy. As I said, excess vitamin B or C is eliminated in the urine; excess A, D, or E can be

stored, but sometimes with unhappy results. Too much vitamin D affects calcium levels and can retard growth, and megadoses of vitamin A can be lethal. So getting the recommended amount of vitamins is very important, but more is not necessarily better.

Athletes do need more vitamins as they burn more calories, but increased food intake usually takes care of this need. Athletes who are engaged in extremely heavy training or who are losing weight should consider a daily vitamin supplement to ensure that vitamin needs are met. But even then the supplement should not exceed the recommended daily allowance for the vitamin. Vitamin supplements will not benefit the health or performance of an athlete already eating an adequate diet.

Minerals

Iron, zinc, calcium, magnesium, iodine, and phosphorous are some of the minerals considered essential for good nutrition.

Iron is particularly important to athletes, both female and male. Much of the iron absorbed by the blood goes into producing hemoglobin for the red blood cells. The iron in hemoglobin helps carry oxygen from the lungs to the working muscles. Athletes who are deficient in iron risk anemia and poor performance.

Only 10% to 20% of the iron in food is absorbed into the bloodstream, so an athlete must take in up to 10 times the amount the body needs. Athletes from low-income families are more likely to be iron deficient, perhaps because they eat less lean meat, which is rich in iron. Females lose iron during menstruation, and all athletes are subject to iron loss or reduced absorption during hard training. Dates, prunes, apricots, raisins, beans, and meats contain iron. If you are concerned about an athlete's iron intake, encourage consumption of iron-rich foods. If problems persist, encourage medical evaluation of the athlete's iron status.

The mineral zinc has received recent attention among athletes because of its role in growth and tissue repair. Zinc is needed for growth, enzyme reactions, blood cell formation, and tissue repair. But athletes need not waste money on expensive supplements; they can obtain ample zinc simply by eating whole-grain foods.

Calcium intake is important because it relates to a condition called *osteoporosis,* a loss of bone density that predisposes bones to fractures. Hard training, weight loss, and inadequate calcium intake have increased the risk of osteoporosis and stress fractures, especially in female athletes. To help athletes avoid this risk, keep training sensible, encourage athletes to maintain healthy body weights, and recommend that they get ample servings of skim milk and dairy products rich in calcium.

Key vitamins and minerals are listed in Table 13.3 along with their importance, recommended daily allowances, and sources. Review this information as you strive to improve nutrition without turning to supplements.

Balanced Diet

Good nutrition means eating a *variety* of foods from the food groups (see Figure 13.1). Diets that concentrate on one food or exclude a food group are likely to spell trouble. Most athletes can meet their nutritional needs by eating a balanced diet, with an emphasis on complex carbohydrates. Extra calorie needs due to training can be met by increasing food intake. A good daily food plan can be developed from Figure 13.1. Remember that nutritional problems can arise from fad diets, uneducated vegetarianism, a lack of food variety, and rapid weight loss.

Pregame Meal

Much too much has been made of the pregame meal; it isn't a big deal. In fact, if an athlete is already on the high-performance diet, a typical meal is probably adequate. Your major concern for the pregame meal is that it be easily

Table 13.3 Vitamins and Minerals: Functions and Sources

Nutrient	Important Functions	Sources	Recommended Daily Allowance[1]
Fat Soluble Vitamins			
Vit A Beta-carotene	Vision, immune function Cell growth, antioxidant	Milk products Fruit, vegetables	1000/800µg
Vit D	Bones, teeth, calcium	Sunlight, eggs, fish milk products	10/10µg
Vit E	Antioxidant	Vegetable oils, nuts, greens	10/8mg
Vit K	Blood clotting	Greens, cereals, fruits, milk products, meat	65/55µg
Water Soluble Vitamins			
Vit B1 (thiamin)	Energy production	Pork, grains, beans	1.5/1.1mg
Vit B2 (riboflavin)	Energy production	Milk, eggs, fish, meat, greens	1.8/1.3mg
Niacin	Energy production	Nuts, fish, poultry, grains	20/15mg
Vit B6 (pyridoxine)	Energy production Protein metabolism	Meats, grains, vegetables, fruits	2.0/1.5mg
Folate	Red and white blood cells, RNA, DNA, amino acids	Vegetables, beans, nuts, grains, meat, fruit	200/180mg
Vit B12	Blood cells, RNA, DNA Energy production	Meats, milk products, eggs	2.0/2.0µg
Biotin	Fat & amino acid metabolism, glycogen synthesis	Beans, vegetables, meats	30-100µg*
Vit C (ascorbic acid)	Wound healing, connective tissue, antioxidant, immune function	Citrus fruits, vegetables	60/60mg

(continued)

[1] For males/females 15-18 years old. Recommended Daily Allowance (RDA) is based on 1989 standards set by the National Research Council of the National Academy of Sciences.

* Given in form of range.

digested and out of the stomach before competition starts. Athletes should eat at least 3 hours before a contest and avoid lots of fat. They should eat enough to feel satisfied but not stuffed. Nervous athletes may do better with an easily digested liquid meal.

Neither tea and toast nor steak is superior fare for the pregame meal. Rather, the pregame

Table 13.3 *(continued)*

Minerals	Important Functions	Sources	RDA Male/Female
Calcium	Bones, teeth, blood clotting, muscle contraction	Milk products, vegetables, legumes	1200/1200mg
Chloride	Digestion, extracellular fluids	Salt (NaCl) in food	750/750mg
Chromium	Energy metabolism	Legumes, grains, meats, vegetable oils	0.05-0.25µg*
Copper	Iron metabolism	Meats, water	1.5-3.0mg*
Fluorine	Bones, teeth	Water, seafood, tea	1.5-4.0mg*
Iodine	Thyroid synthesis	Fish, milk products, vegetables, iodized salt	150/150µg
Magnesium	Protein synthesis	Grains, green vegtables	400/300mg
Phosphorus	Bones, teeth, acid-base balance	Milk products, meats, poultry, fish, grains	1200/1200mg
Potassium	Nerve transmission, fluid and acid-base balance	Green vegetables, bananas, meats, milk products, potatoes, coffee	2000/2000mg
Selenium	Antioxidant	Seafood, meats, grains	50/50µg
Sodium	Nerve function, fluid and acid-base balance	Salt (NaCl)	1100-3300mg*
Sulphur	Liver function	Dietary protein	Not established
Zinc	Enzyme activity	Meat, poultry, fish, milk products, grains, fruits, vegetables	15/12mg

* Given in form of range.

meal can be compared to the energy supply for your car. A half tank of gas is plenty for a short trip; the car won't run any better on a full tank—and neither will your athletes.

Distance athletes may have various precompetition eating habits—some prefer not to eat before the event, while others eat 3 to 4 hours before competition. A higher than normal carbohydrate meal is not necessary. Drinking water with some carbohydrate is helpful during a long distance event to keep the muscles working after muscle glycogen has been depleted.

Weight Control

Weight gain or loss is mostly a matter of energy balance. If athletes regularly eat more calories than they burn, especially calories from fat, they'll gain weight; if they burn more than they eat, they'll lose weight.

Ideal Weight

Is there an ideal weight for athletes? Yes, but it depends on the athlete's sport, build, age, and sex. The ideal weight for an athlete is most easily determined by finding out how much weight is fat and how much is lean tissue (muscles, bones, and vital organs). It's important to remember that females have a higher percentage of essential fat than males.

In sports like distance running, athletes perform better with a relatively low percent body fat (about 5-7% for males and 12-15% for females). In other sports the percent body fat is not as important, although athletes should never carry excess fat. Well-conditioned male athletes average about 8% to 12% fat; well-conditioned females, 15% to 21%. The percent fat should never drop below 5% for young boys or 12% for girls. The body needs a certain amount of fat to maintain cell membranes, insulate nerves, protect vital organs, and facilitate the metabolic process.

Excess emphasis on body weight and fat has led to eating disorders (anorexia nervosa and bulimia) and other serious health consequences. You can find more specific information on identifying these problems in *Coaches Guide to Nutrition and Weight Control* (Eisenman, Johnson, & Benson, 1990). Professional intervention is most frequently required to help an athlete recover from eating disorders. If you suspect that one of your athletes has an eating disorder, get help immediately. Untreated, these conditions can lead to debilitation and death.

To help athletes achieve the weight appropriate for their body type and sport, you need to be able to estimate their body fat. The most practical of the procedures available measures the fat just beneath the skin using a device known as a skinfold caliper. About half of the body's fat is stored beneath the skin; using a formula appropriate for the age, sex, and activity level of your athletes, you can determine percent fat with reasonable accuracy. Teaching you to take skinfold measurements and to determine percent body fat is beyond the scope of this book. Although the method is relatively simple, applying it requires knowledge of the correct skinfold sites and skill in using the calipers. For information on skinfolds, see the following books: *Coaches Guide to Sport Physiology* (Sharkey, 1986), *Coaches Guide to Nutrition and Weight Control* (Eisenman, Johnson, & Benson, 1990), or *Anthropometric Standardization Reference Manual* (Lohman, Roche, & Martorell, 1988); or watch an actual demonstration and explanation of the skinfold-measuring procedure on the video *Measuring Body Fat Skinfolds* (Lohman, 1987).

Without skinfold calipers or some other method to estimate percent body fat, you will have to rely on your judgment to decide whether athletes need to gain or lose weight (excess emphasis on weight loss has led to serious eating disorders in athletes). Ideal weight is the one that feels good, looks good, and allows the athlete to perform well. If weight or fat are too low, the athlete will become weak and listless. When weight is too high, it interferes with performance and could become a health problem. Now let's see how to gain and lose weight safely.

Weight Gain

For many of us, gaining weight is easy—too easy. But for some athletes, especially those interested in sports like football, weight gain can be a challenge. Here are some guidelines you can use to help your athletes gain lean tissue (muscle).

- Ensure that weight gain is slow and gradual, with caloric intake increased no more than 500 calories above daily needs. At least 15% of additional caloric intake should be good quality protein.
- Combine increased calorie consumption with a strength training program so that muscle is gained rather than fat. If possible, monitor body fat with the more accurate underwater weighing technique.
- Increase caloric consumption by 3,500 calories for each pound of weight to be gained.

- Be sure athletes avoid eating extremely large meals; instead, recommend that they eat small meals more often (e.g., three balanced meals and two nutritious snacks).
- Suggest that athletes consume the largest portion of their calories early in the day.
- Direct athletes to increase protein intake but to avoid excessive amounts of animal fat, salty foods, and empty calories.
- If possible, cut back on calorie-burning endurance training.
- Do not permit athletes to use drugs (such as androgenic hormones or anabolic steroids) to promote weight gain.
- Keep records of body weight, percent body fat, and weight training.
- Stop the weight gain program when the ideal weight is reached.

Achieving one's ideal weight is healthy; excess weight, whether fat or muscle, is a health risk. Extra weight sometimes means elevated blood pressure and blood fats (cholesterol, triglycerides), and that means a higher risk of heart disease. Carefully consider whether an athlete *needs* to gain weight. If so, remember this: *Any coach who allows or encourages athletes to gain extra bulk is responsible to help those athletes return to healthy body weights following the season.* This responsibility may call for a postseason weight loss program that emphasizes calorie-burning exercises like running or cycling. As a coach and teacher you cannot shirk this responsibility.

Weight Loss

Although weight gain takes effort, weight loss is even more difficult. The four approaches to weight loss are

- exercise,
- dieting (calorie restriction)
- exercise and dieting combined, and
- behavior therapy

Exercise. The single most effective way to lose weight is to exercise. Exercise burns off more fat and conserves muscle protein, compared with dietary restriction, which leads to a greater loss of protein and water and a smaller loss of fat. Moderate aerobic exercises, like run-

ning, cycling, swimming, or cross-country skiing, are good ways to burn off 10 calories per minute. Other sports like tennis, which burn 7 to 8 calories per minute, are also good because they can be continued for an hour or more. Brisk walking, at 5 to 7 calories burned per minute, is another good alternative.

Dieting. One good way to avoid the problem of excess weight is not to eat extra calories in the first place. Skip the giant burger, fries, and shake and you avoid the need to burn off 1,300 unnecessary calories (13 miles of running at 100 calories per mile). The weight loss diet does not mean eating more or less of any one food, just eating fewer calories, especially from fat—and less junk food, snacking, and nonnutritious calories. When dieting is combined with vigorous training for weight loss, a vitamin supplement may be helpful. And when significant weight loss accompanies serious training, ensure adequate protein intake to prevent loss of tissue protein.

Dieting

Dieting, without exercise, is a cause of overweight and obesity. Dieting leads to loss of muscle tissue and a drop in the metabolic rate. With less muscle and a lower metabolic rate, weight loss becomes more difficult, and many regain even more fat than they lost. Combine dieting with exercise in a sensible weight loss program.

Exercise and Diet. Together, exercise and dietary control will speed weight loss and enhance the development of good, lifelong health habits. The calorie deficit (the difference between the calories you eat and those you burn) should not exceed 1,000 calories per day. For example, an athlete who burns 3,000 calories and consumes 2,500 has a deficit of 500 calories. Over a 7-day period, this deficit adds up to 3,500 calories, a 1-pound weight loss. If the athlete increases exercise by 500 calories per day, the deficit becomes 1,000 calories. In 7 days, a 7,000-calorie deficit would yield 2 pounds of weight loss. Weight loss should never exceed 2 pounds a week, or 1,000 calories a day. Athletes who lose weight faster than this rate will find it hard to engage in practice or competition.

Behavior Therapy. Eating is a learned behavior that often needs modification. Behavior therapy uses record keeping and goal setting to help individuals recognize eating problems and take steps to improve them. The first step is to document the behavior and identify problem areas. Overweight athletes should eat only at mealtimes, seated at a table. They should avoid eating junk food at fast-food restaurants and nibbling on snacks while watching television. At meals they must learn to put less food on their plate and to eat one serving only. Behavior therapy usually involves a reward system for good behavior, such as a monetary or material reward for each pound of weight lost. Breaking bad eating habits requires the same type of discipline that is necessary for success in sport. Help your athletes develop self-discipline—and be sure you are a good example!

Weight Loss Guidelines

Consider the following guidelines as you assist athletes in losing weight:

- Determine ideal body weight by measuring percent body fat (don't use standard height and weight charts).
- Monitor progress, both in weight and percent body fat.
- Remember, it takes a calorie deficit of 3,500 calories to lose 1 pound, and the deficit should never exceed 1,000 calories a day; thus, weight loss should not exceed 2 pounds a week.
- Encourage athletes to eat balanced meals.
- Help athletes identify and change troublesome food-related behaviors.

Fluids and Hydration

The body has an elaborate system to maintain optimal fluid balance in cells, body fluids, and blood. Disrupting the system may have serious, even life-threatening, consequences.

Dehydration

Water weighs about 2 pounds per quart. Athletes can sweat at the rate of 2 quarts an hour during vigorous effort in a hot environment, and it is common for them to lose 2 to 4 quarts (4 to 8 pounds) during practice in hot conditions.

Even moderate water loss (2-3% of body weight) has a noticeable effect on performance, and dehydration over 5% brings a risk of heat exhaustion. Dehydration not only rids the body of needed water, it also alters the balance of electrolytes. Electrolytes, such as sodium and potassium, are charged molecules of minerals located in the fluid inside and outside of cells. When dehydration alters the electrolyte balance, nerve conduction and muscular contraction are affected and strength and endurance decrease. Endurance is further affected by the drop in blood volume resulting from water loss. When athletes intentionally dehydrate to "make weight," they risk diminished strength and endurance, and more.

When combined with a low-calorie diet, dehydration can have serious health consequences. To guard against dehydration problems in the heat, weigh athletes before and after practice. The amount of weight loss will indicate how much fluid needs to be replenished. At the start

of the next practice, athletes should weigh within 2 pounds of their previous day's prepractice weigh-ins. If they do not, don't allow them to participate that day.

In sports where athletes must "make weight," try to avoid the need to rehydrate before a contest. Help athletes to select sensible target weights early in the preseason and to achieve those weights gradually rather than using dehydration to temporarily shed a few extra pounds. Remember that young athletes are growing; they need energy, essential nutrients, and water. Deprive them of these essentials and you could affect their health and their growth. No sport is worth that!

Heat Stress

When exercising in hot conditions, the body can usually maintain a safe temperature through the evaporation of sweat. It is not the sweating but the evaporation of sweat that cools the body. If sweat drips off the body, it doesn't have time to evaporate, and the body loses only fluid instead of excess heat.

Remember that athletes can lose up to 1 to 2 quarters of sweat in every hour of practice or competition. This water must be replaced or the body becomes dehydrated, and a dehydrated body doesn't function well. Hydration can be maintained in most sports by drinking one or two 8-oz glasses of water before practice or competition, taking frequent drinks during the activity, and continuing to drink afterward (the body's thirst mechanism underestimates fluid needs).

Some electrolytes (sodium and potassium), necessary for efficient muscular function, are lost in sweat. However, the loss of sodium (salt) is not that great. Ordinarily, the salt in meals will replace any sodium they have lost in sweat. Any potassium depletion can also be easily remedied if athletes eat potassium-rich foods, like citrus fruits and juices, potatoes, and bananas.

Some coaches like to use commercial carbohydrate/electrolyte drinks. These drinks encourage fluid replacement since flavored beverages lead to greater fluid intake. The important thing is to provide plenty of fluid (water) during practice and competition and

schedule practices and games for the cooler parts of the day. Carbohydrate drinks are important for longer duration events (over one hour), and electrolytes help reduce urinary fluid loss.

When you will be competing in the heat, you can prepare your athletes in several ways.

- *Fitness*—Aerobic fitness enhances the circulatory system, which is responsible for heat transfer. And because fit individuals start to sweat sooner, they are less likely to overheat.
- *Acclimation*—Four to 8 days of practice in the heat will prepare athletes for competition in a hot environment.
- *Clothing*—Select uniforms and equipment that allow sweat to evaporate. Avoid dark uniforms that absorb heat from the sun.
- *Fluids*—Make sure athletes practice good hydration habits; they should drink before, during, and after practice or competition.
- *Electrolytes*—Encourage athletes to drink carbohydrate/electrolyte beverages and to eat potassium-rich foods.

Key Points to Remember

1. Athletes may need 3,000 calories or more per day to meet their energy needs.
2. The high-performance diet for best athletic performance and good health is 20% fat, 15% protein, and 65% carbohydrate.
3. Good nutrition results when athletes select a variety of foods from the food groups, with an emphasis on low-fat, high-carbohydrate foods.
4. Vitamins are essential for helping convert food into energy. A well-balanced diet provides the vitamins and minerals an athlete needs, unless the athlete is on a weight loss diet.
5. Athletes should eat the pregame meal at least 3 hours before competition.
6. Weight gain or loss is a matter of energy balance. If athletes eat more calories than they burn (especially fat calories), they gain weight; if they burn more than they eat, they lose weight.

7. To gain weight wisely, athletes should increase calorie consumption (especially protein) gradually and engage in strength training.

8. Weight loss is best achieved by a combination of exercise and calorie restriction (dieting) and by modifying poor eating behavior.

9. Depriving athletes of water during exertion in the heat risks poor performance, heat exhaustion, and other serious consequences.

10. Water is the best fluid replacement; athletes should drink frequently when exercising in hot conditions.

11. Athletes should replace electrolytes at mealtimes, by eating potassium-rich foods, and with carbohydrate/electrolyte beverages.

12. Coaches should be role models for fitness, body weight, eating behavior, and fluid replacement.

Part V

Sport Management

Chapter 14
TEAM MANAGEMENT

Chapter 15
RISK MANAGEMENT

Chapter 16
SELF-MANAGEMENT

You've developed a sound coaching philosophy, you understand the psychology of coaching, you're becoming a master teacher of sport skills, and you've gained valuable insight into training and fueling your athletes' bodies. Now you are ready to coach; you're eager to put this knowledge to use. But before you leap up and race to the playing field or gymnasium, you'll want to learn more about the major management functions you are likely to have as a coach.

Sport management, from your perspective as a coach, is the process by which you provide leadership so that your team can achieve its goals efficiently and effectively. Your coaching responsibilities include ensuring that the necessary human and material resources are available and can be used effectively to achieve the team goals. One of those resources is you, and in chapter 16 I'll discuss managing yourself—your fitness, your stress, and your time.

Managing any enterprise involves at least five major functions. Applied to coaching, these functions are the following:

- *Planning.* As you learned in Part III, you are responsible for establishing the team's instructional goals and the methods for achieving them. You also may be responsible for planning other functions associated with the team.

- *Organizing.* As a manager, you will be responsible for developing the team structure among the players, and you may be responsible for developing the structure of your support organization as well.
- *Staffing.* Staffing involves selecting players, assistant coaches, and others who may help your team achieve its goals, as well as training, assigning specific duties, and providing a favorable work environment.
- *Directing.* As the coach, you will be responsible for leading the team by making good decisions to successfully achieve the team goals. Directing is guiding others—especially your players and assistant coaches—to help you achieve these goals.
- *Controlling.* You must monitor the process of achieving the team goals and make necessary adjustments when situations change or problems arise.

As a coach your management responsibilities will depend substantially on the organization for whom you coach. At one end of the spectrum, you may be the organization. If this is true, then you have broad management responsibilities. On the other hand, you may be a coach in a large high school with a well-organized athletic department. In this case the athletic director will have many management responsibilities for the larger organization, and your responsibilities will be limited to your team and assistant coaches. Most coaches appreciate limited management responsibilities because they can focus more time on coaching their athletes. In Part V we will consider those management functions most commonly expected of coaches, assuming you have some management support from your organization.

In Part V, I cover three vital topics of management. In chapter 14, team management—the many duties of looking after things before, during, and after the season—is reviewed. In chapter 15, you'll learn essential information about risk management: you'll want to manage risk not only to avoid lawsuits, but also to provide a safe environment for your athletes. And in chapter 16 we turn from managing your team to managing yourself.

Chapter 14

Team Management

Coaches' many responsibilities beyond coaching their players are a common source of complaint. Coaches wish they had fewer of these management responsibilities so they had more time to actually coach. But such is not the case for most coaches. These team management functions are part and parcel of the job. The purpose of this chapter, then, is to help you identify these management responsibilities and be prepared to carry them out. The more efficiently you do so, the more time you will have to coach your athletes.

The list of team management responsibilities is so extensive that I cannot adequately discuss it in entirety here. These responsibilities also vary greatly depending on the sport you coach and the organization for whom you coach. For example, you may be the coach of a shooting club that has only 10 members or a ski jumping team of 6 teens. You have no assistants or outside funds and very limited facilities. The management of every aspect of the team is your responsibility. On the other hand, you may be a coach in a large, urban high school with a highly organized athletic department. Your management functions are substantially fewer and are clearly specified in your job description.

Despite the wide differences in coaching situations, you will find this chapter valuable to review whatever management responsibilities you hold. I have compiled from many sources a list of common management functions; some apply to almost every sport, and others are applicable only to particular sports. Select what applies to you, and use the information as a checklist to determine your management responsibilities and prepare for them.

It is not possible in one chapter for me to identify and discuss show to carry out each management function in light of the specific requirements of your sport and organization. I have focused on what needs to be managed and have written little on how to manage it. I encourage you as you continue your coaching education to take the ASEP Sport Administration Course to learn more.

The four major sections of the chapter are

- preseason management,
- in-season management,
- postseason management, and
- managing relationships.

In the first three sections the major team management functions are identified and briefly explained, and then questions are presented for you to consider. As you read through the list of functions, determine if each activity is one for which you will have management responsibility. If so, then answer the questions for your sport, organization, team, and unique situation. If not, be sure you know who is responsible for this management function. Although a given responsibility may not be yours, if a function is not managed well it is likely to adversely affect your team. Thus, you need to know who to see if problems arise.

This chapter also lists activities that involve risk management, which are then discussed in-depth in chapter 15. Where I thought an example or additional information about a management function would be helpful, you will find it in a sidebar.

The chapter concludes by addressing your relationships with the people you work with most. This part of coaching is far more challenging than any other aspect of team management. I'll provide some guidelines that I hope will help you in your work with these people.

Preseason Management

The following section describes the gamut of team management responsibilities. The more you address the functions you are responsible for now, the fewer management hassles you will have during the season.

Review Your Coaching Philosophy

Before each season it's good to think through your coaching philosophy again. I highly recommend you reread Part I of *Successful Coaching* as you reexamine your answers to two crucial questions:

- What are your coaching objectives?
- What coaching style will you adopt to achieve these objectives?

Develop Your Season Instructional Plan

You simply can't do the best coaching of which you are capable if you don't plan the instructional sequence for the season. And the right time to develop or modify that plan is during the preseason. To develop your season plan you need to answer three questions:

- What are your instructional goals for the season?
- What subject matter will you teach to achieve each goal?
- What's the best way to organize this subject matter for instruction?

Selecting and Training Staff

Your involvement in selecting and training staff will depend, of course, on your particular situation. You may be the only staff, or you may be responsible for selecting and training a number of people to help you manage these team responsibilities. Or you may be responsible for training but not selection. Whatever your situation, you may need to answer a number of questions.

- Are you responsible for selecting all your staff?
- Are you responsible for training your staff?

Assistant Coaches. Will you have any assistant coaches? Are you responsible for selecting them or is someone else?

- What will you look for in an assistant coach?
- How many assistants will you have?
- What will be the duties of each?

Other Positions. What other positions do you want or need? Your situation may provide for formal paid positions or you may create positions that will be staffed by volunteers. Parents of athletes, students in your school, and friends who care about the sport are good sources for volunteers. In school settings volunteers may need to be approved by an administrator—be sure to check with your athletic director. These individuals will report to you, but you must coordinate all activity with the athletic director. (See the support positions chart for a list of positions you might want to consider.)

In finding people to fill those positions, ask yourself the following questions:

- What personal qualities will you want in the people who fill each of the additional positions you select?
- Once you select your staff, will you provide each a written list of duties?
- What must you do to help train each?

SUPPORT POSITIONS

You may find the following positions helpful.

- Team manager
- Certified athletic trainer
- Student athletic trainer
- Team physician
- Financial manager
- Publicity manager
- Team statistician
- Transportation coordinator

- Do you need a preseason meeting with all staff?
- What would be the agenda of this meeting? (See "Preseason Staff Meeting Agenda.")

The agenda provided here has worked well for many coaches. Feel free to adapt it for your own purposes.

PRESEASON STAFF MEETING AGENDA

- Staff introductions
- Organization and team philosophy
- Organizational structure of staff
- Staff responsibilities
- Staff conduct
- Budget (funds, salaries, equipment, etc.)
- Problem-solving procedures
- Athlete roster and eligibility
- Emergency medical procedures
- Athlete-staff relations
- Athletes' conduct
- Parental issues
- Plans for initial preseason team meeting
- Plans for meeting with athletes' parents
- Season practice and game schedules
- Travel procedures
- New information (training, game strategy, etc., from clinics, literature, or other sources)

Player Preparation

You will be much better prepared to work with your players when the season starts if you plan ahead. Consider the following questions to help you manage your team better.

Recruiting Players. Are you responsible for recruiting or finding your players? How do you let potential athletes know about your team? What can you do to encourage participation? Are there recruiting regulations you must follow?

Communication System. How will you communicate with players throughout the season? Are the procedures for communication clear? (See the sample communication tree.)

SAMPLE COMMUNICATION TREE

A team is often a complex organization, comprising many personnel in addition to the head coach and players. For such an organization to function efficiently and productively it needs orderly internal communication. A sample communication arrangement is shown here:

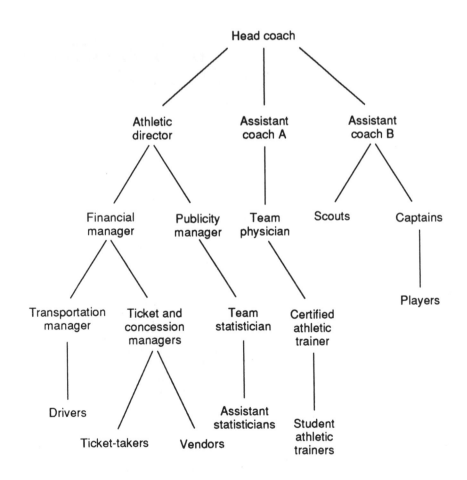

In this communication tree, the head coach makes only three calls. Each of the assistant coaches contacted by the head coach then make two or three calls. From there, others are involved until everyone in the organization has been informed. It is likely that the team captains would further break down their calling responsibilities. The structure of this division is dependent upon the sport involved.

Your situation may be very different. Examine your needs carefully. Be sure to include administrators to whom you are responsible in the tree.

Do you have an easily accessible bulletin board where you can post announcements? Do you have a communication system for cancellations or last-minute changes? Do you have communication procedures for emergencies? If you want to stay in touch with your team and staff during the off-season, do you have a communication system for doing so?

Eligibility. Do you know the eligibility requirements for your players? Do your players know and understand them? Do your players meet any requirements that exist for age, weight, sex, years of participation, skill level, or academic standards? If your players must meet academic requirements, do you have a way to monitor their grades during the course of the school year?

Team Rules. Do you want a set of team rules? If so, what should they be? (See "Topics to Consider for Team Rules.") I recommend providing a written copy of team rules to all athletes and their parents.

TOPICS TO CONSIDER FOR TEAM RULES

- Players' language
- Attendance at practices and games
- Behavior at practices and games
- Interactions with officials
- Discipline for misbehavior
- Behavior when traveling
- Locker room behavior
- Dress when practicing, competing, traveling
- Protecting valuables
- Safety guidelines

- Visitors at practice
- Reimbursement for expenses
- Drug and alcohol use
- Curfews
- Criteria for awards
- Trouble with the authorities

Team Notebook. Do you need a team notebook for each player? What should be in this notebook? (See "Potential Content of a Team Notebook.")

POTENTIAL CONTENT OF A TEAM NOTEBOOK

- Summaries of team tradition, outstanding team and individual accomplishments, and the preceding season
- Statement of staff's philosophy
- Goals and objectives for the season
- Eligibility requirements
- Team rules and consequences for violating them
- Guidelines for conduct in school and during practices and games
- Use and care of equipment and facilities
- Medical examination and insurance requirements
- Expectations of health maintenance (diet, sleep, etc.)
- Explanation of the inherent risks of the sport
- Injury prevention, treatment, and rehabilitation practices
- Suggestions for mental practice
- Schedules and telephone numbers of staff members
- Practice schedule and protocol
- Season schedule (with brief report on opponents, if possible)
- Schedule of planned team social events
- Criteria for evaluating and selecting team members
- Method for selecting team captain(s)
- Awards and criteria for selection
- Space to add more information as the season progresses

Preseason Team Meeting. Do you need to meet with your team before the first practice? What will be the meeting agenda? (See "Sample Agenda for Preseason Team Meeting.")

SAMPLE AGENDA FOR PRESEASON TEAM MEETING

- Overview of program
- Introduction of coaches and their responsibilities
- Coaching philosophy
- Introduction of players
- Eligibility requirements
- Team rules
- Expectations for player conduct
- Risks of the sport
- Importance of following staff directions
- Season goals and objectives
- Training and practice sessions
- Player selection (for team and starting positions)
- Season practice and competitive schedules
- Contingency plans for bad weather for outdoor sports
- Team social functions
- Pregame meals
- Fund-raising events (needs and options)

Initial Skill and Knowledge Evaluation. Have you developed evaluation tools to determine your players' skills and knowledge as discussed in chapter 7? When will you evaluate your players? For what purpose will you evaluate players—to plan their instruction, to classify them into categories, to assign them to positions? Will you cut players based on their evaluations? Do you document your evaluations so you can justify selection decisions?

Team Captain. Should you have any team captains? Who should make the selection— you or the team? What are the responsibilities of a team captain? (See "Sample Duties of Team Captains.")

SAMPLE DUTIES OF TEAM CAPTAINS

- Discuss player concerns with the coach.
- Present player ideas and suggestions.
- Organize team activities away from athletic environment.
- Show leadership on and off the field.
- Model hard work, academically and athletically.
- Be a team player.
- Demonstrate sportsmanship.
- Encourage other players.
- Abide by team rules and code of conduct.
- Maintain a positive attitude.
- Help make practices fun.
- Intervene in conflicts between team members.
- Confront players who violate team rules and inform coaches of violations if necessary.
- Communicate effectively with officials.

Award System. Will you have an award system? For what purpose? How will the award system work? (See "Sample Award Systems.")

SAMPLE AWARD SYSTEMS

- Decals for various types and levels of achievement
- "Player of the Week" or "Player of the Month" recognition
- Letters for team members meeting certain criteria over the course of the season
- Specific performance honors for each game, match, or meet (e.g., the highest percentage of good first tennis serves)
- Publicly spotlighting the athlete who demonstrates the most effort in practice each week
- Publicizing the most valuable reserve player in the school newspaper each week
- Allowing a "practice player of the day" to have input into the next practice session

---

Scheduling

Scheduling may not be your responsibility. But even if you don't make the schedule, you'll want to doublecheck that it is complete. If scheduling is your job, here are some questions to guide you.

Foremost, do you know who schedules contests (including scrimmages and exhibitions), practices, facilities, and officials? If you are responsible for scheduling contests, do you know the regulations governing length of season and number of contests? How many contests do you want to schedule, and with whom, when, and where? How soon should you start the scheduling process? Do you need contracts or are verbal agreements sufficient? Do you need to schedule the facilities where contests will be played? Are you responsible for scheduling preseason contests? If you must schedule officials, how do you identify qualified individuals and what procedures must be followed? Do you need contracts with officials? Are they volunteers or paid? What records do you need to keep? Will your daily planner (discussed in chapter 7) meet your record-keeping need?

Facilities

The coach usually is not responsible for facilities for practice and competition, except perhaps to schedule them. Answer these questions, though, to make sure that you know what you should.

What facilities are needed for practice and contests? Are you responsible for scheduling them? Must you prepare the practice facility for your use? Do you regularly inspect facilities for hazards (see the facility inspection checklists in chapter 15)?

Are you responsible for preparing the contest facility? If so, what must be done to prepare it? If not, whom do you contact if it is not properly prepared? What alternatives do you have during bad weather if you rely on outdoor facilities for regular practice?

Equipment and Supplies

Coaches often purchase their equipment, or they give considerable input to the process. Consider the following questions in managing equipment and supplies.

Are you responsible for purchasing equipment and supplies? What is the present inventory and state of repair of your equipment? Are there existing procedures for uniform rotation,

equipment replacement, or large equipment purchases? What equipment and supplies do you expect to need for the season? Do you have a sufficient budget to buy them? Do you need someone's approval to actually make the purchase? What equipment must athletes buy? Do you need to give them instructions on what to buy, where to buy it, and how much to spend? Where will you buy the items you need? Are there any factors to consider besides quality, cost, and service in making the purchases? Is the equipment properly identified? Do you have procedures for issuing equipment and uniforms? How will you ensure that equipment is properly fitted and athletes know how to use it correctly? What audiovisual equipment will you need during the season? How do you arrange to have it available? What supplies will you need? How large a stock of supplies do you need on hand? Have you adequate record keeping for equipment and supplies?

Fiscal Management

Perhaps you'll have little responsibility for financial matters, other than approving expenditures and submitting receipts for reimbursements. However, many coaches are responsible not only for all the expenses to be incurred, but also for raising the money to be spent. Here are some questions for you to consider regarding financial responsibilities.

Are you responsible for securing any or all team funds? If so, how will you acquire them? Will you develop and maintain the team budget? (See "Sources of Funding for Sport Teams.")

If you are not responsible for fund-raising, do you know your budget? Do you understand the system for approving and making all expenditures? Who holds the money and how do you get to it? What record keeping is required when you spend money? Who can spend it?

Risk Management

You have many duties to properly manage the risk your players and staff may face. Although you may be able to delegate some of the day-

---

SOURCES OF FUNDING FOR SPORT TEAMS

- Budget from sponsoring organization
- Fund-raising events or projects
- Participation fees
- Booster donations
- Gate and concession receipts
- Parking fees
- Advertisement sales (ads in programs, on backs of tickets, etc.)
- Student activity fees
- Personal solicitation for donations

---

to-day management activities, you are responsible as head coach to see that the delegated functions are carried out.

Do you plan every practice based on a master plan for the season? Do you keep up-to-date on new coaching techniques for your sport? Do you provide clear, complete, and concise instructions to your athletes? Do you regularly inspect your facilities for potential hazards and take steps to eliminate them? Do you inspect personal and other equipment regularly and arrange for necessary repair? Are you alert to the dangers of mismatched competition? Are you trained to provide first aid for sport injuries? Do you keep appropriate medical forms on record? Do you provide general supervision for all facilities your athletes use and specific supervision for activities with increased risk or injury? Do you inform parents and athletes of the inherent risks of your sport? Do you have an emergency plan to direct activities when a serious injury does occur?

Chapter 15 explains each of your legal duties and suggests how to fulfill them. A variety of sample forms are also provided to help you document the performance of your legal duties.

Parent Orientation Program

You will want to meet with your athletes' parents prior to the season. This will allow you to set up a communication system, express your objectives for the team, alert parents to the inherent risks of the sport, and let them know what you expect of them. Appendix B outlines a complete explanation of a parent orientation program.

In-Season Management

At last the season arrives. You've carefully planned for it, and now you're eager to coach your team and play the games. But your management responsibilities are not complete. This section will help you determine your in-season management responsibilities.

Player Management

You have a number of ongoing responsibilities in managing your players during the season. These functions all comprise the sometimes not-so-glamorous job of coaching.

Do you know your duties for supervising athletes during the season? This is part of your responsibility to manage risk. These supervisory functions are discussed in detail in chapter 15. (See "Coaches' Supervisory Responsibilities.")

What will you do if a player on your team gets into trouble with the law during the season? Are you prepared to discipline athletes who break team rules or otherwise misbehave? Are you prepared to deal with substance abuse problems?

COACHES' SUPERVISORY RESPONSIBILITIES

- Collecting player medical examination forms
- Inspecting playing facilities
- Guaranteeing that players are matched by size, physical maturation, and ability
- Ensuring that each player is properly fitted with equipment and knows how to use it
- Being aware of all safety standards for equipment involved
- Frequently inspecting equipment and facilities to ensure safety
- Teaching skills in the proper sequence
- Verifying before participation that each athlete knows the rules of the sport and how to use any apparatus involved
- Forbidding athletes to perform any potentially dangerous activities or use any potentially dangerous apparatus without supervision
- Requiring athletes to comply with the rules of the sport at all times
- Allowing only healthy and uninjured athletes to participate
- Refusing to hold practice sessions when weather conditions may be harmful to players' health
- Ensuring that athletes perform proper and sufficient warm-up and flexibility exercises before participating

---

Practice Planning

You know about the need for developing practice plans, but now that you are into the season, are you allocating sufficient time to develop them? Consider these questions as you plan.

Are you following your season plan but making adjustments based on the progress of your players? Are you seeking input from your players and assistants? Are you developing practice plans that work? Are you keeping a notebook of those plans for future reference?

Equipment and Supplies

Here are a few more management concerns for dealing with equipment and supplies as the course of the season progresses. Have you answers to these questions?

Who is responsible for maintaining equipment? Do you regularly inspect protective equipment and other equipment that may cause injury? Who is responsible for cleaning uniforms and other equipment and how often? What are the procedures for replacing broken, lost, or stolen equipment? Who monitors the use of supplies and determines when to reorder?

Fiscal Management

Hopefully you are not burdened with raising money during the season. But you do have some ongoing responsibilities. Check that you are fulfilling your duties by answering these questions.

Are you watching the budget and staying within it? Are you following the system for making expenditures? Are you keeping the records you or the organization will need?

Scouting

You may not be so competitive that you will scout your opponents, but it is a common activity in many sports. Here are some questions to consider if you plan to scout.

Who will do the scouting? Who will cover your practice if you scout? What contests will you scout? Do you have a standard scouting form? How will you use the information you collect? Will you scout by observing opponents directly or by watching videos? What is the cost of scouting? Is it a justified expense? Can you build the expense into your budget? Are there regulations or unwritten ethics that impose restrictions on your scouting?

Transportation

Transporting athletes and others associated with your team is another activity with considerable risk. Thus, you'll learn more about how to manage this risk in chapter 15. But as you identify your team management functions, answer these questions about transportation.

Are you responsible for arranging transportation? Will you use privately owned vehicles or public transportation? Who will drive? Are the drivers properly licensed and insured? Are people other than the players permitted to travel with the team if you use public transportation? Are you aware of your legal responsibilities when transporting athletes? Will you allow players to travel to or from games with family or friends? If so, what procedures will you follow?

Contest Management

Before, during, and after the contest you may have many management responsibilities. By answering the questions below, you can check to see that you are prepared to meet them.

For a more detailed look at managing contests, see ASEP's book *Event Management for SportDirectors* (Human Kinetics, 1996).

General Preparation. Have you arranged for the facility? Have you verified the attendance of officials and arranged for someone to greet them and take them to their dressing area? Have you arranged for janitorial service, ticket takers, ushers, scorekeepers, announcers, and any other personnel needed to conduct the contest? Have you made arrangements to assist the press in covering your contest? Have you arranged to have programs prepared for the contest? Have you briefed your staff on their duties? If your sport is a collision sport, have you arranged for a physician and ambulance to be present? Have you made arrangements for the visiting team, including someone to greet them and take care of their needs? If you expect a large crowd, what crowd control steps do you need to take? Is all contest equipment ready for use?

Precontest Preparation. Have you developed your strategy for the contest? Have you selected the starting lineup and planned for substitutes? Have you prepared your players for the precontest routine you wish to follow, including the warm-up? Will you meet with your team before the contest? If so, what do you want to say?

During the Contest. Are you prepared to manage your own behavior so that it positively influences your players and represents your organization favorably? Are you prepared to manage your staff and players' behavior so they represent your organization well? What do you do if an official makes an error? If a player is hurt? If players get in a fight? If the crowd is acting ugly? How will you observe the contest to best make tactical decisions? How will you record your observations about the team and individual players for later instructional use? What do you do with the team between periods?

Postcontest Activities. What messages do you want to communicate to players for a win? A loss? Who will supervise the locker rooms?

Who will pay the officials? What do you do with the departing visiting team? Who do you need to thank? What responsibilities do you have with the media?

Publicity

Most sport teams want publicity, but you need to decide what is appropriate publicity for your team. Then you need to manage the publicity process so that you get what you want. The following questions will help you manage this aspect of coaching.

How much and what type of publicity do you want for your team? Do you want a publicity manager? How do you get media coverage? (See "Guidelines for Working With the Sports Media.")

Do you want to set up policies about how the media is to make contact with your team? Do you desire additional publicity, such as speaking to local groups, a team brochure or media kit, posters, and so on? How do you arrange such publicity?

GUIDELINES FOR WORKING WITH THE SPORTS MEDIA

- Provide the media with player information (name, height, weight, position, etc.) and a forecast of the team's prospects before the season.
- Invite the media to a preseason "picture day."
- Be accessible—let the media know when and where you can be reached.
- Offer reporters insights they may not be familiar with regarding tactics or strategies of your sport.
- Encourage players to give interviews at times that are convenient for both the athletes and the media.
- Instruct athletes on how to communicate appropriately with the media.
- Be available to and cooperative with reporters following a contest.
- Contact local and even national media to promote noteworthy player or team achievements.
- Make certain press passes are arranged before each game and that they will be honored.
- Try to ensure adequate space and comfort for the media at contests.
- Assign someone familiar with the spellings and pronunciations of players' names to help writers and broadcasters.
- Suggest appropriate human interest stories concerning various team members.
- Arrange for copies of official game statistics to be delivered promptly to the press after the contest.

Postseason Management

The last contest is played, the season is over—but not for you yet. You have several postseason management responsibilities, which can be readily done by responding to the following functions.

Program Evaluation

Foremost of all postseason activities, you need to evaluate your program. Consider the areas listed in "Sample Program Evaluation Considerations" to help you fulfill this function.

SAMPLE
PROGRAM EVALUATION CONSIDERATIONS

Area of evaluation	Poor	Fair	Good
• Ability to meet team goals/objectives	☐	☐	☐
• Adequacy and enforcement of team rules	☐	☐	☐
• Coach-player relations	☐	☐	☐
• Players' performance	☐	☐	☐
• Players' attitude	☐	☐	☐
• Assistant coaches' contributions	☐	☐	☐
• Staff time management	☐	☐	☐
• Communication between staff members	☐	☐	☐
• Season schedule/opponents	☐	☐	☐
• Practice procedures	☐	☐	☐
• Conditioning methods	☐	☐	☐
• Injury prevention and care	☐	☐	☐
• Scouting system	☐	☐	☐
• Travel methods and procedures	☐	☐	☐
• Status of budget	☐	☐	☐
• Facilities and equipment	☐	☐	☐
• Equipment supply and distribution	☐	☐	☐

Do you have a systematic way to evaluate your players? (Remember that chapter 7 provides one.) Do you have a systematic way to evaluate your staff? Will you review your instructional goals now while you remember the events of the season well? How can you best record the changes that you wish to make in your program for next year?

Player Management

As your players depart for the off-season, you will want to take care of several matters. The questions below will help you plan for these activities.

What will be the agenda of your final team meeting? (See "Sample Agenda for Postseason Team Meeting.")

SAMPLE AGENDA FOR POSTSEASON TEAM MEETING

- Season summary
- Review of goals and objectives
- Recognition of players' efforts during the season
- Farewell to departing players
- Staff personnel changes
- Prospectus for next season
- Planned changes in training or strategy for next season
- Off-season camps and clinics
- Off-season fund-raising events or projects
- Planning an off-season outing
- Off-season conditioning
- Appointments for individual player-coach consultations

When will players return their equipment? When and how will you present each player's final evaluation? Will you outline goals for the player to work on during the off-season? Will you prescribe an off-season fitness program? What, if any, involvement will you have with your players' academic progress? Will you help graduating players obtain scholarships? Will you ask players to evaluate the program? (See "Sample Program Evaluation Form for Players.")

Facilities and Equipment

If you have responsibilities here, then you will want to develop efficient ways to deal with

---

SAMPLE PROGRAM EVALUATION FORM FOR PLAYERS

Please answer the following questions honestly, expressing your true feelings about each topic. This evaluation is important to the success of our program, so we need feedback that accurately reflects the job we are doing in each phase of the program. There is no need to sign your name to this form. Simply respond honestly to each item and return the form as soon as possible. We appreciate your time in completing this inventory and your contribution to the program as a player.

	No	Yes	Comments

1. Did the program
   a. help you develop physically?
   b. develop your skills?
   c. teach you strategies?
   d. increase your desire to play?
   e. allow you to have fun?
   f. improve your self-confidence?
   g. distribute awards fairly?
   h. provide proper and safe equipment?
   i. show concern for injured players?
   j. provide good injury care?
   k. have appropriate and fair team rules?
   l. require too much from players?

2. Were the coaches
   a. organized?
   b. good teachers?
   c. fair?
   d. worthy of your respect (good models)?
   e. easy to talk with?
   f. flexible?
   g. good at giving praise you deserved?
   h. honest?
   i. reasonable in their demands?
   j. concerned about each player?

Please provide more comments about any of the above.

Please offer any other additional comments about the program.

---

them. Here are some questions to help you manage this postseason function.

What do you need to do to close the facility? To whom do you report any needed repairs?

What is the procedure for returning equipment? Who is responsible for checking the equipment for repair and recording what needs to be done? Who is responsible for repairing equipment?

Where is the equipment stored? Who prepares the final inventory and where is it kept until needed next season?

Record Keeping

Throughout this chapter you have been urged to keep records. Now that the season has ended you need to make certain the records are complete and then submitted to the right person or filed safely. Consider these questions in performing this management function.

Are your player records complete, including current addresses, so you can communicate with players during the off-season? Have you retained all medical examination records? Have you made copies of all accident reports? Do you have copies of all requests for fixing unsafe facilities or damaged equipment? Have you updated all eligibility records? Have you summarized and organized all participation, individual performance, and team outcome records? Have you recorded an accurate inventory of all equipment and supplies? Have you balanced the budget and prepared all needed financial reports? Do you need to update any other records? Where will you store your records?

Awards and Kudos

Before the season you decided whether you would offer awards of any type to your players.

If you decided you would offer awards, you now must follow through. These questions will help you plan for this task.

Who will compile the records to determine who receives what rewards? Will you have a postseason awards banquet? (See "Awards Banquet Program Ideas.")

AWARDS BANQUET PROGRAM IDEAS

- Host the team and coaches at your home
- Have parents and members of the community put on a potluck dinner in the school cafeteria
- Hold a catered buffet funded by a civic or booster organization with the team and coaches as guests of honor
- Schedule a popular speaker, such as a college coach
- Plan a reunion with former team members
- Sell tickets to pay for trophies, food, a guest speaker, and the use of a facility
- Barter with a favorite restaurant to use its banquet room in exchange for free advertising the following season
- Create a videotape of season highlights
- Have the captain or another team member recap the season
- Combine with other teams for a conference or an all-sports banquet
- Develop a tradition for passing responsibilities from the seniors to the other players (such as a senior will or legacy)

Who will organize and pay for this banquet? Who besides the players do you wish to acknowledge and how?

Managing Relationships

It takes no genius to see that managing a team involves multiple tasks. You can be a more successful coach by recruiting people to help you and then working effectively with them. Managing inventory or arranging transportation is comparatively easy to the challenge of working with other people. In this closing section I give a few guidelines for working with your assistant coaches, administrators, officials, medical staff, and parents. These guidelines focus on the special nature of your relationship with each of these people.

Your objective is to develop positive working relationships, so that individuals not only do their jobs effectively, but enjoy what they are doing and feel a sense of satisfaction. That's an easy objective to state, but often very hard to accomplish. You'll find it easier to develop these positive relationships if you adopt the cooperative style I discussed in chapter 2 and work with your staff in the same way I have urged you to work with your athletes. Build these relationships on a foundation of mutual respect.

Assistant Coaches

Many people begin coaching as assistants, in positions that serve as apprenticeships for learning the many roles of a coach. The relationships you establish with your assistants will have great impact not only on what they can do for your team, but on how well you help them learn the coaching profession. Here are a few guidelines to help you establish effective relationships with your coaches.

- To the extent possible, assign your assistants to positions they are qualified for and interested in.
- Specify responsibilities clearly and make them meaningful.
- Within reason, help prepare your assistants for their duties. Be certain they understand your coaching philosophy and that you expect them to adhere to it.
- Involve your assistants in as much decision making as possible. Their views may be helpful and they'll learn and be motivated by participating in the process.
- Provide your assistants with formal and informal evaluation throughout the season.
- Don't let situations arise where players attempt to play you and your assistants against each other.
- Recognize your assistants' contributions to the team during and after the season.

Administrators

You may be fortunate to have an athletic director or administrator to help you with many of the management functions outlined in this chapter. If so, you will want to cultivate a cooperative relationship. Here are a few important guidelines for nurturing it.

- Be certain you understand what is expected of you and what procedures you are to follow for various management functions.
- Stay organized; submit your requests for items controlled by the administrator in sufficient time for processing.
- Keep your administrator informed of the team's activities through formal and informal communications, and invite him or her to attend practices and contests.
- Keep requested records and stay within your budget.
- Give credit to your administrator during and after the season for contributions to the team's achievements.
- If an administrator is not fulfilling responsibilities and thus is creating problems for your team, speak directly but politely to him or her about it. Don't start grumbling to others about the problem and allow your views to be communicated through others.
- Avoid going over the administrator's head unless the situation is very poor and you have first tried to solve any problems directly.

Officials

Officials can greatly influence the contest. No coach wants to see a contest officiated poorly because athletes are denied the opportunity to make a fair comparison of their skills. Thus, if you are responsible for selecting officials, choose the very best you can find. Then follow these guidelines in working with them.

- Be prepared for the officials' arrival before the contest. You or someone you designate should greet them, show them their dressing facilities if they need them, and familiarize them with the facility.

- Treat the officials just as you would want to be treated, and require the same from your staff and players.
- Avoid constantly harassing officials from the sidelines. It seldom helps your cause, it distracts officials from performing their duties, and it diminishes your integrity.
- If you question a rule interpretation, express your concern to the official at the appropriate time and in an appropriate way. Many sports specify when coaches can talk with officials and what issues they are permitted to question.
- Avoid intimidation tactics. They set a very poor example for players, staff, and spectators. If you engage in this behavior, you will find it difficult to keep your staff and players from doing the same. Very ugly situations can be the result.
- Help officials in every way possible to enforce the rules that protect the well-being of all players.
- Thank officials for their work after the contest. Even if you feel the officials contributed to a loss for your team, maintain a respectful relationship. If officials perform poorly, do not employ them again, or write a report on their deficiencies to the person responsible for hiring.

Medical Personnel

If you coach a contact or collision sport, you'll definitely want to establish a working relationship with a physician. For many sports, it also is helpful to have an athletic trainer. On the other hand, these support personnel may not be available to you, and you will need a basic knowledge of first aid and athletic training and how to summon emergency care services. If you will have a physician and athletic trainer working with your team, here are some guidelines to keep relationships with them productive.

- You need to understand clearly the qualifications of the medical personnel working with you. In the case of athletic trainers, is the person certified by the National Athletic Training Association, thus having full athletic training skills, or a student trainer with very limited experience? You are responsible to see that athletic trainers do not perform functions beyond their qualifications.
- The medical personnel need to know exactly what their responsibilities are. Do they respond first to all injuries? Who decides if a previously injured player can return to play?
- Do not interfere or try to influence the medical decisions of physicians or athletic trainers when they are functioning within their realms of responsibility. If something clearly seems contradictory to common sense, then seek another medical opinion.
- Ask medical personnel not to interfere with nonmedical issues that are your responsibility, so that they don't improperly offer counseling or attempt to take action that interferes with your management functions. But realize that your medical personnel can be a valuable source of information about team problems.
- Physicians and athletic trainers need to be appreciated, rewarded, and motivated. Give them attention, recognition, and respect and you will find them eager to help your team achieve its goals.

Parents

Some parents want to be extensively involved in their children's participation, perhaps too much so; others don't get involved enough. You need to foster appropriate involvement by giving parents clear guidelines about their roles and your expectations of them. I highly recommend that you conduct a preseason parent orientation program (see Appendix B). You will find an orientation program to be a wise investment in short-circuiting the parent-coach conflicts you often hear about. Here are additional guidelines to help you work effectively with parents.

- Remember that parents are ultimately responsible for their children. They are loaning you their offspring for a certain activity and a designated period of time. Respect parents' ultimate responsibility for the well-being of their children by not being threatened when they inquire about athletes' participation.
- Parents, in turn, need to respect your position. They should expect not to interfere with your coaching unless there is reasonable cause for them to suspect that their son or daughter is being exposed to unnecessary physical or psychological risk or is not being treated fairly.
- Keep parents informed, and involve them

constructively. Parents can fill many of the support roles outlined earlier.
- Don't allow athletes to play you and their parents against each other. You can usually avoid this problem by communicating directly with parents.
- Help parents know their responsibilities regarding equipment, uniforms, fees, pregame meals, transportation, and particularly contest behavior.
- Inform parents directly and immediately if a serious problem arises involving their son or daughter (injury, theft, drugs, ineligibility, or other disciplinary action).
- Not all parents will care much about their son or daughter's participation, nor will they all respond as you would hope, but you still have a duty to inform them and request their help.

Conclusion

This chapter has covered many management functions you may find yourself performing as a coach. It doesn't make for great bedtime reading (unless you are having sleep problems!), but as you prepare for your coaching responsibilities this chapter can be of considerable help to you in meeting them. Consult it periodically as you approach each phase of your season.

Chapter 15

Risk Management

This may be a topic you don't want to read about, but you'd better. Sport, like the rest of our society, is subject to some disturbing trends:

- People are quick to sue each other.
- Individuals seem unwilling to accept responsibility for their own actions and turn to the courts for relief.
- The courts seem less concerned with who is at fault and more concerned with who can best afford to pay damages.

Exposure to risk and liability is inherent in coaching sports, especially contact sports. Consequently coaches are being sued in greater numbers than ever, sometimes for ridiculous and frivolous reasons.

Although you could describe the liability crisis as negative, it has had the positive effect of making sports safer. Your legal duties as a coach, as now prescribed by numerous court rulings, encourage responsible and professional conduct to protect your athletes and others. In this chapter you will learn what your legal duties are and how you can fulfill them. When you take appropriate actions to meet these legal duties you are *managing risk*.

When we hear of frivolous lawsuits filed against competent coaches, and occasionally of a ruling against a coach that defies common sense, we feel outrage against the legal system. A few coaches have thrown in the towel because of our imprudent jurisprudence system. But I recommend an alternative approach to this seemingly inequitable system.

As every coach knows, the best defense is a good offense. So don't focus on protecting yourself from lawsuits. Rather, begin your risk management program by adopting the ASEP philosophy of *Athletes First, Winning Second*. You *want* to manage risk because you want to do what is best for your athletes. Focus on the positive side of helping your athletes play safe and you will be most likely to avoid litigation.

The Legal System

I can't turn you into an attorney, but you should understand the basics of our legal system, and especially negligence. Figure 15.1 shows an overview of the American legal system.

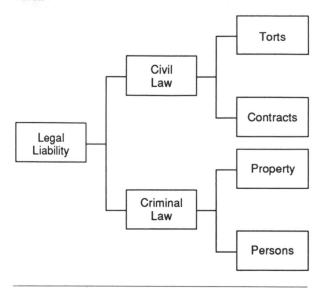

Figure 15.1 The American legal system.

Legal liability refers to the responsibilities and duties between persons that are enforceable by the courts. As you can see in Figure 15.1, legal wrongs may be either civil or criminal. Under civil law, legal wrongs are classified as either *torts* or *contract liabilities.* In this chapter, we do not consider criminal or contract law, but focus on tort law, which is applicable to most litigations involving coaches.

Negligence

Tort law is concerned with determining if a person has failed to conform to a legal duty. As a coach you have certain legal duties to fulfill. If you fail to do so, and this failure results in injury, you can be sued under tort law. The legal term for failing to fulfill your legal duty is *negligence.*

When coaching, you are negligent if you fail to exercise the skill and knowledge normally possessed by fellow coaches in working with those to whom you have a legal duty. Negligence may occur because of an inappropriate act or a failure to act.

Determining Negligence

In our legal system, anyone can sue another person for negligence. If you are sued for negligence and the case goes to trial, the court will determine whether you have been negligent by making a judgment on four key questions.

- Did you indeed have a legal duty to the injured party in this situation?
- Did you fail to fulfill this duty?
- Was there injury to the party to whom you owed the duty?
- Did your failure to fulfill the duty cause the injury?

All four questions must be answered yes for you to be found negligent.

A frequent defense in sport negligence cases is that an injury occurred due to the *inherent* risk in that sport and not a failure on the coach's part to fulfill a legal duty. For example, you have properly instructed a young girl in diving, the board is in excellent condition, and the pool is sufficiently deep. As the girl executes a one-and-one-half inward dive, she strikes her head on the board, sustaining a serious injury. If no other factors are involved, her injury is the result of a risk inherent to diving, not of negligence on your part.

A second common defense is that the injured party, often an athlete, may have contributed to the injury by his or her own behavior, such as failing to follow instructions. It may be that you failed to fully meet your legal duty and that the athlete also contributed to the cause of the injury. This is known as *contributory negligence,* and in many states if an athlete contributed to the negligence in any way you may not be found negligent. Recently, though, more states have adopted *comparative negligence* laws, in which the negligence of each party involved is compared on a percentage basis. Most commonly, a player who contributed to the negligence by 50% or more cannot recover any damages.

Risk Management Process

The objective of risk management is to produce the safest environment possible for your

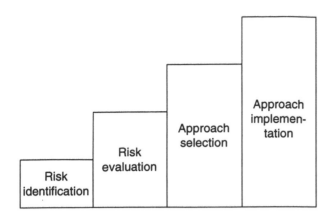

Figure 15.2 A four-step plan for managing risk.

athletes and others and to avoid litigation. The four steps to managing risk are shown in Figure 15.2.

Identify Risk

In this step you determine the likely risks you face when coaching your team. You can determine them by carefully reviewing the nine legal duties discussed on pages 159-176. In broad terms, you need to consider the participant, activity, environment, equipment, and methods of instruction and supervision in identifying risks. As you review these legal duties, make note of those you think are the greatest risks in your situation.

Evaluate Risk

The second step in risk management is assigning a probability to the likelihood that each risk may lead to an injury and the likely severity of that injury. Begin by determining whether an injury is likely to occur *often, infrequently,* or *seldom*. Next, decide whether the severity of the injury and its financial impact are likely to be *high, medium,* or *low,* with *high* representing a severe injury with great financial impact and *low* standing for a slight injury with little financial impact.

Select an Approach

The third step is deciding what approach to take for each risk. See Figure 15.3 for a recommended approach based on how frequently

you determined an injury was likely to occur and how severe the injury and its financial impact would be. To use the chart, first find the column that represents your response to the likely frequency of occurrence (often, infrequently, or seldom). Then find the row that represents your response to the likely severity of injury or impact (high, medium, or low). The box in which the row and column you selected intersect contains a course of action you might want to take for this risk.

For example, if you selected "often" for frequency and "high" for severity, the chart would suggest you consider avoiding or transferring this risk. The meaning of each of these approaches is explained in the next section.

Implement the Approach

The final step is implementing the approach you have selected for each risk. You have at least four options.

- The first option is not included in Figure 15.3. You can eliminate the risk by removing the hazard, by fulfilling your duties competently, or by not engaging in the activity.
- You can *avoid* risk, reducing the likelihood that the risk will become an injury by taking steps to protect athletes from potential hazards. You can do this by padding walls or protruding objects, providing repeated warnings, and giving safety instruction.
- You can accept the risk. If you judge the risk to be minor, you may decide you will live with it. Stated differently, you may determine that the benefits of proceeding with the risk at hand outweigh the potential costs of avoiding it.
- You can transfer the risk in several ways: for example, (a) rather than driving your own car when transporting athletes, you can use the school's vehicle or public transportation, (b) you can transfer the financial risk by being insured for legal liability costs (see pages 180-181 for more information about insurance), or (c) under certain circumstances you can transfer the *inherent* risks through par-

Frequency of occurrence

	Often	Infrequently	Seldom
High	Avoid or transfer	Transfer	Transfer
Medium	Transfer	Transfer or accept	Transfer or accept
Low	Accept	Accept	Accept

Severity of injury or financial impact

Figure 15.3 Selecting an approach.
Adapted, by permission, from Van der Smissen, B., *Legal Liability and Risk Management for Public and Private Entities*, Vol. 2 (Cincinnati, OH: Anderson Publishing), §23.31. © 1990 by Anderson Publishing.

ticipation agreements (see page 176). Because many insurance premiums have become outrageously high, some organizations have had to cancel sport programs because they could not afford sufficient insurance to transfer the risk.

Remember, you cannot transfer your legal duties, but you can transfer some or all of the risk.

Immunity

A 10-year-old New Jersey boy who had played second base during the regular season was transferred to the outfield in preparation for an all-star game. During practice in the outfield the boy misjudged a ball, which hit him in the eye and caused permanent damage. The parents sued the coaches for $750,000, charging them with negligence for placing the boy in a position he was not trained to play.

The coaches were able to document that the boy had played outfield the previous season. Nevertheless, the insurance company decided to settle out of court for $25,000. The immediate consequence was skyrocketing insurance rates and coaches quitting in anger. Eventually the New Jersey legislature passed the first law providing immunity to volunteer coaches against frivolous and ordinary negligence lawsuits.

More than a dozen states have passed similar legislation. In each state this new form of Good Samaritan law provides *volunteer* coaches immunity against frivolous lawsuits, but not against gross negligence. Of course, the courts must decide whether a lawsuit is frivolous or involves either ordinary or gross negligence.

Although the intent of such legislation is positive, these immunity laws raise two important issues. First, they provide immunity only to volunteers, not to paid coaches, and second, most do not require coaches to have any training to secure immunity. In fact, it appears that coaches who are formally trained to coach may not be granted immunity.

You can see the unintended consequence. Coaches who are paid and who seek out formal education to do their jobs are not given the same protection from frivolous lawsuits as coaches who are untrained volunteers. Will this encourage volunteer coaches to remain untrained and thus less capable of managing risks for the athletes in their charge? The answer is yet to be determined.

If Athletes First, Winning Second is your philosophy, then you will want to do all you can to protect your athletes. That requires your becoming the best trained coach possible. Thus, while these new immunity laws may provide some protection against risk, you should not rely on this protection. Instead rely on yourself to provide a safe environment through competent coaching.

Coaches' Legal Duties

Over the past 20 years, through thousands of lawsuits, the courts have defined and continue to define your legal duties as a coach. These duties may vary from state to state and may change as sport litigation continues unabatedly. In this section, I will describe the most well-established duties and at least some of the actions that you can take to fulfill your legal duties as a coach. Actually much of this book advises you directly or indirectly on how to fulfill your legal responsibilities. The case studies that introduce each of the duties are based on actual court cases.

Your Nine Legal Duties

Duty 1: Properly plan the activity.

Duty 2: Provide proper instruction.

Duty 3: Provide a safe physical environment.

Duty 4: Provide adequate and proper equipment.

Duty 5: Match your athletes.

Duty 6: Evaluate athletes for injury or incapacity.

Duty 7: Supervise the activity closely.

Duty 8: Warn of inherent risks.

Duty 9: Provide appropriate emergency assistance.

Duty 1: Properly Plan the Activity

A young gymnastics coach taught a 7-year-old girl how to do a headstand the first day of practice. The girl suffered a serious neck injury when she fell during her second attempt. The coach was sued and found negligent because she failed to prepare the girl with proper strength training and lead-up skills.

Understanding Your Duty. The courts have repeatedly ruled that coaches have a duty to properly plan the activities for the athletes participating under their supervision. You will go a long way toward fulfilling this duty if you do what is outlined in chapter 7, "Planning for Teaching."

Among your essential duties is to teach the skills of the sport in the correct progression. Avoid teaching advanced skills too quickly just because a few of your better athletes are ready or because you are getting bored. Practicing advanced skills can be very dangerous, and you can be found negligent, as the gymnastics coach was, if you don't follow a reasonable progression. "A reasonable progression" will be judged relative to the progression used by other prudent coaches and the readiness of the individual athlete.

To fulfill your planning duty you must consider each athlete's developmental level and current physical condition. You will not fulfill your duty to properly plan activities if you prescribe the same plan for all your athletes. Thus, at least at the beginning of the season, evaluate your athletes' readiness with a test or checklist rating system. Not only is this a good coaching practice for planning practices, it will provide a written record validating your effort to plan your activity properly.

Fulfilling Your Duty

1. Develop a season plan using progressions appropriate for your athletes.
2. Test players to determine their physical capacity and skill level for your sport.
3. Develop written practice plans that adhere to the recommendations in chapter 7.
4. Adapt your plans to the individual needs of your athletes.
5. Don't deviate from your plans without good cause.
6. Keep all records of your planning and testing.

Duty 2: Provide Proper Instruction

Spear tackling, a form of tackling in football in which the tackler's head is "speared" into the ball carrier's chest, was the accepted way to tackle in the 1960s. But many spinal injuries resulted from this technique, and after several studies demonstrated how vulnerable the spine is in this tackle, the technique was no longer recommended, especially for high school players. Unfortunately high school coach Mike Douglas did not know that spear tackling was contraindicated. It was the way he had learned tackling and thus the way he taught it. Using the technique resulted in quadriplegia for his middle linebacker and a $2.8 million lawsuit for Mike and his school.

Understanding Your Duty. You have a duty to teach skills correctly and thoroughly so athletes are not injured and their actions do not injure others. Thorough instruction includes teaching the skills and strategies necessary for proper performance as well as the rules of the game.

In general, the law requires you to teach athletes in accordance with accepted procedures of the sport, allowing for individual variations as long as they are not radical or dangerous. For example, you can use a number of approaches to teach feet-first sliding in baseball, but if you teach head-first sliding and the athlete is injured, you have a good chance of being found negligent. Although many advanced baseball players slide head first, the technique is not accepted as the correct way to teach sliding.

If you are the head coach, your instructional duty cannot be delegated. If you ask assistant coaches or more skilled athletes to teach, you must supervise their instruction and you are responsible for its being correct.

Fulfilling Your Duty

1. Keep abreast of current instructional standards for your sport and use them.
2. Teach skills, strategies, and rules in accordance with customary methods of your sport and the developmental level of your athletes.
3. Make your instructions clear, complete, and consistent. Provide adequate feedback on how your athletes are progressing.
4. Realize that as head coach you remain responsible for supervising instruction to ensure it is proper if you delegate the task of instructing your athletes.

Duty 3: Provide a Safe Physical Environment

After a short but heavy rain the barren softball infield was too muddy to use for practice, so Coach Ellen Archer moved the team to a large grass field. Kelly Smith stepped in a hole, breaking her leg in four places. The resulting litigation found Coach Archer negligent for not properly inspecting the playing facility.

Understanding Your Duty. Playing sports holds an inherent risk in any physical environment, but as a coach you are responsible to regularly and thoroughly inspect the facility. How regularly depends on the activity. The rule of thumb is, The greater the risk the more regular the inspections. If you want to be a good risk manager, I recommend you develop a Facilities Inspection Checklist for your sport, similar to the one on pages 161-164. Adapt the sample to your sport.

Facilities Inspection Checklist

Name of inspector _____

Date of inspection _____

Name and location of facility _____

_____

Note: **This form is an incomplete checklist provided as an example. Use it to develop a checklist specific for your facilities.**

Facility Condition

Circle Y (yes) if the facility is in good condition and N (no) if it needs something done to make it acceptable. In the space provided note what needs to be done.

Gymnasium

Y N   Floor (water spots, buckling, loose sections) _____

Y N   Walls (vandalism free) _____

Y N   Lights (all functioning) _____

Y N   Windows (secure) _____

Y N   Roof (adverse impact of weather) _____

Y N   Stairs (well lighted) _____

Y N   Bleachers (support structure sound) _____

Y N   Exits (lights working) _____

Y N   Basketball rims (level, securely attached) _____

Y N   Basketball backboards (no cracks, clean) _____

Y N   Mats (clean, properly stored, no defects) _____

Y N   Uprights/projections _____

Y N   Wall plugs (covered) _____

Y N   Light switches (all functioning) _____

Y N   Heating/cooling system (temperature control) _____

Y N   Ducts, radiators, pipes _____

Y N   Thermostats _____

Y N   Fire alarms (regularly checked) _____

Y N   Directions posted for evacuating the gym in case of fire _____

Y N   Fire extinguishers (regularly checked) _____

Other (list)

_____

_____

(continued)

Facilities Inspection Checklist *(continued)*

Locker room(s)

Y N   Floor _____

Y N   Walls _____

Y N   Lights _____

Y N   Windows _____

Y N   Roof _____

Y N   Showers _____

Y N   Drains _____

Y N   Benches _____

Y N   Lockers _____

Y N   Exits _____

Y N   Water fountains _____

Y N   Toilets _____

Y N   Trainer's room _____

Other (list)

_____

_____

Field(s)/outside playing area

Surface

Y N   Too wet or too dry _____

Y N   Grass length _____

Y N   Free of debris _____

Y N   Free of holes and bumps _____

Y N   Free of protruding pipes, wires, lines _____

Y N   Line markers _____

Stands

Y N   Pitching mound _____

Y N   Dugouts _____

Y N   Warning track & fences _____

Y N   Sidelines _____

Y N   Sprinklers _____

Y N   Garbage _____

Y N   Security fences _____

Y N   Water fountain _____

Y N   Storage sheds _____

(continued)

Facilities Inspection Checklist *(continued)*

Concession Area

Y N Electrical _____

Y N Heating/cooling systems _____

Other (list)

_____

_____

Pool

Y N Equipment in good repair _____

Y N Sanitary _____

Y N Slipperiness on decks and diving board controlled _____

Y N Chemicals safely stored _____

Y N Regulations and safety rules posted _____

Lighting—adequate visibility

Y N No glare _____

Y N Penetrates to bottom of pool _____

Y N Exit light in good repair _____

Y N Halls and locker rooms meet code requirements _____

Y N Light switches properly grounded _____

Y N Has emergency generator to back up regular power source _____

Exits—accessible, secure

Y N Adequate size, number _____

Y N Self-closing doors _____

Y N Self-locking doors _____

Y N Striker plates secure _____

Y N No obstacles or debris _____

Y N Office and storage rooms locked _____

Ring buoys

Y N 20-inch diameter _____

Y N 50-foot rope length _____

Reaching poles

Y N One each side _____

Y N 12-foot length _____

Y N Metal stress _____

Y N Good repair _____

(continued)

Facilities Inspection Checklist *(continued)*

Guard chairs

    Y N   Unobstructed view _____

    Y N   Tall enough to see bottom of pool _____

Safety line at break point in the pool grade (deep end)

    Y N   Bright color floats _____

    Y N   3/4-inch rope _____

First-aid kit

    Y N   Inventoried and replenished regularly _____

Stretcher, two blankets, and spine board

    Y N   Inventoried and in good repair _____

Emergency telephone, lights, and public address system

    Y N   Accessible _____

    Y N   Directions for use posted visibly _____

    Y N   Powered by emergency generators as well as regular power system _____

    Y N   Emergency numbers on telephone cradle or receiver _____

Emergency procedures

    Y N   Sign posted in highly visible area _____

Track

Surface

    Y N   Free of debris _____

    Y N   Free of holes and bumps _____

    Y N   Throwing circles _____

    Y N   Fences _____

    Y N   Water fountain _____

Other (list)

_____

_____

Recommendations/observations: _____

_____

_____

_____

_____

_____

_____

_____

You also have a duty to notice hazards and to do what you can to reduce their risks. When you cannot eliminate a hazard, such as a protruding rock on a playing field or a wall too close to the end line of a basketball court, you are responsible to try to reduce the hazard and to warn your players of it. You might place a bright cloth over the rock or pad the wall, and warn players to avoid them. Again, you are expected to do what a prudent coach would do in the same situation.

When you encounter a facility that does not conform to the standards set by the governing body of your sport, you have a duty to notify the facility manager that the facility is unsafe and to recommend corrective action. If you and the facility manager are unfamiliar with these standards, you should contact the governing body of your sport (listed for the U.S. in Appendix C).

Remember too that the physical environment can change when you are practicing or competing, whether you are inside or out. Rain-slick playing surfaces, high winds, and lightning can make outdoor environments unsafe quickly. Although changes are less likely indoors, facilities can still become hazardous quickly if there is a loss of lighting, heat, or moisture control. You must continuously monitor a changing environment to determine if it is safe for your athletes and to take appropriate action if not.

Fulfilling Your Duty

1. Note and remedy hazardous conditions through regular inspections of the playing facility and the warm-up, training, and dressing areas.
2. Develop a Facilities Inspection Checklist for the facilities and equipment used in your sport. Use it regularly, and keep these checklists on file.
3. Change any dangerous conditions that you can; reduce the hazard if you cannot remove it. Warn your players of the hazard and notify the facility manager through written recommendations about correcting the hazard.
4. Give precise rules for using the facility. Post the rules, remind the players of them, and enforce them consistently.

5. Monitor the changing environment and make prudent judgments about continued participation if it becomes hazardous.

Duty 4: Provide Adequate and Proper Equipment

Robert Bloom thought he was making a good buy when he purchased new plastic face masks for his hockey team. The masks were mounted in the helmets by the school maintenance man, although no instructions were provided on how to do so. Four weeks into the season Brad Kosnick was hit in the mask by a high stick, shattering the mask and sending a plastic splinter into his left eye. Brad lost the sight of that eye, and in the court trial the mask manufacturer, the coach, and the school were found negligent.

Understanding Your Duty. Your duty here is generally the same as for Duty 3. It is your duty not only to provide adequate and proper equipment, but also to explain its correct use and any unique characteristics. For example, a football helmet is intended to protect the player, but used incorrectly it can be dangerous to both the player and those he plays with. Similarly, gymnastics apparatus are designed to be as safe as possible for specific events, but used incorrectly they can be highly dangerous.

Just as with facilities, you must inspect equipment regularly. If it is worn or broken, it is your duty to remove it from use or have it properly repaired. Use the Large Equipment and Personal Equipment Inspection Checklists on pages 166 and 167 to routinely inspect the team's equipment.

When purchasing equipment you should buy the best you can afford and be sure that it meets the standards of the National Operational Committee on Standards for Athletic Equipment. Equipment should be bought with due consideration given to the age and skill level of the athletes. When equipment is furnished by the player or by the school, you have less legal responsibility for its meeting these standards or being safe.

Large Equipment Inspection Checklist

Date of inspection: _____

Equipment inspected: _____

Current condition: _____

Inspector: _____

	Satisfactory	Unsatisfactory	Comments
Clean	___	___	_____
Free of rust	___	___	_____
Free of splinters or sharp edges	___	___	_____
All parts (original factory parts) in place	___	___	_____
All parts (from manufacturer's repair facility) in place	___	___	_____
All parts in working order	___	___	_____
All repairs done by authorized personnel	___	___	_____
Nuts and bolts tightened appropriately	___	___	_____
Placed correctly for use	___	___	_____
Secured properly for use	___	___	_____
Padding installed according to specifications	___	___	_____

Received by: _____

Date: _____

Repair work scheduled: _____

Date repairs completed: _____

Signature of supervisor: _____

Follow-up inspection date: _____

Much of the responsibility for equipment safety falls on the manufacturers, partly because of the "deep pockets" approach to litigation. Nevertheless, you have a duty to see that equipment fits properly and is used according to the manufacturers' specifications.

You also are responsible for seeing that equipment is properly stored. Leaving equipment, such as weights or springboards, in unlocked and unattended areas invites injury and litigation.

Fulfilling Your Duty

1. Buy the best equipment you can afford, considering the age and skill of your athletes.

Personal Equipment Inspection Checklist

Date of inspection: _____

Equipment inspected: _____

Condition of equipment when issued: _____ New _____ Reconditioned

Condition of equipment now: _____

Inspector: _____

	Satisfactory	Unsatisfactory	Comments
Clean	_____	_____	_____
Free of rust, splinters, and sharp edges	_____	_____	_____
Fits appropriately	_____	_____	_____
Padding in place	_____	_____	_____
All integral parts in place	_____	_____	_____
All integral parts operational	_____	_____	_____
No modification from factory specifications	_____	_____	_____
All repairs done by authorized personnel	_____	_____	_____

Received by: _____

Date: _____

Repair work scheduled: _____

Date repairs completed: _____

Signature of supervisor: _____

Follow-up inspection date: _____

2. Teach your athletes how to fit, use, and inspect their equipment. Encourage them to return any equipment that does not fit or appears defective.
3. Inspect equipment regularly; the more stress placed on the equipment, the more frequently you should examine it.
4. Allow only qualified people to install, fit, adjust, and repair equipment. You may want to insist that a manufacturer's representative fit all the equipment (e.g., helmets, pads, and mouth guards).
5. Warn players of potentially hazardous equipment and give verbal and written instructions on using it.
6. Be aware of changes in equipment by keeping current on accepted standards.

Duty 5: Match Your Athletes

Randy Brooks was a 115-pound football player who irritated Coach Jack Bennis with his continual misbehavior and boasting of unfounded ability. After an hour of Randy's provocations one day, Coach Bennis organized a one-on-one tackling drill and matched Randy with Tom McNab, a 205-pound tackle and the strongest player on the team. In the drill Randy suffered a serious concussion and was hospitalized. The court found Coach Bennis negligent for his imprudent judgment in matching the players.

Understanding Your Duty. This duty is especially pertinent to contact and collision sports, but is also relevant in sports where balls are thrown or hit to other players.

It is common in sport to match athletes by age, under the assumption they will be of similar size and experience. But of course we all know that this is not necessarily true. Two boys, with a chronological age of 12 can differ by 5 or 6 years in biological age (physical maturity). One boy might weigh 60 pounds and have the biological age of a 9-year-old while the other weighs 160 pounds and has a biological age of 15. To match these two players in a contact sport is obviously dangerous, and the courts have found coaches who have done so to be negligent.

Your duty is to see that your players are not placed in situations where they are at such a disadvantage that their risk of injury is increased. Thus, you need to consider more than just age in matching children. You must also consider size, physical maturity, skill, and experience.

You should also avoid having athletes with substantially different conditioning levels compete against each other. If you coach a mixed-sex team you must be particularly careful not to create mismatches. Remember, males and females of the same age are likely to differ in size, maturity, skill, and experience.

Mismatches can occur also when athletes return to competition after serious injuries. Coaches must use good judgment in reintroducing athletes gradually to full intensity practice and competition. Coaches must give similar consideration to any athlete with a disability.

Fulfilling Your Duty

1. Match players in size, maturity, skill, and experience as well as age so that they are not placed in situations where the risk of injury is increased.
2. Enforce eligibility rules; they often are intended to provide equitable competition.
3. Modify the drill or practice structure when mismatches in ability cannot easily be corrected.
4. Be especially alert to mismatches between the sexes, with athletes recovering from injury, and for those with disabilities.

Duty 6: Evaluate Athletes for Injury or Incapacity

Andy Jacobs was knocked unconscious for about 30 seconds when he was slammed to the mat by his opponent in a high school wrestling match. After 15 minutes Andy insisted he was all right and demanded to continue the match. His coach reluctantly agreed. Andy died 20 minutes after the match from a cerebral hemorrhage. The two physicians who testified at the trial stated unequivocally that the coach should not have permitted Andy to return to the mat. The jury found the coach negligent.

Understanding Your Duty. You have three important responsibilities in order to fulfill this duty.

- You must insure that an athlete's health is satisfactory for participation in your sport at the beginning of the season.

WE'VE GOT TO MATCH UP BETTER.

- You must determine if an illness or injury during practice or competition is sufficiently threatening that participation should be stopped.
- You must insure that an injured athlete is ready to return to play.

These responsibilities are not yours solely, but are shared with parents and physicians. In fact, good risk managers transfer as much of the responsibilities as possible to the team physician, but often that cannot be done.

The American Academy of Pediatrics (AAP) recommends that athletes have physicals at least every 2 years. Thus, every athlete may not need a preseason physical for your sport, but he or she should provide evidence of having passed a preparticipation medical examinaton within the past 2 years. A good exam should test for those conditions listed on page 179. You should also be certain that you or the sponsoring agency has on file for each athlete a completed medical history similar to the one shown on pages 171-172. Some states and organizations require that specific forms be completed. Check with your sport director to ensure you are using an appropriate form.

You also must decide whether athletes with special medical conditions can play and whether any restrictions need to be placed on their participation. Table 15.1 (pages 173-174) outlines the AAP guidelines for participation by young people with special conditions. Although this table is useful for reference, it's important that a physician make the decision about whether an athlete with special considerations should participate on your team.

Coaching Athletes With Disabilities.

When considering whether an athlete is physically capable of participating on your team, it's important that you keep in mind the implications of the Americans With Disabilities Act. The Act states

No individuals shall be discriminated against on the basis of disabilities in the full and equal enjoyment of goods, services, facilities, privileges, advantages or accommodations at any place of public accommodation by any person who owns, leases or operates a place of public accommodation. Benefits provided for the disabled cannot be separate or different from those provided for others, unless they are as effective as those provided for others.

At this printing, the specific requirements of the Act are still being debated in the courts. But the Act's intent is to provide individuals with disabilities with the same opportunities for involvement as those afforded to individuals without disabilities. Before you decide to exclude any athlete from participating on your team on the basis of a disability, be sure to discuss the issue with your sport director or chief administrator to consider the implications of the ADA.

Injured Athletes. When athletes are injured during practice or competition, you must judge the risk of returning them to play. When a physician is present you can transfer that responsibility, but often no physician will be present. I highly recommend you complete the ASEP Sport Injuries Course to learn to make better judgments.

The ASEP Sport Rehabilitation Course will help you determine when it is safe for athletes to renew participation. As a general rule, however, if the athlete was treated for an injury by a physician, the physician should certify that the athlete is ready to return to action.

Fulfilling Your Duty

1. Require evidence that all athletes have received preparticipation physical examinations in the past 2 years.
2. Follow the AAP guidelines in determining if and under what conditions persons with special conditions can participate.

Preparticipation Physical Evaluation

Physical Examination   Date _____

Name _____ Age _____ Date of birth _____

Height _____ Weight _____ Blood Pressure _____ / _____ Pulse _____

Vision R 20/ _____ L 20/ _____   Corrected: Y N   Pupils _____

	Normal	Abnormal findings					Initials
Cardiopulmonary							
Pulses							
Heart							
Lungs							
Tanner stage	1	2	3	4	5		
Skin							
Abdominal							
Genitalia							
Musculoskeletal							
Neck							
Shoulder							
Elbow							
Wrist							
Hand							
Back							
Knee							
Ankle							
Foot							
Other							

(Left margin labels: Complete / Limited)

Clearance:

A. Cleared

B. Cleared after completing evaluation/rehabilitation for _____

C. Not cleared for: ❏ Collision

❏ Contact

❏ Noncontact _____ Strenuous _____ Moderately strenuous _____ Nonstrenuous

Due to _____

Recommendation: _____

_____

_____

Name of physician _____ Date _____

Address _____ Phone _____

Signature of physician _____

Medical History

History   Date _____

Name _____ Sex _____ Age _____ Date of Birth _____

Grade _____ Sport _____ _____ _____

Personal physician _____ _____ _____
                              Address   Physician's phone

Explain "Yes" answers below:	Yes	No
1. Have you ever been hospitalized?	❑	❑
Have you ever had surgery?	❑	❑
2. Are you presently taking any medication or pills?	❑	❑
3. Do you have any allergies (medicine, bees or other stinging insects)?	❑	❑
4. Have you ever passed out during or after exercise?	❑	❑
Have you ever been dizzy during or after exercise?	❑	❑
Have you ever had chest pain during or after exercise?	❑	❑
Do you tire more quickly than your friends during exercise?	❑	❑
Have you ever had high blood pressure?	❑	❑
Have you ever been told that you have a heart murmur?	❑	❑
Have you ever had racing of your heart or skipped heartbeats?	❑	❑
Has anyone in your family died of heart problems or a sudden death before age 50?	❑	❑
5. Do you have any skin problems (itching, rashes, acne)?	❑	❑
6. Have you ever had a head injury?	❑	❑
Have you ever been knocked out or unconscious?	❑	❑
Have you ever had a seizure?	❑	❑
Have you ever had a stinger, burner, or pinched nerve?	❑	❑
7. Have you ever had heat or muscle cramps?	❑	❑
Have you ever been dizzy or passed out in the heat?	❑	❑
8. Do you have trouble breathing or do you cough during or after activity?	❑	❑
9. Do you use any special equipment (pads, braces, neck rolls, mouth guard, eye guards, etc.)?	❑	❑
10. Have you had any problems with your eyes or vision?	❑	❑
Do you wear glasses or contacts or protective eye wear?	❑	❑
11. Have you ever sprained/strained, dislocated, fractured or broken or had repeated swelling or other injuries of any bones or joints?	❑	❑

❑ Head   ❑ Shoulder   ❑ Thigh   ❑ Neck   ❑ Elbow   ❑ Knee   ❑ Chest

❑ Forearm   ❑ Shin/calf   ❑ Back   ❑ Wrist   ❑ Ankle   ❑ Hip   ❑ Hand   ❑ Foot

	Yes	No
12. Have you had any other medical problems (infectious mononucleosis, diabetes, etc.)?	❑	❑
13. Have you had a medical problem or injury since your last evaluation?	❑	❑

14. When was your last tetanus shot? _____

When was your last measles immunization? _____

15. When was your first menstrual period? _____

When was your last menstrual period? _____

What was the longest time between your periods last year? _____

(continued)

Medical History *(continued)*

Explain "Yes" answers:

_____

_____

_____

_____

_____

_____

I hereby state that, to the best of my knowledge, my answers to the above questions are correct.

Date _____

Signature of athlete _____

Signature of parent/guardian _____

3. Keep a medical history of every athlete on file.
4. Use extraordinary judgment in identifying athletes who are injured or ill enough that they should not participate.
5. Get parental and physician approval before permitting seriously ill or injured athletes to return to participation.

Duty 7: Supervise the Activity Closely

> High school basketball coach Sue Emmerling was in a practice session working on speed drills when a student assistant called her to the office for an important telephone call. The team continued to practice but became reckless, and the drill degenerated into horseplay. Two players collided; one broke her jaw and knocked out several teeth. Coach Emmerling was sued and found negligent for failing to fulfill her duty to supervise properly.

Understanding Your Duty. Your duty to supervise will require general supervision at some times and more specific supervision at others. *General supervision* is being in the area of activity so that you can see and hear what is happening. General supervision is required of all preparation areas, such as locker rooms, and playing facilities before and after practice. You are expected to be

- immediately accessible to the activity and able to oversee the entire program systematically;
- alert to conditions that may be dangerous to players and to take action to protect them; and
- able to react immediately and appropriately to emergencies.

Specific supervision is direct supervision at the immediate location of an activity and is more action-oriented. You should provide specific supervision when you teach new skills and continue it until your athletes understand the requirements of the activity, the risks involved, and their own ability to perform in light of these risks. Specific supervision is also advised when you notice athletes breaking rules or a change in the condition of your athletes.

As a general rule, the more dangerous the activity the more specific the supervision required. This suggests that more specific supervision is required with younger and less experienced athletes.

As part of your supervision duty, you are expected to foresee potentially dangerous situations and to be positioned to help prevent them

Table 15.1 American Academy of Pediatrics List of Disqualifying Conditions

	Contact			Noncontact	
	Contact/ collision	Limited contact/collision	Strenuous	Moderately strenuous	Nonstrenuous
Atlantoaxial instability *Swimming (no butterfly, breast-stroke or diving starts)*	No	No	Yes*	Yes	Yes
Acute illness *Needs individual assessment (e.g., contagiousness to others, risk of worsening illness)*	*	*	*	*	*
Cardiovascular					
Carditis	No	No	No	No	No
Hypertension					
Mild	Yes	Yes	Yes	Yes	Yes
Moderate	*	*	*	*	*
Severe	*	*	*	*	*
Congenital heart disease	†	†	†	†	†
Needs individual assessment †Patients with mild forms can be allowed a full range of physical activities; patients with mild or severe forms or who are postoperative should be evaluated by a physician*					
Eyes					
Absence or loss of function of one eye	*	*	*	*	*
Detached retina	†	†	†	†	†
Availability of American Society for Testing Materials approved eye guards may allow competitor to participate in most sports, but this must be judged on an individual basis †Consult opthalmologist*					
Inguinal hernia	Yes	Yes	Yes	Yes	Yes
Kidney (absence of one)	No	Yes	Yes	Yes	Yes
Liver (enlarged)	No	No	Yes	Yes	Yes
Musculoskeletal disorders	*	*	*	*	*
Neurologic					
History of serious head or spine trauma, repeated concussions or craniotomy	*	*	Yes	Yes	Yes
Convulsive disorder					
Well controlled	Yes	Yes	Yes	Yes	Yes
Poorly controlled	No	No	Yes†	Yes	Yes††
Needs individual assessment †No swimming or weight lifting* ††No archery or riflery*					

(continued)

Table 15.1 *(continued)*

	Contact			Noncontact	
	Contact/ collision	*Limited contact/collision*	*Strenuous*	*Moderately strenuous*	*Nonstrenuous*
Ovary (absence of one)	Yes	Yes	Yes	Yes	Yes
Respiratory					
Pulmonary insufficiency	*	*	*	*	Yes
Asthma	Yes	Yes	Yes	Yes	Yes
May be allowed to complete if oxygenation remains satisfactory during a graded stress test					
Sickle cell trait	Yes	Yes	Yes	Yes	Yes
Skin (boils, herpes, impetigo, scabies)	*	*	Yes	Yes	Yes
No gymnastics with mats, martial arts, wrestling or contact sports until no longer contagious					
Spleen (enlarged)	No	No	No	Yes	Yes
Testicle (absent or undescended)	Yes*	Yes*	Yes	Yes	Yes
Certain sports may require protective cup					

from occurring. This requires you to know your sport well, especially the rules that are intended to provide for the safety of the athletes.

Failure to adequately supervise is among the most common sources of lawsuits in sport. You cannot take this legal duty lightly. Yet you are not expected to personally observe every action or to guarantee the safety of your athletes. In a lawsuit, the court will consider the activity, the type of supervision provided, and the location and competency of the coach in determining negligence. Remember that the degree of supervision is expected to be proportional to the risk of injury that is known or can be reasonably expected.

Fulfilling Your Duty

1. Always provide general supervision for all facilities and playing areas being used by your team.
2. Provide specific supervision when teaching new skills and when the risk of injury increases.
3. Know your sport so well that you can anticipate potentially dangerous situa-

tions and be positioned to prevent them from occurring.

4. Use posters, notices, and signs to support but not replace your supervision.
5. Do not condone reckless or overly aggressive behavior that threatens the safety of any athlete.

Duty 8: Warn of Inherent Risks

> Bill Edgar, a 16-year-old, was awarded $1.8 million after sustaining permanent paralysis playing baseball. He attempted to score by diving headlong into the catcher. The coach, one of several defendants in the lawsuit, was found negligent for failing to warn that this action could bring serious injury.

Understanding Your Duty. You are responsible to provide instructions regarding the safety of the sport. For example, you are expected to teach your athletes how to react to potentially dangerous situations. When a 10-year-old boy was injured in soccer because he collided with another player, both of whom were going for a loose ball, the court ruled the coach was negligent because he had failed to teach what should be done in this forseeable and potentially dangerous situation.

Although you cannot protect athletes from all risks in the sport, athletes must know, understand, and appreciate the risks *inherent* in the sport to be able to assume them. Just how much understanding is required is not clear, but it appears that one warning may not be sufficient. Your warnings should be thorough, clear, and repeated.

Accepted ways of warning athletes of inherent risks in sports include these:

- Posting signs describing risks and how to properly perform the sport skills
- Meeting with the team to explain the risks, followed by repeated warnings in practices and contests
- Including discussion of risks in team notebooks and parent orientation programs
- Using participation agreements, which are signed by parents and athletes, to explain the risk in specific terms (see page 176 for a sample form)
- Showing films or videotapes that illustrate the risks

Fulfilling Your Duty

1. Warn your athletes of the inherent risks of the sport so they know, understand, and appreciate them.

2. Use written notices, releases, videos, and repeated warnings to make certain your athletes understand the risks and are mindful of them.

Duty 9: Provide Appropriate Emergency Assistance

> Field hockey player Jill Donovan passed out during practice on a hot, sultry day. Coach Ellis failed to recognize the common symptoms of severe heat exhaustion, and so rather than seeking immediate medical assistance instructed Jill to sit under a shade tree while practice continued. When Jill slipped into shock another team member urged Coach Ellis to get help, but the plea fell on deaf ears. The next morning Jill died: Coach Ellis was found negligent in the lawsuit that followed for failing to provide appropriate emergency assistance.

Understanding Your Duty. You have a duty to provide or secure appropriate medical assistance for injured athletes you coach. If medical assistance is not immediately available, you have a duty to provide appropriate first aid. *Every* coach should complete a general first aid course, or better yet a sport first aid course such as the one offered by ASEP.

To meet your duty to provide emergency assistance you should develop a written emergency plan that is readily available. On page 177, I have provided a sample of such a plan, which should include what is done immediately, who contacts emergency medical help and how, how to transport an injured athlete, who contacts parents and school officials, and how to complete an injury report. Know this plan and follow it when an emergency occurs.

Whenever possible, transfer the risk associated with emergencies to more qualified people. Have a team physician on-site whenever possible, and employ an athletic trainer if you possibly can. When an injury occurs provide only the first aid you are qualified to perform and then immediately obtain medical assistance. Do no more and no less.

Explanation of Inherent Risks and Participation Agreement for Soccer

Note: The athlete and both parents or legal guardians (if living) must sign this form before any athlete may participate in interscholastic sport practices or games. If one parent or guardian is deceased, please indicate so on the appropriate line.

Soccer is an exciting sport that often involves forceful contact with the ground or another player. The sport is also frequently played during hot, humid seasons. Because of these conditions inherent to the sport, participating in soccer exposes an athlete to many risks of injury. Those injuries include, but are not limited to, death; paralysis due to serious neck and back injuries; brain damage; damage to internal organs; serious injuries to the bones, ligaments, joints, and tendons; and general deterioration of health. Such injuries can result not only in temporary loss of function, but also in serious impairment of future physical, psychological, and social abilities, including the ability to earn a living.

In an effort to make the sport of soccer as safe as it can be, the coaching staff will instruct players concerning the rules of soccer and the correct mechanics of all skills. It is vital that athletes follow the coach's skill instructions, training rules, and team policies to decrease the possibility of serious injury. Team rules and policies are listed in the team notebook each athlete receives at the preseason meeting.

We have read the information above concerning the risks of playing soccer. We understand and assume all risks associated with trying out, practicing, or playing soccer. We further agree to hold the _____ School District and its employees, representatives, coaches, volunteers, and agents harmless in any and all liability actions, claims, or additional legal action in connection with participation in any activities related to participation on the _____ High School soccer team.

In signing this form, we assume the inherent risks of soccer and waive future legal action by our heirs, estate, executor, administrator, assignees, family members, and ourselves.

Date: _____

Signature of athlete: _____

Signature of mother (or legal guardian): _____

Signature of father (or legal guardian): _____

Fulfilling Your Duty

1. Protect the injured athlete from further harm.
2. Provide appropriate first aid.
3. Attempt to maintain or restore life using CPR when required.
4. Comfort and reassure the athlete.
5. Activate your emergency plan, transferring the treatment responsibility to trained medical personnel.

Other Duties

You have just reviewed the nine major duties required of coaches to help manage the risk of injury to your athletes and risk of legal liability to yourself. There are several additional duties that also warrant your consideration.

Keep Adequate Records

You can reduce your risk of losing a lawsuit by keeping adequate records. Among the most important are injury reports (a sample form is shown on pages 178-179). This form should be completed after any serious injury, meaning any injury that causes the athlete to miss at least one practice.

The records I have suggested you keep regarding your nine legal duties are the following:

- Preseason and periodic player evaluations
- Season and practice plans

Emergency Plan for Field Hockey

Immediate actions:

1. Head coach Joan Ellis will stay with the athlete and keep her calm. She will also keep other nonmedical personnel away from the area.

2. Do not move the injured athlete until the possibility of serious injury (especially head, neck, or back injury) has been ruled out. If Joan Ellis decides that it is safe to move the athlete, she will be moved only after all injuries have been stabilized. Procedures covered in first aid training will be used.

3. Joan Ellis will provide first aid until medical assistance arrives.

4. Assistant coach Anne Phillips will summon the school nurse or contact the emergency medical system (EMS) immediately.

If the EMS is activated:

1. The EMS phone number is 555-1234 . The physical education office phone will be accessible at all times.

2. Anne Phillips will give the following information to the EMS dispatcher:
    a. Her name, her position, and the school name
    b. The athlete's name, age, and suspected injury
    c. The address of the field and directions for access
    d. Any additional information requested
    Important: Do not hang up until the EMS dispatcher has hung up.

3. Anne Phillips will then go to the school entrance to direct medical personnel to the field.

4. Student manager Carol Fields will pull the athlete's emergency card, which includes phone numbers for parents and important medical history information. She will also note the names of adult witnesses to the injury for the injury report form.

5. Joan Ellis will contact the parents as soon as the medical personnel have examined the athlete and prepared her for transport to a medical facility. The athlete will be transported to the medical facility only in an EMS vehicle. School or personal vehicles will not be used.

6. Joan Ellis will then inform the athletic director of the activation of the emergency plan.

In any injury situation:

1. Joan Ellis will complete the injury report. Names of adult witnesses were previously taken by Carol Fields . This information should be included on the report.

2. File copies of the injury report form with the athletic director, principal, and school nurse. Keep one copy on file with the team records and another as a personal record.

3. Joan Ellis will follow up with medical personnel to determine any role she will need to play in the recovery and rehabilitation process.

Important phone numbers:
EMS dispatcher: 555-1234
Fire department: 555-5678
Police department: 555-0987
School nurse: Ext. 1621
Principal: 555-1357
Athletic director: 555-2468

Injury Report Form

Date of report _____

1. Name _____ Home address _____

2. Organization _____ Sex M ☐ F ☐ Age _____ Sport _____

3. Time accident occurred: Hour _____ AM _____ PM _____ Date: _____

4. Place of accident: _____

5. Nature of injury: (check)

Abrasion	☐	Concussion	☐	Puncture	☐
Amputation	☐	Cut	☐	Scalds	☐
Asphyxiation	☐	Dislocation	☐	Scratches	☐
Bite	☐	Fracture	☐	Shock (elec.)	☐
Bruise	☐	Laceration	☐	Sprain	☐
Burn	☐	Poisoning	☐	Other (specify)	☐

Part of body injured: (check)

Abdomen	☐	Eye	☐	Other	☐
Ankle	☐	Face	☐	Leg	☐
Arm	☐	Finger	☐	Mouth	☐
Back	☐	Foot	☐	Nose	☐
Chest	☐	Hand	☐	Scalp	☐
Ear	☐	Head	☐	Tooth	☐
Elbow	☐	Knee	☐	Wrist	☐

Description of accident

What object or substance was the source of injury? _____

How did source of injury come into contact with athlete? _____

6. Protective equipment worn? Yes ☐ No ☐ Type of equipment _____

7. Degree of injury: Death ☐, permanent impairment ☐, temporary disability ☐, nondisabling ☐

8. Coach in charge when accident occurred (name) _____

   Present at scene of accident: No ☐ Yes ☐

9. Immediate action taken:

   First-aid steps taken? ☐ By (name) _____

   Sent to physician ☐ By (name) _____

   How transported _____

   Physician's name _____

10. Sent to hospital ☐ By (name) _____

    How transported _____

    Hospital name _____

(continued)

Injury Report Form *(continued)*

11. Was parent or other individual notified? No ☐ Yes ☐ When?_____

How? _____ Name of individual notified _____

By whom? (enter name) _____

12. Restricted activity time _____
_____

13. Corrective actions taken or recommended to prevent future incidents _____
_____

14. Witnesses: 1. Name _____ Address _____

Remarks:

Signed: (Youth Sport Director) _____ (Coach) _____

- Season schedule
- Medical examination clearances
- Emergency plan
- Player participation agreements
- Eligibility records
- Injury reports
- Other safety checklists

Provide Safe Transportation

The best way to transport your athletes in terms of liability is by public carriers. You thus transfer the responsibility to them, and often they offer the safest and most convenient way to travel.

The next best option is to use a vehicle owned by the school or agency for whom you coach. Be certain whoever drives the vehicle has the proper license if a special classification is required.

The least preferred choice is to drive your automobile. If you transport athletes in your car, be certain you are properly licensed and insured and that the vehicle is in good repair. Some insurance policies invalidate the personal liability section of a policy if the driver is compensated for transporting others. If your school or sponsoring agency asks you to drive your car, find out whether any insurance coverage is provided.

Follow Due Process

You are expected to protect the constitutional rights of your athletes, including the following:

- The right to fair treatment and not to be subject to arbitrary or capricious rules
- The right to free expression (meaning you cannot impose unreasonable requirements regarding dress or hair styles, for example)
- The right not to be discriminated against because of race, sex, or religion
- The right to confidentiality regarding medical information

These rights complement and affirm the athletes' Bill of Rights, which was presented on page 6.

Procedural Due Process.   Many state associations and other sport organizations have imposed specific requirements for the procedure you must follow to meet athletes' rights to due process. Check with your sport director for your specific requirements. These procedures commonly consist of the following three steps:

1. Provide athletes with notice of charges or violations and the penalty to be imposed.

2. Allow athletes to present their side of the situation.
3. Provide a written record of findings.

In minor cases, these requirements can be met by telling athletes what rule they have violated and what penalty will be imposed, and by then pausing to allow them to respond. For major violations, you may need to provide a written notice of the violation and the penalty, conduct a formal hearing, and follow up with a written record of findings from that hearing. One of the most frequent problems coaches encounter is reacting too quickly, without giving athletes an opportunity to respond until a penalty has been imposed. You can avoid most problems with due process by making sure you have given athletes a chance to present their side of the situation.

Proper Training of Coaches

By now it is obvious that coaches have a legal responsibility to be properly trained to fulfill their duties. When a coach is not trained, the risk of injury for athletes and lawsuit for the coach and sponsoring agency increases greatly. The courts are telling us that it is no longer acceptable to place an unqualified person into the position of coach to supervise athletes.

As a head coach you also are responsible, along with your sponsoring agency, for insuring that your assistants are qualified. If you use untrained assistants, you must provide close and direct supervision until they demonstrate competency.

As coaching becomes a recognized profession, mandatory training and certification are rapidly approaching reality. Although certification is no guarantee of competency, it is a big step in the right direction. And though certification does not guarantee protection from lawsuits, it will help in defending against them.

Waivers and Participation Agreements

As lawsuits have increased in sport, many sponsoring agencies have turned to using waivers of responsibility to absolve or indemnify (hold harmless) themselves. The waiver or release is a contract signed by participants or their parents that seeks to transfer responsibility from the sponsoring agency to the participant. Waivers have limited legal value for several reasons:

- Minors cannot enter into contracts and parents cannot waive minors' rights to sue.
- The courts reject contracts to waive negligence.
- It is frequently considered a violation of public policy to require a release prior to participation in a sport.

Although waivers may have some psychological value in discouraging individuals who have signed them from suing, don't put confidence in waivers as part of your risk management plan. Instead, consider using *participation agreements*, which are not contracts, but signed documents stating that your athletes

- understand the dangers *inherent* in the sport;
- appreciate the consequences of the risks involved, including the possibility of injury and death;
- know the rules and procedures of the sport and the importance of following them; and,
- knowing all this, request to participate in the sport.

Participation agreements must be stated explicitly, the rules to be followed must be listed, and the possible dangers must be clearly spelled out. Participation agreements cannot prevent lawsuits or absolve you from negligence, but they clearly establish that you fulfilled your duty to warn. Remember, athletes cannot assume risk for something about which they are ignorant; participation agreements spell out the inherent risks in your sport. A sample of such an agreement (for soccer) is shown on page 176.

Insurance

In our litigious society, insurance is essential in managing risk. You simply should not coach without liability insurance, and sponsoring agencies should not permit anyone to coach without it.

Simply knowing that you have insurance is not sufficient. You need to know the specific coverage. Before your next season, find out from your sponsoring agency or school whether it has liability coverage for you and what this coverage is. Get answers to these questions:

- What events are covered?
- What property is covered?
- What activities are covered?
- What locations are covered?
- What losses are covered?
- What amount of loss will the insurer pay?
- What time period is covered?
- What special conditions are excluded?
- What steps must be taken following a loss?
- What is the coverage for transportation when using an agency vehicle? Your own vehicle?

If the sponsoring agency does not have liability coverage or you consider it inadequate, buy your own liability insurance. You have at least three options for doing so.

- You can add this coverage to your homeowner's policy for a relatively small sum.
- If you belong to a professional organization (such as the National Recreation and Park Association, the American Alliance for Health, Physical Education, Recreation and Dance, or a national coaching association), it may offer personal liability insurance at low rates.
- You can purchase a separate personal liability policy.

A policy should provide a minimum of $1 million in coverage as well as pay for the costs associated with the investigation and defense of lawsuits. Review policies carefully, for they differ widely in coverage for the premiums charged.

Also, some policies are only secondary policies, meaning they provide coverage only after any other existing policy pays. While some of these policies are useful supplements, others have so many exclusions that your actual coverage is very limited.

Summary

1. The best way to avoid litigation is to take a positive approach and do what is best for your athletes.
2. Legal liability is a responsibility or duty to others that is enforceable by the court. Negligence is a legal term for failing to fulfill a responsibility or duty.
3. Negligence is determined only when four conditions are met: you have a legal duty; you fail to fulfill a legal duty; there was an injury to someone to whom you had a duty; and your failure to fulfill the duty caused the injury.
4. You should use these four steps to manage risk: identify the risk, evaluate the risk, select an approach, and implement the approach.
5. Some states have immunity laws to protect volunteer coaches. Paid coaches are not currently covered.
6. You have nine legal duties. They include the duty to
   - Plan the activity properly
   - Provide proper instruction
   - Provide a safe physical environment
   - Provide adequate and proper equipment
   - Match your athletes
   - Evaluate athletes for injury or incapacity
   - Supervise the activity closely
   - Warn of inherent risks
   - Provide appropriate medical assistance
7. You can reduce your risk further by keeping adequate records, providing safe transportation, following due process, and getting proper coaching training.
8. Participation agreements are superior to waivers.
9. Be sure that you have at least $1 million of liability insurance.

Chapter 16

Self-Management

Coaching is a helping profession. A cardinal principle for all helping professionals is, Take care of yourself first in order to take care of others. Coaching is a demanding helping profession, and the better your mental and physical condition the better able you will be to help your athletes. After 15 chapters that have encouraged you to take care of your team, this chapter encourages you to take care of yourself. You will evaluate how well you manage your stress, your time, and your health. Then I'll point you in the right direction for improving these skills.

Stress Management

Bill Adler is a high school basketball coach at a large suburban school—and desperately needs help managing his stress. Bill has been modestly successful, if success is defined by his teams' won-lost records. His team won the league championship 2 years ago, but had a very disappointing season last year.

Bill loves basketball, was a good player in college, and worked hard to acquire his current position. People in the community and school are basketball enthusiasts, in some cases maybe too much so. Bill feels that many influential members of the community and the school administration expect more of him than he has delivered. But Bill also expects a great deal from himself, and he too is not satisfied with his record.

Bill has had trouble relating to his players. "They just don't seem to care like athletes used to," grumbles Bill to his wife. The harder he pushes the less they seem to respond. He works long hours, but feels underappreciated by the athletic director and principal as well as key community leaders.

Bill was very uptight most of last season. He worried constantly about whether he was playing the right athletes, what he could do to improve their performance, and how people were judging his coaching. The stress has strained his marriage, and now he feels his wife isn't as supportive as she used to be. "She just doesn't understand the pressure I'm under," Bill tells himself.

Several hours before and during each game Bill is an emotional basket case. He's tense and jittery, and his heart rate and blood pressure shoot up. His temper is short. He is easily irritated whenever something doesn't go right. He finds it hard to concentrate and consequently "chokes" when needing to make important tactical decisions during the contest. Later, when he calms down somewhat, he often second-guesses his tactics, which only renews his stressed feeling.

Bill has let his health deteriorate. He's smoking again after quitting 2 years ago, and he's gained nearly 40 pounds since his college days. He can't find time to work out because he always is behind on projects. He spends a lot of time worrying. In fact, the work of worrying is taking so much of his energy that he has little left for other work. If the truth be known, Bill is no longer enjoying coaching, once his passion.

Bill is clearly stressed—and he's not managing it well. It is a problem endemic to coaching. Over the past 10 years many famous coaches have called it quits because of the relentless pressures they faced. Dick Vermeil, Ara Parseghian, Sonia Hogg, Jack Hartman, John Madden, Al McGuire, and Earl Weaver are a few of the more visible coaches, joined by thousands less known, who were unable to manage stress and consequently were forced to abandon the profession they loved.

Causes of Stress

Bill's life contains many potential sources of threat. Few would question the tremendous demands placed upon coaches in situations similar to Bill's. But not all coaches become so stressed by these same demands. Why then does one coach experience so much stress and another see the demands as a challenge? The answer is in how different individuals perceive their situations.

Bill sees his situation very negatively. He perceives that his players are not relating to him well. He perceives that the administration and community don't appreciate his difficult task. He perceives that his wife doesn't understand his lot. He perceives that. . . . And on and on. But another coach in the same situation might perceive it very differently.

The point here—the most crucial point to understand about stress—is that stress is not caused directly by a demanding situation, but by how the person interprets the situation. In Bill's case, the situation certainly plays an important part in shaping Bill's perceptions, but he has several options for interpreting his circumstances. Bill could see his situation as normal for a basketball coach and disregard the pressure to win more. Or he could see it as the challenge of coaching, and view it positively. The point is, the situation alone does not dictate the stress. Nevertheless, most people who experience stress tend to blame their situations as the cause, not their interpretations of them.

Checking Your Stress Tendency

Before proceeding, consider the following statements to evaluate your own tendency to experience stress and your ability to cope with it. These are not scientifically valid tests; they are merely tools to help you become aware of your tendency to experience stress and your ability to handle it when coaching. Record the number you feel reflects your place on the rating scale for each statement.

Now, sum your scores for each scale. An individual with an average tendency to experience stress and an average ability to manage it would score 30 on each test. The ideal scores would be very low on the Stress Tendency Test and very high on the Coping Ability Test, meaning you tend to feel little stress and you cope quite well with it when you do. Very high scores for stress tendency and low scores for coping ability suggest a need for you to examine the stress

Coaches' Stress Tendency Test

1	2	3	4	5
Rarely true		Occasionally true		Almost always true

_____ 1. I worry that my players won't respect me.

_____ 2. I do not sleep well because of practices and games.

_____ 3. When I coach I worry about making mistakes.

_____ 4. I almost always feel tired during the season.

_____ 5. I have a hard time calming down after games.

_____ 6. My schedule during the season makes me feel overloaded.

_____ 7. I worry that my players are going to mess up.

_____ 8. It upsets me that parents or fans may criticize my coaching.

_____ 9. Before games I am very nervous.

_____ 10. I am on edge when I coach.

Coaches' Coping Ability Test

1	2	3	4	5
Rarely true		Occasionally true		Almost always true

_____ 1. I usually find something good to comment on from a bad practice or game.

_____ 2. I keep my temper and other emotions under control when I coach.

_____ 3. I seldom feel troubled by a coaching matter at home.

_____ 4. I find coaching challenging but not overwhelming.

_____ 5. I don't fly off the handle when a player or an official makes a mistake.

_____ 6. I have confidence that I am doing a good and worthwhile job as a coach.

_____ 7. My colleagues, family, and friends support me and are there when I want to discuss a problem.

_____ 8. I understand that I, as a coach, can't control everything.

_____ 9. When something bad or unexpected happens during the season, I can adjust to it without much difficulty.

_____ 10. I set aside time each day for myself, to exercise, relax, or just be alone.

you experience as a coach. Read the next section to find out what you can do to better manage your stress.

Managing Stress

Coaching will be stressful from time to time for nearly every individual, but it is how one manages that stress that is important. Left unmanaged, stress leads to burnout, which occurs when coaches feel they have no "out," no buffers, and no support system for the stress they repeatedly experience. (You can read more about coaching burnout in *Coaches Guide to Sport Psychology*.)

Let's look at what Bill can do to manage his stress. He has two options. He can change his situation or he can change his perceptions—his interpretation of the situation he faces.

It is rational to try to change situations that you perceive as being negative. Bill could try talking with his administrators, players, and wife to get them to appreciate what he is trying to do. He may find out that they already do, and that he had perceived the situation incorrectly. Or if he chooses not to talk with them, he might look for another job, leave the community, or perhaps leave his wife. These actions may eliminate his stress. On the other hand, because Bill has a tendency to perceive things negatively, he might soon find himself in another situation where he is perceiving events very negatively and once again feeling stressed.

Another option available to Bill is to change the way he interprets his situation. This is not easy to do, but often it is easier than changing the situation. Psychologists have found that the single most effective way to manage stress is to change habitual negative thinking to more realistic and constructive thinking. Many stress management programs are available for people like Bill to learn to change their negative thinking.

It is beyond the scope of this chapter to describe the many, and sometimes complex, methods of managing stress. My purpose is to help you determine if you are having a problem with stress and to direct you in finding help if so. The most important step is recognizing that you are experiencing stress and that the stress is in part caused by how you are interpreting your situation. Once you recognize this, you often can begin changing your perceptions, on your own or through a self-help program.

Here are four sources of help for managing your stress.

- Read the stress management chapter in *Coaches Guide to Sport Psychology*, where I briefly describe some of these techniques and how you can use them with your athletes. In fact, learning to use these techniques to manage your own stress will help you use them more effectively with your athletes. Exercises to get you started are included in the *Sport Psychology Study Guide*.
- Read *New Guide to Rational Living* (Ellis & Harper, 1976). It is a terrific book for helping yourself correct negative thinking.
- Many other books, audiotapes, and videotapes present effective stress management programs. I've listed references to some of the better programs below.
- If your stress is high and you don't think you can solve your problem alone or these self-help programs don't work, then seek professional help. It's not a loss of face to seek trained help when you have a problem. We all can help each other. You can help many young people by being an effective coach, and a psychologist can help you manage your stress. In that way, you can continue helping young people through sport. Remember, you've got to take care of yourself to take care of others.

Books

Benson, H., & Klipper, M.Z. (1976). *The relaxation response*. New York: Avon.

Girdano, D., & Everly, G.S. (1986). *Controlling stress and tension*. Englewood Cliffs, NJ: Prentice-Hall.

Jacobson, E. (1976). *You must relax* (5th ed.). New York: McGraw-Hill.

McGuigan, F.J. (1981). *A guide to stress and tension control*. San Diego, CA: U.S. International University Institute for Stress Management.

Morgan, W.P., & Goldston, S.E. (1987). *Exercise and mental health*. Washington: Hemisphere.

Pelletier, K. (1977). *Mind as healer, mind as slayer*. New York: Dell.

Selye, H. (1975). *Stress without distress*. New York: New American Library.

Selye, H. (1978). *The stress of life*. New York: McGraw-Hill.

Audio-Visuals

Keeping cool: How to deal with stress. Mount Kisco, NY: The Center for the Humanities.

Stress: The time bomb within. Mount Kisco, NY: The Center for the Humanities.

The stress mess. Pasadena, CA: Barr Films.

Other Guidelines for Managing Stress

- Listen to constructive criticism as feedback, but don't let "Monday morning quarterbacks" trouble you.
- When a problem arises, address it quickly instead of letting it be a source of ongoing concern.
- Do not panic and blow difficult circumstances out of proportion.
- Plan periodic "fun days" when you and the team break away from the normal practice routine.
- Learn to laugh and not be so serious about your role.
- Join in relaxation sessions with your players.
- Set aside time for yourself daily. It's amazing how having your own time and space can rejuvenate you.

Time Management

You'll never meet a more delightful, helpful person than Sandy Gross, a computer programmer for the local electric utility in Medford. Sandy is also the swim coach at Medford High School and in the summer at the Medford Swim Club, positions she has held the past 2 years. Sandy is unmarried, but regularly dates Rick, whom she often works out with playing racquetball or tennis.

Sandy's life is full, or it would be more accurate to say chaotic, because of her poor time management skills. Sandy can't say no when she is asked to help out, which results in her having more to do than she could possibly complete, even if she managed her time well. In addition to her full-time job and nightly practices from 4:30 to 6 p.m., this week Sandy is speaking at the local junior high school and refereeing a club volleyball game because they couldn't find anyone else.

Because Sandy does not teach at the school, her swimmers and the athletic director call her at work when problems arise. Computer programming requires intense concentration, and these calls, which occur often because of her poor time management, usually disrupt her work significantly. Consequently she is having trouble meeting her deadlines, and last week her boss expressed concern about her job performance. Sandy hopes to solve the problem by putting in more hours rather than stopping the phone calls, because she feels she needs to be available to her team. But where will she find the extra time?

Sandy is so busy she takes no time to plan her days well. Last night she got a call from Rick, who was miffed because she stood him up for yesterday's lunch date. She missed lunch because the athletic director had called to report that Sandy had failed to prepare the registration forms on time for the upcoming quadrangular meet. So she rushed over to the school on her lunch hour to take care of them. Although he didn't say anything, the athletic director was obviously unhappy; it cost the school an extra $100 for late registration and cost him his lunch period to solve Sandy's oversight.

Sandy's practice sessions are never formally planned. They closely follow the practice sessions of her former collegiate coach. She tries to get everyone swimming, and then responds to problems. She almost never has formal teaching sessions: she watches for mistakes or waits until a swimmer asks for help and then attempts to correct the problem. This unstructured approach leaves her swimmers and assistant not knowing what to do.

In fact, Sandy has never given her assistant, Pat, specific responsibilities. Pat knows Sandy is overworked and tries to help by asking how she can help. But Sandy is so disorganized that she can't effectively delegate work to Pat. In her constant rush, Sandy fails to see how Pat is growing alienated through frustration at the lack of direction.

Cause of Poor Time Management

Sandy is an intelligent person who wants to be successful. Why then can't she manage her time better? Experts have identified five common causes of poor time management.

Relying on "Mythical Time." This is the mistaken belief that you will have more time later so you procrastinate the work before you. When you rely on mythical time, you are inclined to squander the real time available to you for completing the work.

Underestimating Demands on Time. You continually think you can do more than you actually can because you are less efficient than you think or have less free time than you recognize. You fail to realize that much of your day is committed to routine tasks; you fail to expect the unexpected. You don't plan for telephone calls, paperwork, conversations with athletes and assistants, and requests for information, but all are part of a coach's daily routine.

Task Creeping. You fail to complete the task before agreeing to take on another. As you creep from one task to the next you get farther and farther behind, failing to meet your commitments. When desperate, task creepers begin rushing through their work, making mistakes and sometimes costing others time, money, and opportunity.

Task Hopping. You jump from one task to another because of poor concentration, too many deadlines to meet, and little sense of priority. You get a good idea, but lose it because you don't write it down and your mind is too full to remember it.

Ignoring Reality. You fail to recognize your limitations. You want to be involved in everything; when people request your services you are flattered and you see your involvement as an opportunity for personal advancement or to help others. You also ignore the reality of how your poor time management adversely affects others.

Evaluate Your Time Management Skills

Poor time managers, like Sandy Gross, create environments that are unproductive and unrewarding, not only for themselves but for those who work with them as well. To determine how well you manage time, complete the self-evaluation questionnaire in this section. You can estimate your effectiveness at managing your time by answering forthrightly the questions on page 189.

Time Management Scale

1. To what extent do you plan your time?

1	2	3	4	5
Always	Frequently	Sometimes	Seldom	Never

2. To what extent do you set priorities and stick to them?

1	2	3	4	5
Always	Frequently	Sometimes	Seldom	Never

3. To what extent do you waste time on the telephone?

1	2	3	4	5
Never	Seldom	Sometimes	Frequently	Always

4. To what extent do you lose time because of unnecessary visits and nonproductive conversations?

1	2	3	4	5
Never	Seldom	Sometimes	Frequently	Always

5. To what extent do you waste time in meetings?

1	2	3	4	5
Never	Seldom	Sometimes	Frequently	Always

6. To what extent do you lose time because of inefficient processing of paperwork?

1	2	3	4	5
Never	Seldom	Sometimes	Frequently	Always

7. To what extent do you overcommit yourself?

1	2	3	4	5
Never	Seldom	Sometimes	Frequently	Always

8. To what extent do you avoid decisions and procrastinate?

1	2	3	4	5
Never	Seldom	Sometimes	Frequently	Always

9. To what extent do you delegate work?

1	2	3	4	5
Always	Frequently	Sometimes	Seldom	Never

10. To what extent do you engage in task hopping?

1	2	3	4	5
Never	Seldom	Sometimes	Frequently	Always

Now total up your score on the 10 items and compare yourself to the scale on page 190. Use the comparison as a guide to determine the need to develop your time management skills further.

If you scored high on your ability to manage time, you are to be congratulated. Coaches who know the importance of time always are seeking even small ways to improve. So read on. You may pick up one or two points of value, or you may be reminded of some you already know but have neglected lately. If you scored lower than you would like, study carefully the following guidelines for improving

Range	Time management skill
10 to 15	Outstanding
16 to 20	Superior
21 to 25	Good
26 to 30	Average
31 to 50	Weak

your time management skills. You also should consider taking the ASEP Time Management Course, which teaches you much more about how to become a better manager of your time.

Improving Your Management of Time

- Set aside time regularly to plan. Any effort to manage time stems from planning.
- Now plan by clearly defining your goals for the immediate future. Write down your weekly plans and review them at least once a day. Mark off those tasks that have been completed.
- Set realistic goals. It's good to shoot high, but not so high that your goals become impossible to achieve. Be realistic not only in the number of tasks you take on, but the time you allocate to each task.
- Determine what tasks *must* be done and how much time each will take. Put all other tasks at a lower priority, working on them only when the "must do" tasks are completed. Watch out when prioritizing tasks; people tend to avoid tasks that are important but that they dislike.
- Set limits. Do not take on more work unless you know that you will have spare time after completing your "must do" tasks.
- Develop systems for completing routine work efficiently.
- Control your time to the extent possible. Create periods where you are inaccessible except for an emergency. Inform others that this is your time to complete work that will help you help them.

- Develop concentration skills. Planning and efficient processing of routine work demand that you be able to concentrate.
- Help yourself concentrate better by organizing a work area free of self-distractions. If possible, use this area only when you are working so that you associate it with work. Put other work out of sight so you are not tempted to task hop.
- Record important details by writing them down.
- Set and keep deadlines.
- Delegate tasks to others when possible. Make certain they know what to do and when it is to be done. Monitor what you delegate so you are certain it will be completed on time.
- Encourage others not to waste your time. Learn how to close conversations in person and on the phone. In turn, don't waste other people's time.
- Learn to make quick transitions between tasks.
- Manage your stress; it will improve your use of time. Manage your time effectively; it will reduce your stress.
- Slow down and regroup when you feel overwhelmed. Reestablish your goals, develop your plans, and prioritize your work.
- Find time for yourself. Maintain your health; it will help you manage your time and stress.

Health Management

Paul Horn lives to coach wrestling; it puts meaning into his life. He coaches 30 or more 10- to 15-year-olds for the Greenville Wrestling Club, an organization affiliated with USA Wrestling. But Paul won't be finishing the season; he is recovering from a heart attack he suffered 2 weeks ago at the grocery warehouse where he works.

Paul never thought it would happen to him, especially at age 41. He's not an uptight, Type A personality. In fact, he's quite laid-back and enjoys the good life—too much so. When Paul wrestled he weighed 154 pounds; now he has 240 pounds on a 5-foot, 10-inch frame. Once

Paul quit competing he stopped all activity, and because he always had been cutting weight, he began eating all the things he had deprived himself of for years.

Paul not only likes his food, he enjoys his beer. It's not uncommon for him to drink a six-pack in an evening. The wrestlers tease him about his beer belly, which he uses well when casually wrestling with some of the boys. But he doesn't wrestle often with them, first because his weight risks injury to the smaller boys, and second because he becomes exhausted from less than a minute of exercise.

Paul has smoked two packs of cigarettes a day for nearly 20 years. Although Paul didn't know it until his heart attack, he has high blood pressure and a cholesterol level of 275, well above the recommended maximum of 200.

Paul knew he wasn't taking care of himself like he should, but as a former athlete he just didn't think a heart attack would hit him. For years now, he has been telling himself he ought to quit smoking and lose some weight, but he also likes his lifestyle. Now the doctor told him he must change, that he was fortunate that this attack was not fatal.

Cause of Poor Health Management

You don't need a medical degree to have forecasted what would happen to Paul Horn. You could see the heart attack coming, yet Paul didn't, nor do thousands of other Pauls. People think it just won't happen to them. Of the two million deaths in the United States in 1988, 49% were due to coronary heart disease—primarily heart attacks, strokes, and hypertension-related disorders.

Those nearly one million people weren't randomly selected to get coronary heart disease. Some of them died even though they managed their health quite well. They were among the unfortunate who inherit a propensity for coronary heart disease. But many of these people didn't manage their health well. In fact, they abused their bodies by not managing three primary causes of coronary heart disease:

- Smoking
- High blood pressure
- High cholesterol

All this "good" living increased their heart attack risk 5 times and their stroke risk 11 times higher than among those who managed these three health factors.

If you would like to further increase your odds of being one of those one million deaths each year, eat so that you are substantially overweight, remain physically inactive, drink considerable alcohol regularly, and be frequently stressed. Your chances of having a heart attack or stroke will increase 21 times over normal.

The good news is that it doesn't need to happen to you. You can adopt a healthy lifestyle, which consists of

- regular exercise,
- eating the high-performance diet,
- maintaining a moderate weight level,

- controlling blood pressure,
- not smoking,
- drinking alcohol in moderation, and
- managing stress.

Perhaps you believe coronary heart disease only needs to concern you when you get much older. In studies of U.S. Vietnam War casualties, 45% of more than 1,300 autopsies revealed symptoms of the disease, and 5% had severe coronary heart disease. If you are over 20 and smoke, and have high blood pressure and high cholesterol—even if you have no symptoms now—you are probably developing coronary heart disease. This disease does not suddenly strike old people; it is a disease of your cumulative lifestyle.

Many coaches manage their health very well. They are models of the healthy lifestyle, to not only their athletes but the community. You are to be applauded if you are among these coaches. But if you are not, you can become so by learning to *manage* yourself. Coaches describe various reasons for slipping into poor health habits below. Understanding these reasons may help you recognize yourself and encourage you to adopt a healthier lifestyle.

Coaches' Reasons for Not Managing Their Health

"I really didn't realize how rotten I was treating my body. Now that I've quit smoking, lost weight, and am exercising regularly, I see how good I can feel and how lousy I used to feel."

"It's the way everyone around me lives, and what I've done for most of my life. I just don't think I can change all those habits."

"I hadn't thought much about my own fitness until my brother commented on my loss of muscle tone. I've been so busy making sure our athletes are fit that I've neglected myself. I guess somehow I thought my getting them fit would rub off on me. Dumb, huh?"

"The only time I have when I could train is right before or after practice. But I don't want to work out then because I'd hate to have my team see how out of shape I am."

"I was a tough athlete and have a strong body. I don't need to worry about my health."

"I want to lose weight, give up cigarettes, and cut back on the booze, but I just can't seem to change myself. I guess this is how I am and that's the way it is."

These are all reasons why some coaches don't change to active lifestyles. The reasons may not be good enough to justify coaches' damaging health or risking death, but they are powerful enough that coaches do not change to healthier lifestyles. If you are going to manage your team, your stress, and your time, why not also manage your most important possession—your health. The evidence is unequivocal: The healthy lifestyle adds not only years to your life, but life to your years. Through better management of your health, you will be able to coach for more years and have more energy to coach successfully.

I also want to encourage you to manage your health well because you are a powerful role model for your athletes. When coaches let themselves become unfit, their mismanagement of themselves suggests to their athletes that health and fitness are only important when one is training for competition. Athletes may think that when they no longer are required by their coach to be fit, then they too can let themselves slip into unhealthy habits. Of course, this is not the message you want to convey; but if you caution athletes to continue taking care of themselves after they complete their organized sports participation, remember that your actions will speak louder than your words.

Evaluate Your Health Habits

If you have studied this book carefully, you have thought a lot about yourself and how you will coach. I want you to think about your health now and evaluate yourself. Be honest. Rate your health habits as you typically behave on the form on page 193.

Total up the scores in each category and write those numbers in the three "category score" blanks. Then record the total of the three category scores on the "total score" blank. Finally, look at the following scales and find your scores. Is there one category that you scored particularly low in? Perhaps this aspect of health is one that you need to work on.

Evaluation of Coaches' Health Habits

1	**2**	**3**	**4**	**5**
Not true	Seldom true	Sometimes true	Often true	Very true

Exercise and physical fitness

_____ 1. I do regular calisthenics and stretching exercises.

_____ 2. I engage in vigorous exercise for 20 to 30 minutes or more at least three times a week.

_____ 3. I am rarely tired or out of breath because of normal daily activities.

_____ 4. I try to fit time for some physical activity into each day.

_____ 5. I usually walk, climb stairs, or ride a bike to places that I could get to without exercising.

_____ Category score

Diet and weight control

_____ 1. I eat a balanced diet.

_____ 2. I usually choose fresh and natural foods that are low in calories.

_____ 3. Most of the food I eat is nutritious, not junk food high in sugar, fat, and salt.

_____ 4. I seldom eat the fried and greasy foods at fast-food restaurants.

_____ 5. I am within 10 pounds of my ideal weight.

_____ Category score

Addictions

_____ 1. I do not smoke.

_____ 2. I rarely drink more than 1 or 2 ounces of alcohol in a day.

_____ 3. I do not tend to take medicine unless a doctor says it is necessary.

_____ 4. I limit my intake of coffee, colas, and other sources of caffeine.

_____ 5. I do not use drugs.

_____ Category score

_____ Total score

Category score	Health status	Total score	Health status
25-21	Fantastic	75-63	Robust
20-16	Fine	62-48	Reasonable
15 and below	Feeble	47 and below	Run-down

Improving Your Health

If the assessment of your health habits indicates that you have room for improvement, the first step is deciding you want to do something about it. Do you care enough about yourself to give up excessive alcohol consumption? Do you have enough self-discipline to quit smoking? Can you manage yourself along with your team so that you will live longer and better?

The prescriptions for achieving a healthier lifestyle are straightforward. The challenge is to accept the most difficult management task of all—managing your self. Meet that challenge successfully by following these guidelines to better health.

• Eat three meals a day at regular intervals, consuming no more calories than what you expend during the day.

- Eat a nutritious breakfast.
- Follow the high-performance diet: 20% fat, 15% protein, and 65% carbohydrate. It's especially important to limit your fat intake.
- Engage in regular exercise at least three times a week for 20 to 30 minutes of vigorous activity.
- Get 7 to 8 hours of sleep each night.
- Lose weight so your body fat is no more than 19% for males and 25% for females.
- Quit smoking. It causes cancer and stimulates coronary heart disease.
- Control your blood pressure, keeping it below 140/90.

How to follow some of these guidelines is obvious. Others may require you to learn more, so I've listed the best references I know.

Healthy Lifestyle References

Carlson, B., & Seiden, O.J. (1988). *Health-walk*. Golden, CO: Fulcrum.

Dickman, S.R. (1988). *Pathways to wellness*. Champaign, IL: Life Enhancement Publications.

Johnson, P.B. (1988). *Fitness and you*. Philadelphia: Saunders College Publishing.

Katch, F.I., & McArdle, W.D. (1988). *Nutrition, weight control, and exercise* (3rd ed.). Philadelphia: Lea & Febiger.

Miller, D.K., & Allen, T.E. (1982). *Fitness: A lifetime commitment* (2nd ed.). Minneapolis: Burgess.

Sharkey, B.J. (1997). *Health and Fitness* (4th ed.). Champaign, IL: Human Kinetics.

Wilmore, J.H. (1986). *Sensible fitness*. Champaign, IL: Leisure Press.

Summary

As you manage yourself better—your stress, time, and health—you'll manage your team better, and thereby become a Successful Coach. Review the following management points to stimulate your memory.

1. Your perception, not the actual demands, of a situation is the key to whether you will experience stress.
2. You can manage stress by changing the situation and your interpretation of it and by using relaxation techniques.
3. Five major causes of poor time management are relying on mythical time, underestimating demands on time, task creeping, task hopping, and ignoring reality.
4. A healthy lifestyle includes regular exercise; proper diet; control of weight, blood pressure, and stress; limited alcohol intake; and no smoking.
5. If healthy, you will not only live longer and have more energy to coach successfully, you will also provide a good role model for your athletes.

Appendix A

American Sport Education Program and the National Federation Interscholastic Coaches Education Program

History

The American Coaching Effectiveness Program (ACEP) began in 1976 when Dr. Rainer Martens, then a professor at the University of Illinois, launched it through the university's Office of Youth Sports. The effort involved examining coaching education programs, surveying coaches, consulting national sport agencies, and synthesizing research in the sport sciences. The first version of the ACEP curriculum was released in 1981, focusing on youth sport. Instructors originally conducted the clinics using a slide-and-lecture format.

When feedback indicated the need for easier presentation, ACEP updated its initial course, releasing an instructional video in January 1987. This second edition of the ACEP Level 1 curriculum proved popular, and more and more high school and national organization administrators turned to ACEP for help in adequately preparing their coaches.

Since then, we have been continually working to improve the quality and scope of our offerings. In 1990 the National Federation of State High School Associations (NFSHSA) selected ACEP as the official education program for the National Federation Interscholastic Coaches Association (NFICA). A special version of ACEP's Leader Level curriculum was released as the National Federation Interscholastic Coaches Education Program (NFICEP), improving further the quality of coaching throughout the United States. To meet the needs of coaches for education in providing an initial emergency response to injured athletes, the ACEP/NFICEP collaboration soon added a Sport First Aid Course, and ACEP continued to expand its program offerings to meet coaches' wide ranging needs.

In 1994, ACEP expanded its mission beyond coaching education, to include programs for parents and sport administrators. Accordingly, ACEP became the American Sport Education Program (ASEP). ASEP and NFSHSA continued to work together, and in the summer of 1996, we released a new course, the Drugs and Sport Course. This course was developed in response to the growing need among coaches and sport administrators to help bring effective prevention messages to our nation's athletes.

This publication marks still further collaboration between ASEP and NFSHSA. The original ASEP and NFICEP coaching course is now the Coaching Principles Course (this updated second edition of *Successful Coaching* serves as the course text), and the recently updated edition of *Sport First Aid* represents revision of the Sport First Aid Course. Both these updated courses reflect the latest in sport science and sports medicine, helping ASEP and NFSHSA to provide state-of-the-art education for coaches.

NFICA

The National Federation Interscholastic Coaches Association (NFICA), formed in 1981 as a professional organization of the National Federation of State High School Associations, now serves some 40,000 members. A small annual membership fee brings many benefits, including liability insurance, opportunities to serve on rules committees, and a subscription to the National Federation Coaches' Quarterly—a new publication designed specifically for high school coaches. NFICA affords important leadership involvement to its state coaches associations and holds an annual spring leadership conference to help coaches develop able state leaders.

ASEP Curriculum

ASEP's mission has always been to provide safe, meaningful, and enjoyable sport experiences for athletes by educating coaches in the areas of coaching philosophy, sport science, sports medicine, and sport techniques and tactics. Sport administrators and parents also play vital roles in shaping sport experiences, and ASEP's curriculum is designed to provide educational resources for all these key players—coaches, parents, sport administrators, and soon, officials—to help them better fulfill their roles.

ASEP's curriculum is available to coaches, administrators, and parents for programs involving youth, interscholastic, and club sport and beyond. This multilevel curriculum is presented in the chart on page 197.

For up-to-date information on the availability and prices of curricular and other resources, call the ASEP National Center at 800-747-5698, write to us at P.O. Box 5076, Champaign, IL, 61825-5076, or e-mail us at asep@hkusa.com. You may also visit ASEP on the World Wide Web at http://www.asep.com/.

The American Sport Education Program

Sport Coach

Master Level (advanced/continuing education)

- Sport Psychology
- Sport Physiology
- Sport Law
- Sport Rehabilitation
- Nutrition and Weight Control
- Teaching Sport Skills
- Sport Administration
- Time Management
- Sport Injuries
- Sport Mechanics

Sport Director

Leader Level (inter-scholastic and club sport)

- Program Evaluation
- Event Management
- Promotion
- Facilities and Equipment Management*
- Personnel Management*

* in development

- Coaching Principles Course*
- Sport First Aid Course*
- Drugs and Sport Course*
- Sport Techniques and Tactics resources

* These courses also comprise the NFICEP.

Sport Parent

Volunteer Level (youth sport)

- SportParent Course

- Youth SportDirector Workshop

- Coaching Youth Sport Course

"Athletes First • Winning Second"

Appendix B

A Parent Orientation Program

Developing good working relationships with your athletes' parents is almost as important as those you have with the athletes themselves. With a little effort you can have parents working with you and appreciating your efforts. The key is informing them about your program and listening to their concerns. I have found that many of the traditional problems between parents and coaches can be avoided when coaches hold a preseason parent orientation program. This program can serve a number of useful purposes:

- Enabling parents to understand the objectives of the program
- Allowing parents to become acquainted with you, the person responsible for their daughter or son
- Informing parents about the nature of the sport and its potential risks
- Explaining team rules, regulations, and procedures
- Letting parents know what is expected of the athletes and of them
- Enabling you to understand parents' concerns
- Establishing clear lines of communication between you and the parents
- Obtaining help from parents in conducting the season's activities

Neglecting parent orientation is tempting for overextended coaches. You may feel uncomfortable speaking to an adult group. And you signed on to coach, not cater to adults, right? But in spite of the hassle or your reluctance, parent orientation is important and valuable. Veteran coaches know the importance of open, honest communication with parents to a successful and enjoyable sport program. This chapter offers ideas for planning and implementing your own parent orientation program.

Planning the Program

When Should the Meeting Be Held?
If you have identified most of your athletes, schedule the meeting before the season. If not, hold it as soon after the first practice as possible. Choose a time when most parents can attend, and invite them individually by phone or personal letter. You might even consider making the meeting mandatory given all the important information you will be covering.

How Long Should the Meeting Be?
Two hours or less should be adequate to accomplish the stated objectives.

Should Athletes Attend the Meeting?
Coaches have mixed opinions about this. Some think it inhibits communication between parents and coach, whereas others believe that it promotes communication between parents, coach, and athletes. This is a decision to make based on your coaching philosophy.

Where Should the Meeting Be Held?
Select an accessible location. Be sure the room is suitable for your purposes, is well lighted, and has enough space and comfortable seating.

How Should the Meeting Be Conducted?
First, be well prepared and organized. Get started on time and keep the program moving along. Based on interviews with parents and coaches, we have developed the following format—you may wish to use it in conducting your parent orientation program. Adjust the outline to meet the needs of your situation, adding or deleting topics as appropriate.

Parent Orientation Program Agenda

Introductions (10 minutes)

Introduce yourself and any assistant coaches. Give a little background about yourself—why you're coaching, your experience in the sport, what you do for a living—to tell parents what qualifies you to receive their trust. Have your assistant coaches describe their responsibilities to help parents get to know their roles and feel comfortable with them.

Coaching Philosophy (10 minutes)

A brief review of your philosophy of coaching will be helpful. You might want to reread Part I of this book to prepare. Be sure to discuss at least the following points:

- The value of your sport; that is, how you hope it will benefit the athletes.
- The methods you use to teach skills; you might describe a typical practice.
- The emphasis you give to winning, having fun, and developing physically and psychologically.
- What you expect of each athlete; you might discuss any team rules or guidelines you have.

Demonstration (25 minutes)

Parents may not know much yet about your sport. To help them understand and appreciate it, give a demonstration and explanation of the skills, scoring, and rules. Use the entire team or select a few players to assist you in the demonstration. Keep the demonstration simple, showing how the sport is played and scored. If you cannot arrange a demonstration, perhaps you can locate a good film or video. Many national sports agencies have resources that you could borrow.

The demonstration is an opportune time to discuss the equipment for your sport. Emphasize safety when discussing equipment and the rules, and don't forget to mention the role of the referee in ensuring athletes' safety.

Potential Risks (20 minutes)

Be sure parents know the potential risks of participating in your sport. No one likes to hear about injuries, but it is your duty to inform parents of the inherent risks. They must make informed decisions about their child's participation. One video that addresses the inherent dangers of sports is *Warning—It Could Happen to You*. This multisport video is available from the Athletic Institute (200 Castlewood Dr., North Palm Beach, FL 33408). You might consider it as part of your orientation. Be sure, though, to get specific about the dangers of your sport. Keep your discussion upbeat by telling parents what precautions you take to minimize the probability of injury.

Specifics of Your Program (15 minutes)

Now you are ready to describe the specific program you will be conducting. Here are some things parents will want to know. You may think of others.

- How much time will their sons or daughters be with you?
- How often and when does the team practice?
- How long is the season?
- How many contests will there be?
- How do you decide who plays and who doesn't?
- How frequently does the team travel and who pays the expenses?
- What equipment does each athlete need to purchase?
- Where is equipment available and how much does it cost?
- What rules have you established?
- What school, league, or organization rules influence participation?

- How will you discipline your players?
- What is your policy concerning family trips during the season?

Other specific details of your program can also be discussed at this time. You may wish to talk about drug issues, insurance, and fundraising projects, for example.

Question-and-Answer Session (20-45 minutes)

You've been doing most of the talking up to this point. Now let the parents ask some questions. A number of important questions are listed here. If parents don't raise these questions, you should. We have provided a few comments for each question to help you prepare your answers. Keep in mind that not every question pertains to every sport.

Are Medical Examinations Necessary for Children to Compete?

Most schools and organizations have a policy on this. If yours does not, you should develop one. Most medical organizations recommend an examination at least every 2 years. More frequent exams may be required for individuals with specific medical problems.

Ask parents to tell you about any condition their child has that is not covered on the medical history form (e.g., only one kidney, previous loss of memory). Explain that your interest is *not* in keeping the child out of activity, but in ensuring safe participation.

Who Decides When an Athlete Is Ready to Play After an Injury?

A physician should be consulted for any serious injury. The physician then must release the athlete to return to participation. As the coach you also have the right to withhold athletes from competition if you believe they are not ready. Encourage parents to discuss rehabilitation progress and concerns with you.

What Expectations Should We Have for Our Son or Daughter?

Coaches play significant roles in helping parents develop reasonable expectations for their children. All too often problems result if parents and coaches hold different expectations. Parents sometimes overestimate their children's capabilities, and when athletes don't achieve what their parents would like, parents may look to blame the children or the coach. The topic you'll probably discuss most with parents during the season is your mutual expectations for athletes concerning skill development and playing time.

Should We Attend Practice Sessions and Contests?

Let parents know your policy about their watching practice sessions. Certainly under normal circumstances you want them to attend contests. If you question whether a particular parent should come to contests, set up a meeting to discuss your concerns. Your goal is to help both the parent and the athlete interact positively in competitive situations.

Should We Talk With Our Son or Daughter During Contests?

This question opens the door to the broader issue of parental behavior during competitive meets. Consider developing some guidelines for parental behavior, perhaps suggesting that they refrain from coaching athletes and yelling negative remarks from the sideline and that they praise the effort, not the outcome.

Does My Child Need Any Special Pregame Meal?

Athletes should eat a well-balanced meal at least 3 hours before competition, avoiding high-fat foods (see chapter 13).

Can We Do Anything at Home to Facilitate Our Child's Physical Development or Learning of Sport Skills?

You will need to decide whether you wish to have parents attempt to supplement what you are doing. Many coaches oppose this unless parents are specifically qualified because they may teach skills incorrectly, making the coaching task more difficult.

What Do We Do When Our Child Loses? Wins?

Parents play an important role in helping children interpret their sport experiences. Parents can help a young person understand the significance of winning and losing, the experience of frustration in learning, and the need for developing self-confidence, a desire to achieve, and self-appreciation. Sport experiences can open channels of communication between parent and child if parents show interest in their child's participation. Help parents understand the intense emotions associated with sport. Some children may cry when they lose.

What Are Your Expectations of Us?

Convey to parents what assistance you will need from them during the season. You will need their support and reinforcement of your program objectives. If you have not already done so, specify what you consider appropriate parental behavior at contests. Note the vital role that parents play in encouraging children during the season and in helping children understand the significance of winning and losing and the emotions associated with competitive sports.

What Expectations Can We Have of You?

In part you will have answered this throughout the evening, but you may wish to summarize what the parents can expect from you. Remember that throughout the season parents will observe you, either directly or indirectly through their child, and will compare what you say with what you actually do.

How Do We Contact You If We Have a Concern?

Tell parents how they can get in touch with you. You may want to plan additional meetings. Some coaches like to hold individual midseason meetings with parents to discuss athletes' progress and then host a postseason banquet to recognize all youngsters' accomplishments.

A Final Suggestion

At the end of the season, invite each parent to evaluate you and the program. Ask them to point out things that went well and suggest what might be improved. The following evaluation form is one tool to consider. Give copies to all parents and ask them to return them to you. Their feedback could help you become a better coach!

Postseason Parent Evaluation Form

A. Evaluate the degree to which you believe your son or daughter achieved the following (Circle one):

	Very much		Somewhat		Not at all
My child had fun.	1	2	3	4	5
My child learned the fundamentals of the sport.	1	2	3	4	5

B. Evaluate the degree to which you believe your child changed on the following characteristics (Circle one):

	Improved/ Increased	No change	Declined/ Decreased	Don't know
Physical fitness	I	NC	D	DK
Learning to cooperate	I	NC	D	DK
Self-confidence	I	NC	D	DK
Desire to continue to play this sport	I	NC	D	DK
Development of self-reliance	I	NC	D	DK
Learning specific skills of this sport	I	NC	D	DK
Leadership skills	I	NC	D	DK
Sportsmanship	I	NC	D	DK
Development of initiative	I	NC	D	DK
Learning to compete	I	NC	D	DK

C. How did the coach do on the following items? (Circle one):

	Excellent	Good	So-So	Weak	Poor	Don't know
Treated your child fairly	E	G	SS	W	P	DK
Kept winning in perspective	E	G	SS	W	P	DK
Took safety precautions	E	G	SS	W	P	DK
Organized practice and contests	E	G	SS	W	P	DK
Communicated with you	E	G	SS	W	P	DK
Was effective in teaching skills	E	G	SS	W	P	DK
Encouraged your child	E	G	SS	W	P	DK
Recognized your child as a unique individual	E	G	SS	W	P	DK
Held your child's respect	E	G	SS	W	P	DK

D. Please give any additional comments in the space below and on the back. Perhaps you have some constructive criticism or praise you want to offer.

Appendix C

Directory of National Sport Organizations

Sport-Specific Organizations

The following groups are active in providing information to develop their sports. The names of national governing bodies of Olympic sports are printed in bold letters.

Archery

National Archery Association
One Olympic Plaza
Colorado Springs, CO 80909
719-578-4576

National Field Archery Association
31407 Outer I-10
Redlands, CA 92373
909-794-2133

Badminton

United States Badminton Association
One Olympic Plaza
Colorado Springs, CO 80909
719-578-4808

Baseball

American Amateur Baseball Congress
118-119 Redfield Plaza
Marshall, MI 49068
616-781-2002

American Legion Baseball
P.O. Box 1055
Indianapolis, IN 46206
317-630-1213

Babe Ruth Baseball
P.O. Box 5000
1770 Brunswick Pike
Trenton, NJ 08638
609-695-1434

Dixie Boys Baseball
P.O. Box 193
Montgomery, AL 36101-0193
334-263-7529

The George Khoury Association of Baseball Leagues
5400 Meramec Bottom Rd.
St. Louis, MO 63128
314-849-8900

Little League Baseball
P.O. Box 3485
Williamsport, PA 17701
717-326-1921

National Amateur Baseball Federation
P.O. Box 705
Bowie, MD 20718
301-262-5005

National Baseball Congress
300 S. Sycamore
Wichita, KS 67213
316-267-3372

Pony Baseball
300 Clare Dr.
Washington, PA 15301
414-225-1060

USA Baseball
2160 Greenwood Ave.
Trenton, NJ 08609
609-586-2381

Basketball

USA Basketball
5465 Mark Dabling Blvd.
Colorado Springs, CO 80918-3842
719-590-4800

Youth Basketball of America
P.O. Box 3067
Orlando, FL 32802-3067
407-363-9262

Biathlon

U.S. Biathlon Association, Inc.
421 Old Military Rd.
Lake Placid, NY 12946
518-523-3836

Boating

U.S. Sailing Association
P.O. Box 1260
Portsmouth, RI 02871
401-683-0800

Bobsled

**United States Bobsled & Skeleton
  Federation, Inc.**
P.O. Box 828
Lake Placid, NY 12946
518-523-1842

Bowling

USA Bowling
5301 S. 76th St.
Greendale, WI 53129-0500
414-421-9008

Boxing

USA Boxing
One Olympic Plaza
Colorado Springs, CO 80909
719-578-4506

Canoeing/Kayaking

U.S. Canoe & Kayak Team
Pan American Plaza
201 S. Capital Ave., Ste. 610
Indianapolis, IN 46225
317-237-5690

Curling

United States Curling Association
1100 Centerpoint Dr.
Stevens Point, WI 54481
715-344-1199

Cycling

USA Cycling
One Olympic Plaza
Colorado Springs, CO 80909
719-578-4581

Diving

United States Diving, Inc.
Pan American Plaza
201 S. Capital Ave., Ste. 430
Indianapolis, IN 46225
317-237-5252

Equestrian

American Horse Shows Association
220 E. 42nd St.
New York, NY 10017-5876
212-972-2472

Fencing

U.S. Fencing Association
One Olympic Plaza
Colorado Springs, CO 80909
719-578-4511

Field Hockey

U.S. Field Hockey Association, Inc.
One Olympic Plaza
Colorado Springs, CO 80909
719-578-4567

Football

Pop Warner Football
586 Middletown Blvd., Ste. C-100
Langhorne, PA 19047
215-752-2691

U.S. Flag and Touch Football League
7709 Ohio St.
Mentor, OH 44060
216-974-8735

Frisbee

World Flying Disc Federation
c/o Bill Wright, President
200 Linden
Ft. Collins, CO 80524
970-484-6932

Golf

American Junior Golf Association
2415 Steeplechase Ln.
Roswell, GA 30076
770-998-4653

National Golf Foundation
1150 South U.S. Hwy. 1
Jupiter, FL 33477
407-744-6006

Gymnastics

United States Association of Independent
    Gymnastics Clubs
(USAIGE)
235 Pinehurst Rd.
Wilmington, DE 19803
302-656-3706

USA Gymnastics
Pan American Plaza
201 S. Capital Ave., Ste. 300
Indianapolis, IN 46225
317-237-5050

Handball

United States Handball Association
2333 N. Tucson Blvd.
Tucson, AZ 85716-2726
520-795-0434

Ice Hockey

USA Hockey
4965 N. 30th St.
Colorado Springs, CO 80919
719-599-5500

Ice Skating

Amateur Speedskating Union of the U.S.
1033 Shady Ln.
Glen Ellyn, IL 60137
708-790-3230

Ice Skating Institute of America
355 W. Dundee Rd.
Buffalo Grove, IL 60089-3500
708-808-7528

U.S. Figure Skating Association
20 First St.
Colorado Springs, CO 80906
719-635-5200

**U.S. International Speedskating
    Association**
P.O. Box 16157
Rocky River, OH 44116
216-899-0128

In-line/Roller Hockey

National In-line Hockey Association
999 Brickell Ave., 9th Fl.
Miami, FL 33131
800-358-6442

Judo

United States Judo Association
21 N. Union Blvd.
Colorado Springs, CO 80909
719-633-7750

United States Judo, Inc.
P.O. Box 10013
El Paso, TX 79991
915-565-8754

Karate

USA Karate Federation
1300 Kenmore Blvd.
Akron, OH 44314
216-753-3114

Luge

U.S. Luge Association
35 Church St.
Lake Placid, NY 12946
518-523-2071

Modern Pentathlon

U.S. Modern Pentathlon Association
530 McCullough Ave., Ste. 619
San Antonio, TX 78215
210-246-3000

Racquetball

American Amateur Racquetball Association
1685 W. Uintah St.
Colorado Springs, CO 80904-2921
719-635-0685

Rodeo

National Little Britches Rodeo Association
1045 W. Rio Grande
Colorado Springs, CO 80906
719-389-0333

Roller Skating

U.S. Amateur Confederation of Roller Skating
4730 South St.
Lincoln, NE 68506
402-483-7551

Rowing

U.S. Rowing Association
Pan American Plaza
201 S. Capitol Ave., Ste. 400
Indianapolis, IN 46225
317-237-5656

Rugby

USA Rugby Football Union
3595 E. Fountain Blvd.
Colorado Springs, CO 80910
719-637-1022

Sailing

U.S. Sailing Association
P.O. Box 1260
Portsmouth, RI 02871
401-683-0800

Shooting

USA Shooting
One Olympic Plaza
Colorado Springs, CO 80909
719-578-4670

Skiing

Bill Koch Youth Ski League (cross-country)
1500 Kearns Blvd., Bldg. F
Park City, UT 84060-0100
801-649-9090

U.S. Skiing
1500 Kearns Blvd., Bldg. F
Park City, UT 84060
801-649-9090

Soap Box Derby

All-American Soap Box Derby
P.O. Box 7233
Akron, OH 44306
216-733-8723

Soccer

American Youth Soccer Organization
5403 W. 138th St.
Hawthorne, CA 90250-6496
310-643-6455

Soccer Association for Youth
4903 Vine St.
Cincinnati, OH 45217
513-242-4263

Soccer in the Streets
211 Porter Ln.
Jonesboro, GA 30236
770-477-0354

United States Soccer Federation
1801-1811 S. Prairie Ave.
Chicago, IL 60616
312-808-1300

U.S. Youth Soccer Association
899 Presidential, Ste. 117
Richardson, TX 75081
214-235-4499

Softball

Amateur Softball Association
2801 NE 50th St.
Oklahoma City, OK 73111-7203
405-424-5266

Bobby Sox Softball
P.O. Box 5880
Buena Park, CA 90622
714-522-1234

Cinderella Softball League, Inc.
P.O. Box 1411
Corning, NY 14830
607-937-5469

National Softball Association
P.O. Box 23403
Lexington, KY 40523
606-887-4114

Sports Acrobatics

United States Sports Acrobatic Federation
P.O. Box 8158
Riverside, CA 92515-8158
909-785-2293

Squash

United States Squash Racquets Association
P.O. Box 1216
Bala-Cynwyd, PA 19004-1216
610-667-4006

Swimming

United States Swimming, Inc.
One Olympic Plaza
Colorado Springs, CO 80909
719-578-4578

Synchronized Swimming

U.S. Synchronized Swimming, Inc.
Pan American Plaza
201 S. Capitol Ave., Ste. 510
Indianapolis, IN 46225
317-237-5700

Table Tennis

USA Table Tennis
One Olympic Plaza
Colorado Springs, CO 80909
719-578-4583

Taekwondo

United States Taekwondo Union
One Olympic Plaza
Colorado Springs, CO 80909
719-578-4632

Team Handball

United States Team Handball Federation
One Olympic Plaza
Colorado Springs, CO 80909
719-578-4582

Tennis

United States Tennis Association
70 West Red Oak Ln.
White Plains, NY 10604
914-696-7000

Track and Field

USA Track and Field
One RCA Dome, Ste. 140
Indianapolis, IN 46225
317-261-0500

Triathlon

Triathlon Federation/USA
3595 E. Fountain Blvd., Ste. F-1
Colorado Springs, CO 80910
719-597-9090

Twirling

United States Twirling Association
P.O. Box 24488
Seattle, WA 98124
206-623-5623

Volleyball

USA Volleyball
3595 E. Fountain Blvd., Ste. I-2
Colorado Springs, CO 80910-1740
719-637-8300

Water Polo

United States Water Polo, Inc.
Pan American Plaza
201 South Capitol Ave., Ste. 520
Indianapolis, IN 46225
317-237-5599

Water Skiing

American Water Ski Association
799 Overlook Drive S.E.
Winter Haven, FL 33884-1671
941-324-4341

Weightlifting

U.S. Weightlifting Federation
One Olympic Plaza
Colorado Springs, CO 80909-5764
719-578-4508

Wrestling

USA Wrestling
6155 Lehman Dr.
Colorado Springs, CO 80910
719-598-8181

Multisport Organizations

Amateur Athletic Union (AAU)
The Walt Disney World Resort
P.O. Box 10000
Lake Buena Vista, FL 32830-1000
407-363-6170

American Alliance for Health, Physical
Education, Recreation and Dance (AAHPERD)
1900 Association Dr.
Reston, VA 22091
703-476-3400

Baptist Sunday School Board
127 Ninth Ave. N.
Nashville, TN 37234
615-251-2000

Boys and Girls Clubs of America
1230 W. Peachtree St., NW
Atlanta, GA 30309
404-815-5700

Catholic Youth Organization (CYO)
1011 First Ave.
New York, NY 10022
212-371-1000

Jewish Community Centers Association
15 East 26th St.
New York, NY 10010
212-532-4949

National Association of Intercollegiate
Athletics (NAIA)
6120 South Yale, Ste. 1450
Tulsa, OK 74136
918-494-8828

National Collegiate Athletic Association
(NCAA)
6201 College Blvd.
Overland Park, KS 66211-2422
913-339-1906

National Exploring Division, Boy Scouts of
   America
1325 W. Walnut Hill Ln.
Irving, TX 75038
214-580-2433

National Federation of State High School
   Associations
11724 N.W. Plaza Circle
Kansas City, MO 64195-0626
816-464-5400

National Junior College Athletic Association
   (NJCAA)
1825 Austin Bluffs Pkwy., Ste. 100
Colorado Springs, CO 80918
719-590-9788

National Police Athletic Leagues
618 N. U.S. Hwy 1, Ste. 201
North Palm Beach, FL 33408
407-844-1823

National Recreation and Park Association
2775 S. Quincy St., Ste. 300
Arlington, VA 22206-2204
703-820-4940

United States Armed Forces Sports
Hoffman Bldg. #1, Rm. 1456
2461 Eisenhower Ave.
Alexandria, VA 22331-0522
703-325-8871

United States Olympic Committee
One Olympic Plaza
Colorado Springs, CO 80909
719-632-5551

Women's Sport Foundation
Lannin House, Eisenhower Park
East Meadow, NY 11554
516-542-4700

YMCA of the USA
101 N. Wacker Dr.
Chicago, IL 60606
312-977-0031

YWCA of the USA
726 Broadway
New York, NY 10003
212-614-2700

Sport Organizations for Special Populations

American Athletic Association for the Deaf
3607 Washington Blvd., Ste. 4
Ogden, UT 84403
801-393-8710
TTY: 801-393-7916

Disabled Sports USA
451 Hungerford Dr., Ste. 100
Rockville, MD 20850
301-217-0960

Wheelchair Sports, USA
3595 E. Fountain Blvd., Ste. L-1
Colorado Springs, CO 80910
719-574-1150

Special Olympics International, Inc.
1325 G St. N.W., Ste. 500
Washington, DC 20005-4709
202-824-0300

United States Association for Blind Athletes
33 North Institute
Colorado Springs, CO 80903
719-630-0422

United States Cerebral Palsy Athletic
   Association
3810 West NW Highway, Ste. 205
Dallas, TX 75220
214-351-1510

References

American Sport Education Program. (1996). *Event management for sportdirectors*. Champaign, IL: Human Kinetics.

Bump, L.A. (1989). *Sport psychology study guide*. Champaign, IL: Human Kinetics.

Dintiman, G.B., & Ward, R.D. (1988). *Sportspeed*. Champaign, IL: Leisure Press.

Eisenman, P.A., Johnson, S.C., & Benson, J.E. (1990). *Coaches guide to nutrition and weight control*. Champaign, IL: Leisure Press.

Ellis, A., & Harper, R.A. (1976). *A new guide to rational living*. North Hollywood, CA: Wilshire.

Fleck, S.J., & Kraemer, W.J. (1997). *Designing resistance training programs* (2nd ed.). Champaign, IL: Human Kinetics.

Lohman, T.G. (1987). *Measuring body fat using skinfolds* [Videotape]. Champaign, IL: Human Kinetics.

Lohman, T.G., Roche, A.F., & Martorell, R. (1988). *Anthropometric standardization reference manual*. Champaign, IL: Human Kinetics.

Martens, R. (1987). *Coaches guide to sport psychology*. Champaign, IL: Human Kinetics.

Pryor, K. (1984). *Don't shoot the dog*. New York: Simon & Schuster.

Radcliffe, J.C., & Farentinos, R.C. (1985). *Plyometrics: Explosive power training* (2nd ed.). Champaign, IL: Leisure Press.

Sharkey, B.J. (1986). *Coaches guide to sport physiology*. Champaign, IL: Human Kinetics.

Index

About the Author

Rainer Martens has participated in sports all his life. He has coached at the youth, high school, and collegiate levels and has studied sport as a research scientist. The chief executive officer and president of Human Kinetics, he also is the founder of the American Sport Education Program. An internationally recognized sport psychologist, Martens is the author of more than 80 scholarly articles and 15 books, including *Coaching Young Athletes*, *Joy and Sadness in Children's Sports*, *Competitive Anxiety in Sport*, *Youth SportDirector Guide*, and *Parent Guide to Little League Baseball*. He has also been a featured speaker at more than 100 conferences around the world and has conducted more than 150 workshops and clinics for coaches and athletes at all levels.

After receiving his PhD in Physical Education from the University of Illinois at Champaign-Urbana in 1968, Martens was a member of its faculty for 16 years. The current president of the American Academy of Kinesiology and Physical Education, he has been recognized for his contribution to children's sport by SAY Soccer and the National Recreation and Park Association. Both Emporia State University in Kansas (where he earned a bachelor's degree) and the University of Montana (where he earned a master's degree) have honored Martens with a Distinguished Alumni Award.

Leader Level

American Sport Education Program

National Federation Interscholastic Coaches Education Program (NFICEP)

In addition to the Coaching Principles Course for which *Successful Coaching* (Updated Second Edition) serves as the text, NFICEP/ASEP Leader Level provides the following training courses and resources for coaches in interscholastic or club sport:

Drugs and Sport Coaches Course

This course, based on the text *Coaches Guide to Drugs and Sport*, consists of a 4-hour clinic. After the clinic, coaches study the text and take an open-book test.

Drugs and Sport Course Package

(Consists of *Coaches Guide to Drugs and Sport,* clinic study guide, test packet, and processing)

Item ACEP0093 • $40.00 per coach

Coaches Guide to Drugs and Sport

Contents

Chapter 1. The Presence of Drugs in Sport
Chapter 2. Making the Choice to Use or Not
Chapter 3. Setting a Positive Example
Chapter 4. Establishing and Enforcing Rules
Chapter 5. Using Opportunities to Teach
Chapter 6. Involving Athletes and Parents in Prevention

Chapter 7. Responding Effectively
Chapter 8. The Student Assistance Approach
Chapter 9. Responding to Students' Needs
Chapter 10. Finding Help in the School and Community
Chapter 11. Selecting Educational Resources
Chapter 12. Drug Testing

Sport First Aid Coaches Course

This course, based on the text *Sport First Aid*, consists of a 4-hour clinic. After the clinic, coaches study the text and take an open-book test.

Sport First Aid Course Package

(Consists of *Sport First Aid,* clinic study guide, test packet, and processing)

Item ACEP0082 • $30.00 per coach

Sport First Aid

Contents

Chapter 1. Introduction to Sport First Aid
Chapter 2. Basic Sport First Aid Skills
Chapter 3. Sport First Aid for Specific Injuries

For more information on NFICEP or ASEP's Leader Level, call TOLL-FREE 1-800-747-5698.

American Sport Education Program

P.O. Box 5076 • Champaign, IL 61825-5076 • Fax: 217-351-1549
www.asep.com

The Coaching Successfully Series

The books in ASEP's *Coaching Successfully Series* explain how to teach fundamental sports skills and strategies as well as how to apply principles of philosophy, psychology, and teaching and management methods to coaching. Each sport-specific book shows you not only what to teach athletes, but also how to teach it.

1992 • Paper • 240 pp
Item PWOO0446
ISBN 0-88011-446-0
$19.95 ($29.95 Canadian)

1997 • Paper • 216 pp
Item PCHA0942
ISBN 0-87322-942-8
$19.95 ($29.95 Canadian)

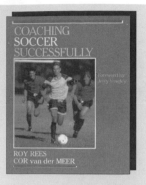

1997 • Paper • 240 pp
Item PREE0444
ISBN 0-87322-444-2
$18.95 ($27.95 Canadian)

1994 • Paper • 192 pp
Item PREA0518
ISBN 0-87322-518-X
$19.95 ($29.95 Canadian)

1995 • Paper • 200 pp
Item PUST0461
ISBN 0-87322-461-2
$19.95 ($29.95 Canadian)

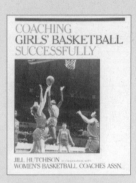

1989 • Paper • 288 pp
Item PHUT0343
ISBN 0-88011-343-X
$20.00 ($29.95 Canadian)

1995 • Paper • 176 pp
Item PHAN0492
ISBN 0-87322-492-2
$19.95 ($29.95 Canadian)

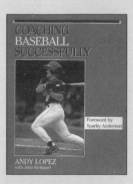

1996 • Paper • 216 pp
Item PLOP0609
ISBN 0-87322-609-7
$18.95 ($27.95 Canadian)

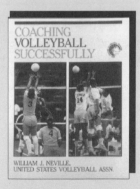

1990 • Paper • 224 pp
Item PNEV0362
ISBN 0-88011-362-6
$19.95 ($29.95 Canadian)

HUMAN KINETICS
The Premier Publisher for Sports & Fitness
www.humankinetics.com

2335

Prices are subject to change.

For more information, U.S. customers call **TOLL-FREE**
1-800-747-4457. Customers outside of the U.S. use the appropriate
telephone number/address shown in the front of this book.